Fresh Fro

the Bible for a change
2015

IBRA
International Bible Reading Association

Help Spread the Word

Thank you for purchasing a copy of Fresh from the Word. We trust it will guide you on your journey through year 2015.

You surely want to help a needy person benefit from these notes by picking an additional copy for him or her. This will do more than what any other Christmas or New Year present could do for such a loved one, because you would be spreading the word in your own small way.

God bless you as you do this.

For bulk purchases contact

Asempa Publishers
Box GP 919, Accra
or No. 8, 13th Street Close
Atomic Gate, Haatso, Accra

Telephone: 028 9672514

E-mail: gm@asempapublishers.com

FRESH from the WORD

the Bible for a change

Foreword by Terry Waite

Edited by Nathan Eddy

Fresh From the Word aims to build understanding and respect for different Christian perspectives through the provision of a range of biblical interpretations. Views expressed by contributors should not, therefore, be taken to reflect the views or policies of the Editor or the International Bible Reading Association.

The International Bible Reading Association's scheme of readings is listed monthly on the Christian Education website at http://shop.christianeducation.org.uk/about-ibra/ and the full scheme for 2015 may be downloaded in English, Spanish and French.

Cover design by Christian Education Publications
Editor: Nathan Eddy

Published by:
The International Bible Reading Association
1020 Bristol Road
Selly Oak
Birmingham B29 6LB
United Kingdom

Charity number: 1086990
ISBN 978-1-905893-81-2
ISSN 2050-6791

Typeset by Wordsense Ltd, Edinburgh: www.wordsense.co.uk
Printed and bound in the UK by Mosaic Print Management

Contents

Foreword

by Terry Waite

The Bible is not necessarily the easiest book to read. In fact it is a library in itself: there are songs and poems, as well as exciting accounts of the adventures of individuals and whole groups of people. Many of the stories in the Old Testament tell of how men and women have gradually gained a deeper understanding of the great mystery that is God. Sometimes they have attempted to use God for their own selfish motives. At other times they have made serious attempts to penetrate the mystery and have found love and compassion.

The New Testament records an even more complete picture of the love and compassion that lies at the heart of mystery. One might say it puts a human face on the great power that lies behind the universe, and teaches the reader that the individual is important and must never be seen as a mere cog in a vast machine.

The Bible contains many truths about human nature and the nature of God, and such truths are revealed by careful and diligent study, not by random selection. Such a varied and complicated volume needs explanation, and this is where *Fresh From the Word* can be so helpful. Day by day, people who have studied the Bible suggest a reading and offer an interpretation. Their words are intended to stimulate further, thorough reflection and understanding, but are not to be taken as the final word. There will always be room for a deeper level of understanding to be gained from the Bible.

Across the generations, thousands of men and women have been encouraged and inspired by reading and studying these ancient texts. Those who have contributed to this guide hope that this may be your experience also. Like all disciplines, one has to persevere, and often the benefits of study do not come quickly. If you approach these readings with an open mind, you may find that you are drawn closer to the great mystery that is God, the fount of love and compassion. A daily reading is not simply an academic exercise – it can be a life-changing experience and, as lives are changed, so this sad and troubled world may become a place of peace and harmony. As co-creators with God we have our part to play, and the Bible can become one of the many tools to assist us in this process.

Terry Waite

Terry Waite

How to use *Fresh From the Word*

How do you approach the idea of regular Bible reading? It may help to see daily Bible reading as spiritual exploration. Here is a suggestion of a pattern to follow that may help you develop the discipline but free up your mind and heart to respond.

- Before you read, take a few moments – the time it takes to say the Lord's Prayer – to imagine God looking at you with love. Feel yourself enfolded in that gaze. Come to scripture with your feet firmly planted.

- Read the passage slowly before you turn to the notes. Be curious. The Bible was written over a period of nearly 1000 years, over 2000 years ago. There is always something to learn. Read and reread.

- 'Read' yourself as you read the story. Be attentive to your reactions – even trivial ones. What is drawing you into the story? What is repelling you? Observe yourself 'sidelong' as you read as if you were watching a wild animal in the forest; be still, observant and expectant.

- What in the scripture or in the notes is drawing you forward in hope? What is closing you down? Notice where the Spirit of Life is present, and where negative spirits are, too. Follow where life is leading. God always leads into life, even if the way feels risky.

- Lift up the world and aspects of your life to God. What would you like to share with God? What is God seeking to share with you?

- Thank God for being present and offer your energy in the day ahead, or in the day coming after a night's rest.

Introduction from the Editor

Its ambition was breathtaking: by this year, halving extreme poverty; halting HIV/Aids; providing universal primary education. The United Nations Millennium Goals have seen some achievements – the number of children out of school has dropped by half since 1990, for example. But many of its goals are unmet.

The Bible says we must work for justice for the poorest of the poor, but it is still rare to find these issues on the table in Bible reading notes and in local churches. It is easy to forget the poor when we read the Bible with a roof over our heads and food nearby (although we might be reading the Bible in a house without walls; see Samoan Alesana Pala'amo's notes beginning 12 April).

We chose the UN Millennium Development Goals as a theme this year in Lent (see 18 February) because we aim to read scripture together with others' needs in mind, not just our own. We aim to read the Bible in order to change lives, beginning, but not ending, with our own. So we have a rich variety of themes for you in *Fresh From the Word* this year: Tears and Rejoicing in the Bible, Attentiveness, Birds in the Bible, and the virtues of being small (Small is beautiful). We will look at the theme of work and at a variety of biblical books (as different as Jonah and the Song of Songs). We have many returning writers, like Ethiopian activist Jember Teferra, Kate Hughes and Nicola Slee; and we have new writers, like workplace chaplain Stephen Willey and Pentecostal pastor Bola Iduoze.

One feature of *Fresh From the Word* is the tradition of both tracing themes through the Bible and giving large chunks of continuous readings from single books. This year the story of Jesus' feeding of the five (or four) thousand in the wilderness is included in both its versions in Mark, and its version in John. We think it works, but we'd like to hear from you.

We are joined in one fellowship by our humanity, by our hope in Jesus Christ, and by our commission to work for the sake of the world. I hope the Holy Spirit dancing in the words in this book takes you further on that journey this year. Please get in touch with us and tell us how it has.

Nathan Eddy

Acknowledgements and abbreviations

We are grateful to the following copyright holders for permission to use quotations from the New International Version of the Bible in the following territories:

Within the UK, EU and EFTA
Scripture quotations taken from the Holy Bible, New International Version Anglicised. Copyright © 1979, 1984, 2011 Biblica, formerly International Bible Society. Used by permission of Hodder & Stoughton Ltd, an Hachette UK company. All rights reserved. 'NIV' is a registered trademark of Biblica. UK trademark number 1448790.

Within the US and Canada
Scriptures taken from the Holy Bible, New International Version®, NIV®. Copyright © 1973, 1978, 1984, 2011 by Biblica, Inc.™ Used by permission of Zondervan. All rights reserved worldwide. www.zondervan.com The "NIV" and "New International Version" are trademarks registered in the United States Patent and Trademark Office by Biblica, Inc.™

Within all other territories worldwide and for all electronic versions of this text
Scriptures taken from the Holy Bible, New International Version® Anglicized, NIV® Copyright © 1979, 1984, 2011 by Biblica, Inc.® Used by permission. All rights reserved worldwide.

Note
Some writers use the abbreviation CE and BCE to indicate Common Era/before the Common Era according to modern convention. No disrespect is intended.

Illumination
1 A lamp to my feet

This week's notes are by **David Bartlett**

David Bartlett is Professor Emeritus of New Testament at Columbia Theological Seminary in Decatur, Georgia. He is Lantz Professor of Christian Communication Emeritus at Yale University Divinity School. He is Theologian in Residence at Trinity Presbyterian Church, Atlanta, Georgia, and is ordained in the American Baptist church. He is passionate about preaching and the life of the church and is co-editor of the major lectionary commentary *Feasting on the Word* (Westminster/John Knox). He and his spouse Carol Bartlett, an early-childhood educator, are co-authors of *Feasting on the Word: Guide to Children's Sermons*.

Thursday 1 January
A book of possibilities

Psalm 119:97-105

Your word is a lamp for my feet, a light on my path. (verse 105)

There is a kind of cartoon version of the law that suggests that biblical law, especially in the Old Testament, is all about the 'shalt nots' – the long list of prohibitions. Sometimes it is said the prohibitions make us anxious: Are we breaking any laws? Sometimes the prohibitions make us guilty: 'Oh no, we broke another law.'

But, for the Hebrew Bible and for many Jews and Christians the law, the Torah, is not so much a book of prohibitions as a book of possibilities. Maybe 'instruction' is a better translation of the Hebrew word 'Torah' than 'law' is. For all of us life is a kind of pilgrimage through a land full of surprises and even dangers. We all need a map, a guidebook, to help us find our way faithfully.

For the psalmist, the Torah is a lamp on a sometimes darkening way. It is a delight and not a threat. It is the dessert that crowns our meal, not the obligatory vegetable we love to hate. Or, more accurately, the law is both our essential nutrient and our lasting delight.

† Lord, let us delight in your instruction, day and night, throughout this coming year.

Friday 2 January
The gift of scripture

2 Timothy 3:14-17

All scripture is God-breathed and is useful for teaching, rebuking, correcting and training in righteousness, so that the servant of God may be thoroughly equipped for every good work. (verses 16-17)

This epistle is written as a farewell letter from the apostle to one of his disciples. Like many other farewell letters between older friends or relatives and younger, the letter is full of advice. The letter is also written at a time when the earliest followers of Jesus are passing away and the author is concerned that the new generation might hold fast to the faith that they have been taught.

Central to this faith is scripture though, of course, this early in the church's life there is no New Testament, so the scripture that the letter commends is our Old Testament. 2 Timothy declares that all scripture is inspired, but it notably does not try to explain exactly how that inspiration works.

The letter also claims that, whatever else scripture may be – inspired, divine, holy, grace filled – it is also useful. That seems like a modest claim, but it is a very strong claim indeed. Think about the teachings, the books, the movies, the plays or television programmes that mean the most to you. They have been useful, not because they give you quick answers to every question, but because they shape your life.

Some wise Christians have suggested that the Bible works for us as a pair of glasses or contact lenses might work. When the world seems fuzzy, complicated and contradictory, scripture provides the lenses through which we can see life more clear and true.

† Open our eyes, kind God, and focus them through your word.

For further thought
• Think of a book or poem or movie that has helped change your way of looking at the world and at yourself. How might the Bible do the same?

Saturday 3 January
Spiritual songs

Colossians 3:16-17

Let the message of Christ dwell among you richly as you teach and admonish one another with all wisdom through psalms, hymns, and songs from the Spirit, singing to God with gratitude in your heart. And whatever you do, whether in word or deed, do it all in the name of the Lord Jesus, giving thanks to God the Father through him. (verses 16-17)

I once met with a group of theologians for a semi-annual seminar. We read papers on important biblical and philosophical topics and other members responded. At the end of the last paper of the day, a distinguished theologian, who had written much and taught long and was now retired, closed his paper by doing something unheard of in that heady gathering: he played a gospel song for the group to hear. Oddly, amazingly, one by one other members of the group contributed a verse or two of a hymn or spiritual song that guided them in their lives of faith and inquiry. Whether we had moved from left brain to right brain or from intellect to spirit or from mundane life to Spirit, for a few minutes we moved from inquiry to gratitude.

Every pastor I know testifies that, when people are seriously ill and sometimes even seriously confused, what they can hold on to are the songs and hymns that they have loved. Listening, humming, singing along even those facing the end of life take on new life in the presence of holy song.

Colossians knows that what sustains faith is not just preaching or reading or thinking, but singing. Colossians knows that music is itself a deep and abiding form of thanksgiving, a deep and abiding prayer.

† Sing in our hearts, God of beauty, and turn us to delight in you, this day and every day this year.

For further thought
• Quick, what's the first hymn that comes to your mind? What does it say? How does it sound? Why do you think this hymn is important to you?

Illumination
2 The mystery made known

This week's notes are by **David Bartlett** (see page 1).

Sunday 4 January
God for the world

Isaiah 60:1-6

See, darkness covers the earth and thick darkness is over the peoples, But the Lord *rises upon you and his glory appears over you. Nations will come to your light, and kings to the brightness of your dawn.* (verses 2-3)

On this Sunday our churches may be celebrating Epiphany, the day the magi arrived from the East, or at least we are getting ready to celebrate Epiphany on its official holy day, 6 January.

Our text is full of details that we will see reflected in Matthew's Epiphany story. But this passage is an Epiphany text for another reason, too. Epiphany is that season when we celebrate the fact that the good news of God's love is not reserved for Israel and Judah alone but becomes a gift to all the nations, including all the Gentiles. For Christians, the promises of Isaiah are fulfilled when Jesus comes to be not only Son of David, but Son of God and Saviour of the World.

When we read the prophets talking about Israel we imagine a great kingdom. A look at the map will indicate that our Holy Land was just a little backwater among the far more powerful empires. The astonishing thing is not that God made Israel a 'great' nation but that God took a small nation to do great things. The astonishing assurance is that Israel's hope – for God's just and peaceful reign – is now a hope extended to all the world.

† We are deeply grateful, kind God, that your mercy has embraced Israel and then the whole world – including us.

Monday 5 January
The mystery of God

Ephesians 3:1-12

[God's] intent was that now, through the church, the manifold wisdom of God should be made known to the rulers and authorities in the heavenly realms... (verse 10)

We often think that the mystery of God is entirely divorced from the all too mundane and unmysterious reality of the church. For some of us, church identity is given with birth and we take it with some of the same indifference with which we take other accidents of birth – our height, the colour of our eyes. For some of us, church membership represents a choice, a deliberate intention to become part of a community.

Like every community, however, the church can get caught up in the apparent trivia and obsession with institutional self-preservation. All those committees; all those more or less obligatory gatherings. At the church where I serve, the minister blessedly decided to postpone all meetings for December until next year, while worship and fellowship went on.

But the church lives under a mandate and a promise. The mandate is to be a steward of the manifold mysteries of God. The promise is that the church will not live out its light in vain. When the sacraments (the 'mysteries') are celebrated gladly, and scripture is read and preached faithfully, that quirky little church family to whom we belong is a guardian of God's grace for the sake of the world.

And the mysteries of grace are so great that our apparently small observances and affirmations shake the powers on earth and the very powers of the heavens.

† Gracious God, in our ordinary church gatherings we want to live out the mystery of your love in our communities. Make it so, day by day.

For further thought

• If you attend a church regularly, what in your life together promotes the mandate in the verse quoted above? What gets in the way of it?

Tuesday 6 January (Epiphany)
Adored and adoring

Matthew 2:1-12

On coming into the house, they saw the child with his mother Mary, and they bowed down and worshipped him. Then they opened their treasures and presented him with gifts of gold, frankincense and myrrh. (verse 11)

Last Christmas friends sent us a Christmas card that included a reproduction of a Christian carving from about the sixth century. The carving was obviously a picture of the first Epiphany, the visit of the magi to the infant Jesus. But it was equally obvious that the artist depicted not three wise men, but four.

The tradition of three wise men is apparently based on the fact that there were three gifts – gold, and frankincense and myrrh – but Matthew himself does not elaborate. Matthew does remind us that they come from far away, and they thus become the first persons from outside the Jewish nation to bring gifts and adoration to the child. In that sense they foretell the good news that the good news is not intended for any one people or any one nation alone – but extends to the ends of the earth.

Notice, too, that Herod plays a role in this story and, in the Gospel that follows, he and his ilk always lurk in the shadowy background of the plot. We are reminded that God's greatest gifts to humankind always arouse opposition, resistance and danger.

Soon enough we shall be reminded that the gifts that the three or four or dozen magi bring to Jesus will be confirmed and eclipsed by the greater gift he gives to all the world – his own life, given in love upon the cross. Now we see not only the adoration of the magi, but the astonishing adoration of our Lord for the world that is his own.

† We bring our varied gifts into the presence of your Son, O God. Accept them and accept our lives as signs of our gratitude.

For further thought
• You might read T S Eliot's poem 'The Journey of the Magi' as a reminder of the way in which the birth and death of Jesus come together as part of one story of redemption and mercy.

Wednesday 7 January
The size of the Spirit

Luke 2:25-32

For my eyes have seen your salvation, which you have prepared in the sight of all nations: a light for revelation to the Gentiles, and the glory of your people Israel. (verses 30-32)

Luke is the Gospel writer most concerned with the life of the Holy Spirit. In Luke's Gospel Jesus begins his ministry by declaring that 'the Spirit of the Lord is on me' (Luke 4:18). In the second volume of his two-volume work, Luke tells us that the Spirit of God falls upon the believers in Jerusalem, in the great moment of Pentecost.

But now, before Jesus has said a word in Luke's Gospel, and before the church has begun its ministry, the Spirit appears. The Spirit appears upon a righteous Jew who knows that salvation is coming but does not yet know the fullness of the gospel. Yet God's Spirit is the Spirit that inspires Israel as well as the church – something we would do well to remember in the twenty-first century as in the first.

But when the Spirit appears, the role of the Spirit is to open up the gift of salvation so that it extends beyond Israel to be visible to all the nations, to Israel first but to the Gentiles, too. We are all tempted to make the Spirit of God too small, the exclusive possession of just a few of us. The Spirit refuses to be confined; the Spirit is God's witness to all the peoples of the world. The light does not belong under a basket, is not confined to a corner, but breaks out to illumine all creation.

† Shine on us, Holy Spirit, and in your light let us see your whole creation illuminated, groaning toward redemption.

For further thought

• Where are the places where we try to limit the working of the Spirit? Where do we see the Spirit breaking through beyond our rules or even our imaginations?

Thursday 8 January
Witness to love

John 1:29-34

Look, the Lamb of God, who takes away the sins of the world! (verse 29)

The Gospel of John is a record of witnesses. The Father bears witness to Jesus, Jesus bears witness to himself, the Spirit bears witness to Jesus and, for the readers of John, the Gospel of John itself becomes a witness to Christ.

John the baptiser is the first major witness in John's Gospel. John 1:7-8 tells us that John comes as a witness, and our passage for today shows John witnessing to Jesus. John's witness tells us two great mysteries of faith. First, in John's Gospel, Jesus himself replaces the Passover lamb who, according to Jewish custom, was killed as a sacrifice for the sins of the people. John does not meditate here or elsewhere on how that sacrifice is effective for our sins and for the sins of the whole world. What he does emphasise is that the cross of Christ is not only the demonstration of God's love, but also the acting out of God's love. On the cross, God doesn't just talk about love. God does it.

The second mystery is that Jesus Christ provides the Holy Spirit, who continues to speak for him in the church of the first century and in our churches, too. God has sent the Spirit upon Christ; Christ will send the Spirit upon the believers and through them to the world.

An epiphany is an appearance, a revelation. John reminds us that the Epiphany of Christmastide will continue through the whole year, and through all the years to come. It continues today.

† Spirit of God, descend upon our hearts. Bear witness to the saving love of the Son.

For further thought

• Think of the role of witnesses in mystery novels, plays and television programmes. How do they help us reflect on the role of the Holy Spirit and the Gospels as witnesses to the deeper mysteries of faith?

Friday 9 January
Gift-giving Spirit

1 Corinthians 2:9-16

What we have received is not the spirit of the world but the Spirit who is from God, so that we may understand what God has freely given us. (verse 12)

In many ways 1 Corinthians is the most informative of Paul's letters, because it tells us not only a good deal about Paul but a good deal about the churches in Corinth. Paul even quotes their letters to him in order to answer their questions or (he is sure) correct their misunderstandings.

One of the pervasive misunderstandings among the Corinthians is a misunderstanding of the Spirit. They rightly perceive that God's Spirit not only is a gift in itself but that God's Spirit provides gifts to believers. What they wrongly think is that there is some kind of rank among the spiritual gifts, and that the Spirit loves people who speak in tongues more than those who give homilies in Greek, or vice versa.

What Paul insists is that the Spirit is God's gift to bring us together, not God's trick to tear us apart. Not only is the Spirit outside us, as witness and illumination, but God's Spirit is also within us as faithfulness and response. God's transcendent Spirit reaches out to the spirit in each of us. And we know that the spirit within each of us is God's Spirit just to the extent that the Spirit brings us together.

That is why, later in the letter, after he has gone through the long list of spiritual gifts, Paul can sum up the unmistakable signs of the true Spirit of God – above us and within us. 'And now these three [gifts] remain: faith, hope and love. But the greatest of these is love' (1 Corinthians 13:13).

† Holy God, in this blessed Epiphany season, when we recognise your Spirit, illumine and cleanse our spirits by your inspiration that we may more perfectly love you and one another and glorify your holy name.

For further thought

• Opening yourself to the Spirit, meditate for a few minutes on what gifts the Spirit has given you as a believer.

Saturday 10 January
Priceless

Psalm 36:5-10

For with you is the fountain of life; in your light we see light. (verse 9)

The superscriptions – the little notes written at the beginning of our psalms, were almost certainly written some time after the psalms themselves and represent some later priest's or committee's best guess on why the psalm was written. But I like to think that this superscription catches the mood and mode of the psalm. David the singer of songs dedicates this song to the director of music in whatever congregation David attended.

All through this season of Epiphany we have thought of mystery, of poetry, of light. When James Joyce wrote his nearly autobiographical *Portrait of the Artist as a Young Man*, he referred to the moments of insight that his hero received as 'epiphanies' – for Joyce, perhaps, best presented in art and best understood by artists.

Notice the artistry with which our psalmist today adds picture to picture, celebration to celebration. God's mystery touches our imaginations and transcends our imaginations.

For Christians, inspiration – inspiriting – is always the gift of the Holy Spirit but it also always exceeds the capacity of our minds fully to understand or our words fully to describe. Thank God for music, poetry, visual art – the ways in which small epiphanies point us to the great Epiphany. Christ in the manger; God's Spirit speaking to our spirits; God's light lightening our hearts.

How priceless is God's unfailing and inexpressible love.

† Light of God, illumine our lives. Lighten the dark places. Shine on the places of beauty. Lead us on.

For further thought
• When next you are in a worship setting, be open to the ways in which the architecture, the music, and the poetry touch your imagination, enriching your thoughts.

Readings in Mark (1)

1 The beginning of the good news

This week's notes are by **Sister Christopher Godden OSB**

The wide-open skies over the coastal village in her native Lancashire have given Sister Christopher a great love of space and silence. Following her schooling she attended a College of Education for 18 months before moving into the electricity industry. Thirteen years later, having become a Catholic in the intervening years, she entered the Benedictine Monastery at Talacre, remaining with the same Community when it moved to Chester.

Sunday 11 January
With wild animals

Mark 1:1-13

At once the Spirit sent him out into the wilderness, and he was in the wilderness for forty days, being tempted by Satan. He was with the wild animals and angels attended him. (verses 12-13)

It's not unusual these days for people to make a fresh start in life with a change of career some years after being in their chosen field of employment. We do not know what Jesus had been doing up until now but it's clear things were about to change after his baptism.

St Mark tells us Jesus was sent into the desert (not led as in Matthew 4:1 or Luke 4:1). He needed to be alone, away from distractions, getting space to work out, plan and prepare himself for what lay ahead.

Again, unlike Matthew and Luke, St Mark is very brief when he describes this time. He uses just one sentence: 'he was with the wild animals'. Lions, tigers, wolves around outside, but what about the 'wild animals within'? We all have them: negative, destructive feelings going on inside us and which we'd much rather were not there.

How to deal with them? There are times when all we can do is stand back in trust and allow God's grace the space to work quietly, constantly and unceasingly within us, changing and re-forming our inscape. Sometimes the most surprising angels are sent to help.

† Lord, help us so to discipline our minds that all we say or do can be put towards the building of the kingdom of God.

Monday 12 January
A complete change of scene

Mark 1:14-20

'The time has come,' he said. 'The kingdom of God has come near. Repent and believe the good news!' (**verse 15**)

Jesus illustrates his parables about the kingdom by using examples of the people, events and work of the everyday life in Galilee, illustrating how life can be seen at different and deeper levels and inviting both his listeners and ourselves to do the same. Our world of computers, IT etc., plus the pace at which we live may be very different from the world of first-century Galilee but our attitudes and the way we go about daily life are pretty similar. We get up, work a little, perhaps, if we are lucky, relax a bit and then go to bed. But do we ever question what we are really doing or what life is really all about? Jesus suggests we ask ourselves these questions and maybe find different answers from the ones we are used to trotting out. It is easy to feel overwhelmed and think 'what difference can one person make?' The answer to that is you don't know and never will unless at the very least you make an effort at trusting in God and leave the rest to him.

Jesus chooses some ordinary fishermen, wise in the way of their present occupation, as his first disciples and suggests they learn to work together with him and go after a different sort of fish and a bigger catch. He asks us the same question, inviting us to play our part in making God's kingdom become something real and not just words. All or no skills are needed, just willing workers. Does that sound like you?

† Let us pray for all starting a new job today and for all for whom this is the first day of being out of work with no prospect of employment on their horizon.

For further thought
• Is it better to do what you are asked or only what you feel you can?

Tuesday 13 January
A new way to live

Mark 1:21-28

The people were all so amazed that they asked each other, 'What is this? A new teaching – and with authority! He even gives orders to evil spirits and they obey him.' (verse 27)

It's not hard to understand why Jesus' preaching and teaching made such an impact on, and aroused such enthusiasm in, those who heard him. Here was something new, exciting and *real*, not like the dry, dusty, repetitive lessons on the law they were usually given. Jesus suggested a new way of living that had a freshness and appeal and was not bound up with rules and regulations. Though, of course, there were some of the latter but not, it seemed, all that many.

Suddenly there was an interruption as the man possessed by a demon began to shout aloud. We know the words of the man were actually true, but those at synagogue that day would have heard them as sheer and utter blasphemy.

In his Gospel, Mark does not refer, as Matthew and Luke do, to the explicit temptations faced by Jesus when in the desert, all of which deal with the misuse of power. In this scene, Jesus, faced by such an issue, deals promptly and sternly with it, dealing directly with the demon, not the man, and expelling the evil spirit, leaving the man healed, whole and ready to make a new start in life. When faced with evil it can be difficult to work out quickly the best and right approach. Caution may be needed but evil should never be ignored. In today's passage Mark portrays Jesus as a man of authority in his words and actions, someone with a strength of mind and purpose, focused and ready to practise what he preaches – someone you want to know more about, and so are encouraged to read on …

† Lord, help us to look with kindness and compassion on those in society who have fallen on hard times. Teach us not to judge what we do not know.

For further thought
- If someone drunk or high on drugs comes up to you in the street, what is the best way to deal with the situation?

Wednesday 14 January
Grace-full living

Mark 1:29-37

So he went to her, took her hand and helped her up. The fever left her and she began to wait on them. (verse 31)

Jesus never grew old; he died young. He did not live long enough to know the aches and pains, trials and tribulations that ageing brings along. However, in his words and actions he does give lessons on coping with infirmities – be you the carer or the one so afflicted.

Mark gives the impression that, upon hearing of Peter's mother-in-law's affliction, Jesus wastes no time at all in going up to her and then with a lovely gesture takes her by the hand and helps her up. She responds immediately by setting about her duty as hostess to her guest. Jesus heals us so we can serve him; not so much wait on him but, as we have already seen this week, by joining him in making the kingdom of God active, alive and real in the present moment. Every moment passed is a moment lost.

Building the kingdom does not always have to involve great or strenuous activity, nor are we all called to leave our present situation and begin something new. Simply trying to make the best of life as it comes can be enough.

As we grow old, limbs stiffen and sight and hearing decrease, but we cannot expect to be released from our service with Jesus. Ours is a lifelong commitment and what we need now is to learn new ways of serving him. Prayer comes first to mind, but there's also the example we can give by a sense of perspective, humour and balance as well as the care, concern, thoughtfulness and kindness for all around us – especially those trying to help.

† Lord, help us to appreciate we are all growing older every day and there is much unspoken suffering in our world. Help us really to see and appreciate each other.

For further thought
• What are some ways you serve Jesus? What are some new ways you could take on?

Thursday 15 January
The sixth dimension

Mark 1:38-45

Jesus was indignant. He reached out his hand and touched the man. (part of verse 41)

Yesterday, Jesus took Simon's mother-in-law by the hand; today he reaches out and touches a leper even though it means he too will become ritually 'unclean' for a while. Jesus is tactile, not afraid to touch others physically or in the mind. He is sensitive to others too. (In Mark 8:22-26 he leads the blind man at Bethsaida outside his village before he heals him.) He reaches out to us, too, because he cares.

Novelist E M Forster often used the words 'Only connect' but somehow, despite email, texting, mobile phones etc., plus all the many words written and spoken each day, people seem to be drifting apart. We seem less able to make relationships other than at a very superficial level. The result is our cities and towns are becoming dotted with separate wells of loneliness, with people reluctant or too frightened to reach out or become involved. There are times when it is often the touch, hand-to-hand, flesh-to-flesh, in friendship and love, that can mean all when hope seems dim.

'The Lord God said, "It is not good for the man to be alone"' (Genesis 2:18). Although we all do need some personal space, it is also as groups – families, workers, teams – pulling and working together that we can build a better society or world and make it work.

A favourite poem of mine ends:
> There is a moving dependent on chance.
> It is the way a look, a touch, can give an absolute necessity to live.
>
> From 'Six Dimensions' by Alan Bold,
> Penguin Modern Poets 15, 1969:16

I think Jesus was like that.

† Let us remember people who are isolated, lonely, and cut off in the world. Help us to reach out to touch in some way all whom we meet today who need encouragement and hope.

For further thought
• How do we stop society from fragmenting and people becoming so isolated?

Friday 16 January
Getting unstuck

Mark 2:1-14

Which is easier: to say to this paralysed man, 'Your sins are forgiven,' or to say, 'Get up, take your mat, and walk'? (verse 9)

Two men, both stuck and not moving. The paralysed man needed a stretcher and friends who had faith enough to bring him to Jesus. Levi is sitting down, probably alone, as tax collectors were despised and hated by all. By the end of the day both men are back on their feet again and making a new start in life.

The paralysed man is brought by his friends to Jesus; Jesus goes to Levi. We have only to want to know Jesus and he will initiate some way of reaching us. There are as many ways as there are people. (Note there are four stretcher-bearers. Four indicates completeness, e.g. north, south, east, west.)

The roof of our head is our skull. We have to open up our minds to Jesus, enabling him to 'move in', speak, refresh, heal and guide us. 'Do not conform to the pattern of this world, but be transformed by the renewing of your mind' (Romans.12:2).

Sin can paralyse. We become bound by guilt, shame and remorse – feelings that will stop us from moving on. Facing up to faults and responsibilities is at times neither easy nor pleasant. Sometimes our good intentions are misunderstood or misinterpreted, but that should not stop us. It's the only way we can really get going again.

We know Levi became an apostle and through his writing is still reaching out to spread the gospel. We do not know what became of the paralysed man, or even if he became a disciple, but I bet he never forgot Jesus.

† Let us thank the Lord for all our friends, all who have helped us when we needed it and all who stand by us even though they may not agree with us.

For further thought

• For a long time you feel you have been 'going nowhere fast' spiritually. How do you get started again?

Saturday 17 January
Fast or feast?

Mark 2:15-22

Now John's disciples and the Pharisees were fasting... (verse 18)

I wonder why they were fasting. It could not have been one of the traditional fast days, surely, otherwise Levi's dinner would not have been taking place. Why do we fast? Usually for health or religious reasons, though of course there are those who fast daily not because they choose to but because they have no choice.

What is the point of fasting? For Christians it's a discipline to help sharpen our perception, or can be a sort of cleansing activity and refocusing of the mind: a period of preparation for something special.

It is certainly no use fasting if it means your attitude is going to be that of the Pharisees and law teachers in today's passage whose thinly veiled criticism is ably dealt with by Jesus' reply.

We may be questioned as to why we are fasting, like those who were merely puzzled by Jesus' behaviour. This time his answer leaves his questioners with plenty to work out for themselves, just as Mark seems to want us to do as we read on.

At the beginning of this week, Jesus was alone in the desert preparing for his forthcoming ministry. During the week we've met many who have been able to start life afresh. Today we join Jesus celebrating dinner with Levi and some of his friends as they rejoice at their own new beginning.

I once embroidered a sampler with the words 'Today is the first day of the rest of your life' (anon). True for all of us.

† We pray for all who will not get enough to eat or drink today.

For further thought
- Look back at the week. Ask God's forgiveness for where you have failed. Can you do anything to put right what has gone wrong? Then commend everything to him.

17

Readings in Mark (1)

2 The crowds gather

This week's notes are by **Mandy Briggs**

 The Revd Mandy Briggs is a Methodist minister who works in the Bristol area. A former journalist, she worked on newspapers in Weston-super-Mare and Bath before training for the ministry. She continues to be interested in how the church and the media can work together in a positive way.

Sunday 18 January

Never on a Sunday?

Mark 2:23-28

So the Son of Man is Lord even of the Sabbath. (verse 28)

Many words have been used to describe Jesus, but one thing is for sure – boring definitely isn't one of them.

His words and actions often infuriated the religious authorities, so much so that they eventually plotted to kill him.

Over the next week we'll be looking at scenes from Mark's Gospel where Jesus was surrounded by crowds. How did he react to them? What did he say to them? Did it ever get a bit much for him?

We start today, however, with a small drama that takes place before the crowds gather. Jesus is challenged about eating grain on the Sabbath but in his reply to the Pharisees he paints a bigger picture than the one contained in their rule book.

It is not that Jesus doesn't respect the rules but he wants to point out that the law of God must ultimately be about grace, not legalism. He understands the law but also points beyond it. The Pharisees use the law as a trap to catch people out. Jesus' view of the law is different. Living God's way means that the principal law to be followed is the law of love.

† Compassionate God, when I am surrounded by rules and regulations, may I never lose sight of the people I am seeking to serve and love.

Monday 19 January
Needing some space

Mark 3:1-12

Jesus withdrew with his disciples to the lake, and a large crowd from Galilee followed. (verse 7)

As the controversial 'Sabbath debate' continues, Jesus and his disciples decide to withdraw from the heated atmosphere of the synagogue. They head for the calm of the lake, but the tranquil atmosphere does not last long.

When a celebrity is spotted shopping, falling out of a club or tripping over a kerb, it usually isn't long before someone writes about it on social media, alerting others to the incident and where the person has been seen. Of course there are also concerted campaigns online that keenly advertise when someone's next public appearance will be, but that's another story.

Jesus didn't live in our instant world – but everyone seemed to know where he was. He was followed to the lakeside, where so many people came to him in need and want that he had to take practical measures to create a space where God's word could be heard and God's Spirit could work.

Although he was surrounded by people, and by influences from the spiritual realm, it is very clear here that Jesus is in control. Crowds are powerful and it is very easy to get swept up in a surge of emotion. In this situation, however, even the impure spirits give way to Jesus' instructions. He stands out from the crowd, and does not let himself be overpowered by influences and demands.

† God, when I feel overwhelmed and yearn for space and peace, may your Spirit speak calm into my crowded life.

For further thought
• Where do you find calm and space and what do you do to protect those times of quiet?

Tuesday 20 January
A crowded house

Mark 3:13-30

Then Jesus entered a house, and again a crowd gathered, so that he and his disciples were not even able to eat. When his family heard about this, they went to take charge of him, for they said, 'He is out of his mind.'
(verses 20-21)

English comedian Harry Enfield once created a comedy character called Kevin the Teenager who sulked, slammed doors and generally felt that life was unfair and that his parents didn't understand him.

I would never compare Jesus to a spotty teenager, but today we find him in a situation where he is in conflict with not just the teachers of the law but also his family. The family seems to be acting in a spirit of concern, for there are people all around Jesus, even inside the house as he tries to eat a meal. But they are misguided – he has not lost his mind. The teachers of the law also cannot see the truth of the situation: in their opinion, Jesus is possessed by the devil! Jesus has to challenge their misunderstandings firmly.

Much confusion can arise around what Jesus means by 'blaspheming against the Holy Spirit'. In her commentary *The Gospel According to St Mark* (A&C Black, 1991), Morna Hooker writes that this suggests 'the deliberate refusal to acknowledge the activity of God's Spirit in Jesus' ministry ... this forms a permanent obstacle between God and man'.

No one is beyond the reach of God's love; however, these verses seem to suggest that it is easy to put up our own barriers that totally prevent us from recognising God at work. Before we jump to conclusions, let's listen for the whisper of the Spirit, who will lead us into all truth.

† Holy Spirit, dismantle the barriers that I may put up in my life and help me to recognise where you are at work.

For further thought
• Where is the Holy Spirit at work in your community?

Wednesday 21 January
Happy families?

Mark 3:31-35

Whoever does God's will is my brother and sister and mother. (verse 35)

My grandmother was born in 1920 and grew up in a very large family in Bristol. As she was the youngest of 14 children, some of her older siblings had left home by the time she was a toddler. But there was still that sense of being a tightly-knit family even if they did not all share one house.

Family life was extremely important in Jesus' time, too. It was normal for generations to share houses, agriculture and businesses. Family loyalty was also considered a must. As theologian Tom Wright comments in *Mark for Everyone* (SPCK, 2001): 'For Jews, the close family bond was part of the God-given fabric of thinking and living. Loyalty to the family was part of the specific outworking of loyalty to Israel as the people of God.'

But again, Jesus challenges what is seen as the norm. 'Whoever does God's will is my brother and sister and mother,' he tells the crowd, implying that to be in God's family is more important than any other blood ties. I wonder how his family might have felt at this pronouncement. Shocked, upset, confused? This is one of those moments when a hidden camera could prove invaluable!

This reading is not a call to denounce our families, however, but rather to explore the idea that, whatever our relationships are like with our parents, our siblings, our grandparents and our friends, we are challenged to put our relationship with Jesus at the heart of all these connections.

† God, help me value my family and friends and bring healing to any relationships that are currently difficult.

For further thought

- 'You don't choose your family. They are God's gift to you, as you are to them' (Archbishop Desmond Tutu, 1986, Address at his enthronement as Anglican archbishop of Cape Town, 7 September 1986, Wikiquote: www.wikiquote.org).

Thursday 22 January
Only the seeds

Mark 4:1-20

Then Jesus said, 'Whoever has ears to hear, let them hear.' (verse 9)

There is a story of a pilgrim who set off on a journey to look for peace, joy and love. He started his journey feeling positive and optimistic but, as he walked, he saw many negative things: war, famine, arguments and greed. He started to despair that he would never find the good things that he was looking for.

One morning he came to a little cottage by the side of the road. Something about this house attracted the pilgrim. It was as though it was lit up from the inside. He went inside and found it was actually a little shop, with a wise old woman at the counter.

'What would you like?' she asked. 'What do you stock?' asked the pilgrim.

'All the things you most long for,' the woman replied. 'Just tell me what you desire.'

The man hardly knew where to begin. 'I want peace – in my own family, in my native land and in the whole world. I want to make something good of my life. I want those who are sick to be well again and those who are lonely to have friends. I want those who are hungry to have enough to eat and everyone on earth to live in freedom.'

There was a pause, as the shopkeeper reviewed the list.

'I'm sorry,' she replied quietly. 'We don't supply the fruits here. We only supply the seeds.'

(Traditional tale, abridged from Margaret Silf, *One Hundred Wisdom Stories from Around the World*, Lion, 2003)

† God, show me where I can plant seeds of hope, joy and peace today.

For further thought
• Grow some wildflowers from seed and give them away!

Friday 23 January
This little light of mine

Mark 4:21-34

[Jesus] said to them, 'Do you bring in a lamp to put it under a bowl or a bed? Instead, don't you put it on its stand? For whatever is hidden is meant to be disclosed, and whatever is concealed is meant to be brought out into the open.' (verses 21-22)

There is an old proverb that goes something like this: 'If you don't think something small can be effective, you've never been in bed with a mosquito!'

When we consider the size of the world, the billions of people who live in it, and the massive concerns and needs that the planet faces, it is easy to feel as small as a mustard seed. Who am I that I should matter and what can I offer in this huge expanse? How can I shine like a lamp on a stand when sometimes I feel that my own small candle of faith is nothing but a flickering stub?

I have always been inspired by a well-known quote from spiritual activist, author, lecturer and founder of the Peace Alliance, Marianne Williamson.

Our deepest fear is not that we are inadequate. Our deepest fear is that we are powerful beyond measure. It is our light, not our darkness that most frightens us. We ask ourselves, Who am I to be brilliant, gorgeous, talented, and fabulous? Actually, who are you not to be? (from *A Return to Love*, Thorsons, 1996).

She goes on to say that our playing small does not offer anything positive, because we are meant to shine, not shrink back. As we shine we glorify God and it is possible for anyone to do this, not just the chosen few. And as we let our own light shine, permission is given to others to shine too.

† I do not always feel able or willing to shine but, God, help me to make a difference in any small way I can.

For further thought

- The quotation in the notes above is often wrongly attributed to Nelson Mandela. Why do you think that is?

Saturday 24 January
Calming the storm

Mark 4:35-41

*[Jesus] got up, rebuked the wind and said to the waves, 'Quiet! Be still!'
Then the wind died down and it was completely calm.* (verse 39)

A few years ago I was able to visit Israel and Palestine as part of a study tour. The trip provided many unforgettable and challenging experiences. After the intensity of Jerusalem, our group was glad to head out for a few days beside Galilee.

Part of the tour included a boat trip around the lake and it certainly provided a 'wow' moment as we listened to words from the Bible and prayed, all the time thinking, 'Jesus was here!' And the lake was perfectly calm...

My only experience of a storm at sea has been a particularly bumpy ferry crossing from Dover to Calais. Jesus' boat was much smaller and the disciples were definitely more frightened. They had left the hubbub of the crowd behind but now had to face the danger of the storm.

Put yourself in the place of one of the disciples. How do you think you would have reacted? Would you have been sitting calmly or having a bit of a panic? Would you have woken Jesus or would you have taken matters into your own hands?

Again, Jesus demonstrates his authority and, on waking, immediately calms the storm. In their panic, the disciples are still struggling to understand who Jesus is and what he can do. It's another step on their journey of faith and there will be many more steps to come.

† Jesus, when I feel as if I am in the middle of a storm at sea, calm my fears and
direct me back to dry land with a sense of faith, not fear.

For further thought
• What helps you pray when problems and storms hit your life?

IBRA ebooks

Would you prefer to use Bible reading notes on their eReader or computer?

Fresh From the Word 2015 is available as Kindle, ePub and PDF files.

Priced at £7.20 inc VAT they can be purchased from our website: shop.christianeducation.org.uk

Please contact the IBRA office for more details:

International Bible
Reading Association
1020 Bristol Road, Selly Oak,
Birmingham B29 6LB

0121 472 4242

sales@christianeducation.org.uk

Join our online community!

Did you know that we are now on Twitter and Facebook?

For real-time updates on Bible reading, news and views from the Christian community, and to get involved and share your thoughts on *Fresh From the Word* 'Like' us on Facebook and 'Follow' us on Twitter:

www.facebook.com/freshfromtheword

www.facebook.com/internationalbiblereadingassociation

www.twitter.com/IBRAbibleread

We also have some very exciting news: we will be launching our brand new IBRA website very soon, so join our online community to keep up to date with announcements of when this will be going live.

25

History of IBRA and the International Fund

The International Bible Reading Association (IBRA) was founded by the Sunday School Union (SSU) committee under Charles Waters in 1882. At the time Waters was the manager of a bank in King's Cross. As a devout young man and Sunday school teacher, Waters had arrived in London in 1859 to further his career and had encountered the brilliant and inspirational teaching of Charles Spurgeon. He threw himself heart and soul in to working with Spurgeon and the Sunday School Union. In 1882 the SSU wrote to all members in Britain and overseas inviting them to join the newly formed International Bible Reading Association, circulating lists of daily Bible readings, supported by brief commentary notes.

The response was amazing. Readers appreciated that each day they were provided with a portion of scripture that was thoughtfully brief, selected with the utmost care to link to the week's topic. There was a living personal touch which was seemingly the secret of its success.

Charles Waters at his desk

By 1910 the readership had exceeded a million people and was touching the lives of soldiers fighting wars, sailors on long voyages to Australia, colliers in the coal mines of Wales, schools in Canada, Jamaica and Belfast, prisoners in Chicago – people all over the world, alone or in groups, felt comforted and encouraged by the idea of joining other Christians throughout the world in reading the same Bible passages. And they still do!

Today, over 130 years later, this rich history lives on, touching the lives of hundreds of thousands of people across the world. IBRA is now part of the Birmingham-based charity Christian Education and is working to continue the legacy, providing support to our global community of IBRA readers. Our aim is still to enable Christians from different parts of the world to grow in knowledge and appreciation of each other's experience of God through our international contributors and writers.

The original mission continues today and on in to the future!

Readings in 2 Samuel
1 David becomes king of Judah and Israel

This week's notes are by **John Holder**

John Holder is Archbishop of the Anglican Province of the West Indies. John was born in Barbados. He also studied for ministry in Barbados and, later, taught Old Testament in theological college there. He contributed to *The Africana Bible* (Fortress, 2010) and to many other publications. He and his wife Betty have one son.

Sunday 25 January
Lamenting the loss

2 Samuel 1:11-12, 17-27

Then David and all the men with him took hold of their clothes and tore them. They mourned and wept and fasted till evening for Saul and his son Jonathan, and for the army of the LORD and for the nation of Israel, because they had fallen by the sword. (verses 11 and 12)

The passages for this week's reflections are from a collection of stories about conflict and pain, loss and gain during David's rise from an insignificant shepherd to the glories of kingship. The writers of the stories go all out to convince the readers that David was the legitimate heir of all he acquired. They shaped David into the perfect successor to Saul. They heaped upon him some outstanding leadership qualities.

In the passage today, David enters into deep mourning for his king and his prince, who is his best friend. He rises above the animosity of his relationship with Saul and does the honourable godly thing. There is compassion and forgiveness all wrapped up in the agony of loss.

How is a good and gracious God related to the chaos that accompanied the establishment of the monarchy in Israel? It was a question in the minds of the writers we are reading this week, and it is a question for us, too. How do we fit God into our stories of conflict and pain, of loss and gain? The writers assure us that we can. They remind us that God works with us and through us to bring good out of conflict, pain and loss.

† O ever-present God, in times of conflict, pain and loss, grant us your grace to meet the challenges of life with courage, faith and hope.

Monday 26 January
The long and winding road

2 Samuel 2:1-11

He sent messengers to the people of Jabesh Gilead to say to them, 'The LORD bless you for showing this kindness to Saul your master by burying him. May the LORD now show you kindness and faithfulness, and I too will show you the same favour because you have done this. (verses 5 and 6)

The stories that tell of David's rise to kingship teach us that God gives us plenty of space to carve out our path through the world, and asks for our patience. The writers believed that David was in a special relationship with God, but this did not shield him from the trauma and the frustrations of life.

Our passage today continues to reflect on David's painstaking climb to power. It portrays David as a goodly upright person who deserves to be king. He is a good and responsible family man (verse 3). He continues to extend a hand of compassion to those who were close to Saul. He is patient with those who are grieving the loss of Saul: 'Now may the Lord show you true kindness! I also will reward you, because you have done this deed,' he says to the men from Jabesh Gilead (verse 6).

Should not the house of Israel do the same? It does not happen immediately, and David is prepared to wait. David allows Saul's son Ishbosheth to have his time in the sun. David's willingness not to rush in and crush Ishbosheth and take from him what he believed was his reflects the great virtue of patience that is an absolute necessity at all levels of leadership.

† O God, when we are in a mad rush to put it all right in a hurry, grant us patience to take that one step at a time when it is necessary to do so.

For further thought

• How strong is the virtue of patience in your life?

Tuesday 27 January
Reaching the top

2 Samuel 5:1-12

When all the elders of Israel had come to King David at Hebron, the king made a covenant with them at Hebron before the LORD, and they anointed David king over Israel. (verse 3)

It has happened. The long road from 1 Samuel 16 has reached its goal. David has acquired that which the writers claim is his divine gift, the kingship over all Israel. But there are still some obstacles in the way. There is Jerusalem and the Jebusites. The conquest of Jerusalem begins a relationship between David and the city that sets in motion a wave of traditions and theology about the City of David that dominate the Old Testament and spill over into the New Testament.

The traditions around Jerusalem are second only to the tradition of the Messiah. Indeed the two were merged along the way. Jerusalem was David's city, as the Messiah became the descendant of David. The city became closely linked to leadership and security. These two everyday experiences were held together and made into the cornerstone of the faith of the Old Testament community.

In our own context, we are led to reflect on how we connect God's presence to the everyday things that are critical for our survival. Do we find it easy to connect God to food and shelter, to clothing and all the many things that we need to survive in this world?

† O God, who supplies our every need, help us to be thankful for all your goodness.

For further thought

• How can you make your community one of peace for all?

Wednesday 28 January
Focusing on God

2 Samuel 6:1-5, 11-23

Wearing a linen ephod, David was dancing before the LORD with all his might, while he and all Israel were bringing up the ark of the LORD with shouts and the sound of trumpets. (verses 14 and 15)

David has shown great patience and a great level of magnanimity towards the house of Saul. Having captured Jerusalem he moves to make the city not only his military capital but his religious one as well. The story in our reading today is a continuation of the story in 1 Samuel chapters 4 to 6. The latter tells of the loss of the ark to the Philistines, while 2 Samuel 6 tells of its return in triumph to Jerusalem. It is not smooth sailing. There is the death of Uzzah, the angry response of David, and the abandoning of the project itself.

And things between Michal and David are not perfect, either. She is identified as 'the daughter of Saul' (verse 16) drawing back into the picture the failures associated with Saul. Matters descend into a name-calling, finger-pointing family squabble. In spite of the negatives, the ark's presence can generate blessings, as in verse 12. It is with this understanding that it moves into Jerusalem with great celebrations. The success of the venture bestows upon David the two great qualities of commitment to complete what he started, in spite of the setbacks, and the courage to defend his decision to restore the ark to central place in Israel's worship.

How do you cope with the setbacks in your life? Do you have the courage of David to persist in following the path that you are convinced God wants you to follow?

† O God, give us the courage to persist along the Christian way in spite of the setbacks that we may encounter

For further thought

• How do you find the strength to persist in the face of criticism, even from within your own family?

Thursday 29 January
David's special status

2 Samuel 7:1-17

The LORD declares to you that the LORD himself will establish a house for you: when your days are over and you rest with your ancestors, I will raise up your offspring to succeed you, your own flesh and blood, and I will establish his kingdom. He is the one who will build a house for my Name, and I will establish the throne of his kingdom for ever. (part of verses 11-13)

The building of the Temple would have been the crowning of all David's achievements. Why didn't God allow him to build it? The answer is that God instructed David not to do so, but to leave it for his successor (verse 13). The chapter, however, is about far more than a search for an answer to why David did not build the Temple. It reflects a conviction that runs throughout the Old Testament and into the New. It states that there was an extra-special relationship between God and David. Against a background of being landless, and a memory of slavery, David – who secured the land and carved out a country and secured freedom – is accorded a status like no other.

Another dimension to David's success is introduced in 2 Samuel 7: a special covenant relationship – and all David's success and power are viewed through the lens of responsibility.

His power comes with great covenantal responsibility attached. It is not a tool to be used to oppress and exploit. David, in spite of all the glorious and great things attached to him, is to be assessed within the context of covenantal responsibility.

That even David is placed within these restrictions indicates how seriously the Old Testament treats the link between leadership and responsibility. No matter how close we or others think we are to God, we are never excused from responsible behaviour.

Christianity embraces this understanding of leadership. It is one that every Christian should reflect in his or her life. If power is a necessary ingredient of life, it is never to be detached from responsibility.

† Lord, help me to use any power that is available to me, in a responsible and compassionate way.

For further thought
• Jesus of Nazareth is described in the New Testament as the son of David and heir to David's covenant. Was Jesus a powerful person? If so, how?

Friday 30 January
More accolades

2 Samuel 9:1-13

'Don't be afraid,' David said to [Mephibosheth], *'for I will surely show you kindness for the sake of your father Jonathan. I will restore to you all the land that belonged to your grandfather Saul, and you will always eat at my table.* (verse 7)

The positive presentation of David that reached a high point in yesterday's readings continues in today's. He is now the one who has been drawn into a special relationship with God. His actions in chapter 9 reflect this special status.

We have already read of his kindness to the house of Saul, especially to his children. He now engages in a search to ensure that all Saul's relatives are cared for. David invites Mephibosheth to be a regular guest at his table. He is depicted here as the ideal king, accorded some of the qualities that should be present in the life of one called to lead.

And they are qualities that should be present in the life of one who follows that way of God. David's actions relate well to the call made by Jesus many centuries later to love our enemies and to pray for those who persecute us (Matthew 5:44).

The writers of today's passage point out the heavy responsibility of leadership. They demand that we deal with friend and foe in a manner that reflects our experiences of God's goodness and compassion. They hold up to the world the great virtue of forgiveness, cutting through all the pomp and pretence and leading us to share the love of God with those who offend us.

† O God, grant us grace to share your love, especially with those who may offend us.

For further thought
• Is there power in forgiveness, or is it giving in?

Saturday 31 January
Election and vulnerability

Samuel 10:1-14

Hanun seized David's envoys, shaved off half of each man's beard, cut off their garments at the buttocks, and then sent them away. (verse 4)

On the journey from 1 Samuel 16 to 2 Samuel 9, things have worked in David's favour. He has grown in stature and displayed the great qualities of leadership. He stands tall among his people. God draws him into a special covenantal relationship.

He starts in verses 1-2 with all the positives he has gathered along the way still intact. The humiliation of his solders at the hands of the Ammonite king Hanun, however, changes the tone of the story. This is a setback to what so far is David's impenetrable stature as follower of Yahweh, and a king. In a very subtle manner, the writers are reminding us that, in spite of his special relationship with God, David remains mortal, frail and vulnerable. His vulnerability is taken to the extreme in the chapters that follow, the so-called Succession Narrative.

The story of David reflects on faith in God as it relates to human vulnerability. It is never easy to relate God to our most vulnerable moments in life. We often hope and pray that God would shield us from these times. Our faith in Jesus, however, assures us that at our most vulnerable moments God is still present and available.

† Be with us, O Lord, at the most vulnerable moments in life.

For further thought
• Share with Jesus where you feel vulnerable, and listen to what he has to say.

Readings in 2 Samuel
2 The tragedy of David

This week's notes are by **Deseta Davis**

Deseta Davis serves as an associate Pastor of a Pentecostal church. She currently works as a tutor in the Centre for Black Ministries and Leadership at the Queen's Foundation in Birmingham, where she is able to bring the study of theology to a range of people who may never have considered such study. She also works very closely with the prison chaplaincy team, helping to bring hope to those that are incarcerated. Married to Charles, Deseta has two grown-up children and a beautiful granddaughter.

Sunday 1 February
Decisions, decisions, decisions

2 Samuel 11:1-13

Uriah said to David, 'my commander Joab and my lord's men are camped in the open country. How could I go to my house to eat and drink and make love to my wife? As surely as you live, I will not do such a thing! (verse 11)

This week we move to a very dark period in King David's life. We see how a poor decision caused David's actions to cascade out of control. His initial decision led to other poor decisions and, in an attempt to cover up his actions, he destroyed many lives, including that of his son.

Uriah, on the other hand, made an honourable decision that also had major consequences. He decided to remain loyal to the king and his army, a resolve that ultimately cost him his life.

David being the 'all-powerful' king made decisions that affected the lives of his subjects. When David called Bathsheba to him how could she refuse the king? In the same way he calls Uriah, who has no choice but to leave the war efforts and meet with the king.

Since time immemorial people have tried to cover up their wrongs – David the king was no different. This narrative shows us how decisions can affect not only our own lives but the lives of others also. Whether for good or bad, the effects of these decisions can live on for many years.

† Gracious God, be with us in our decision-making and help us to accept the consequences of our actions.

Monday 2 February
Jehovah has the final say!

2 Samuel 11:14-27

But the thing David had done displeased the LORD. (part of verse 27)

An African chorus we sing at church asks the question: 'Who has the final say?' The response comes back: 'Jehovah has the final say!' Sometimes the good decisions we make cost us dearly. Uriah decides to be loyal to the king and the army, and ends up carrying his own death warrant.

David sinks to an all-time low and hatches his plot to kill Uriah. He instructs Joab, the commander of the army, to put him on the front lines where the battle is fiercest. There is no word that Joab asks why Uriah should be killed. Again (as did Bathsheba), Joab follows the powerful king's command and has Uriah killed along with many other Israelite soldiers. David is now 'off the hook'. 'Don't be discouraged,' he says to Joab, 'many are lost in battle!'

David, the powerful king, marries Uriah's widow, Bathsheba. She has a baby son and David can now live in freedom. He has got away with it; or so he thought!

'But the thing David had done displeased the Lord.' God has a way of defending the powerless, even when the powerful seem in control. God always has the final say!

I am sometimes amazed that narratives like this are in the Bible. The great respected patriarch, the apple of God's eye, commits such great sins. It is broadcast to one and all. A public display! What is God saying? Maybe God is telling us that, though we fall, we are not utterly cast down – yet we shall rise (Psalm 37:24).

† Loving God, help us to forgive ourselves when we have done wrong, just as you have forgiven us.

For further thought
• Have you ever tried to cover up your wrong? How can or did you make right?

Tuesday 3 February
You are the man!

2 Samuel 12:1-14

Then Nathan said to David, 'You are the man!' (part of verse 7)

How the tables have turned! Uriah carries his death warrant and David pronounces his own sentence – death and a fourfold restitution.

My culture has an oral tradition – we have many sayings and proverbs, similar to the parables of Jesus. We tell stories that have hidden or different meanings. Some of the most popular stories are about Anansi, the spider-man who tricks everyone to get his own way. Nathan the prophet reminds me of Anansi. He spins the story and allows David to pronounce his own sentence.

This also reminds me of the slaves who would use 'trickery' to trick their masters. The use of songs, stories, codes and spirituals enabled the slaves to speak to each other without their masters knowing what was happening in the background. They were able to plan and arrange events without the masters' knowledge. The masters could have killed the slaves if they found out, just as David could have killed Nathan. Many a king has killed the prophets who have not spoken to the king's delight.

David, however, after condemning himself to death, accepted Nathan's verdict, humbly admitted the fact that he had sinned and took the consequences. It is not easy for the rich and powerful to accept judgement from those that are their subjects or out of their 'class'. It sometimes takes the oppressed and marginalised to stand together and 'trick' the powerful into a fourfold restitution.

† God of justice, fill us with humility to accept the truth – even when it hurts and comes from a person or place that we do not expect.

For further thought

• Name some of the ways you could speak to someone who has done wrong. Reflect on how this could be done with empathy and humility.

The innocent suffer for the guilty

2 Samuel 12:15-25

David noticed that his attendants were whispering among themselves, and he realised the child was dead. 'Is the child dead?' he asked. 'Yes,' they replied, 'he is dead.' (verse 19)

When a child is critically ill or dies, people ask why a loving God would allow a baby to die who has never done any wrong. Many have attempted to answer this difficult question in various ways. I do not purport to know the answer but I am comforted by Jesus' reply after meeting a man who was born blind. When asked: 'Who has sinned?' and 'Why was the man was born blind?' Jesus responded, 'neither this man nor his parents sinned ... this happened so that the works of God might be displayed in him' (John 9:2-3).

In today's text David did not ask why; he accepted the prophecy of punishment from Nathan that the child would die. Due to David's sin the family was now permanently in the presence of death. In one area of the palace the child lies sick, in another area the king lies prostrate on the ground (replicating Uriah who refused to go home and instead spent the night lying on the ground with the palace guards). He weeps, prays and fasts, seeking the grace of God for the child. The innocent child ultimately dies.

Today many innocent suffer and die due to the acts of the guilty. The real injustice is that many times the guilty do not acknowledge the suffering of the innocent as they continue to die through no fault of their own.

We may not know why God allows the innocent to die, but we do know that *we* are God's hands and feet for those who are suffering because of the sins of others.

† God of grace, help us to look at ourselves and how our actions affect others.

For further thought

• Take some time to reflect on society and those who are suffering though innocent. What can you do to stand against these injustices?

Thursday 5 February
The accused

2 Samuel 13:1-19

Tamar put ashes on her head and tore the ornate robe she was wearing. She put her hands on her head and went away, weeping aloud as she went. (verse 19)

The Accused is a film in which a woman was horrifically raped and, after reporting it to the police, she had to fight everyone, including her lawyer, to receive justice. She, like Tamar, was blamed for the crime that was committed against her. The difference is that she wanted her story heard, she wanted justice and fought for it, whereas Tamar, like many women in today's society, did not speak about it. She left weeping but nothing else was said or done.

Tamar was the faceless, voiceless victim of Amnon. He was blind to her face and deaf to her cries. The story reflects the continuing act of the powerful against the weak. Tamar, a young virgin woman of Israel, was the king's daughter who should have trusted her family to keep her safe, but it was at the hands of her stepbrother that she eventually fell. She was deemed the guilty party.

How many women in today's world are begging and crying to be heard – not to be abused, but to be treated with respect? How does society deal with rape and domestic abuse? Why is it that many women do not feel they can report these crimes? Could it be that too many times the victim is blamed?

The writer of Samuel puts this story as one of the consequences of David's sin with Uriah and Bathsheba, but does it seem right that Tamar should also suffer the consequences of her father? Nathan prophesied that David's family would bear the impact. After the death of his son, David's family continues to be dysfunctional.

† Loving God, may we hear the cries of the many women who are being, or have been, abused. Please be their comfort and give us the sensitivity to help in their time of need.

For further thought
• What is God saying to you through this story?

Friday 6 February
The sword shall never depart from your house

2 Samuel 13:20-39

Her brother Absalom said to her, 'Has that Amnon, your brother, been with you? Be quiet for now, my sister; he is your brother. Don't take this thing to heart.' And Tamar lived in her brother Absalom's house, a desolate woman. When King David heard all this, he was furious. (verses 20-21)

The lack of information given regarding Tamar's feelings about being raped by Amnon, her abandonment in her brother's house, not knowing whether she will ever be vindicated, shows how unimportant her thoughts and feelings were considered to be in the eyes of the writer. Written from a man's point of view, Tamar has no say and, even when she is violated, she is told to hold her peace, seemingly dismissing her rape as unimportant. She is even told by Absalom not to take it to heart because Amnon is her brother. All this before she completely disappears off the scene.

How many people are told and expected to hold their peace when wrongs are taking place. David the king says nothing and does nothing, showing only anger. He cannot be excused for his silence. The narrative knows that David himself is compromised by his own past action; could this be the reason he says nothing? Again the powerful person ignores the plight of the powerless.

There is a saying in African Caribbean culture: 'Two wrongs do not make a right.' Absalom bides his time; his hatred of Amnon continues to grow. Ultimately, Absalom kills his brother because of the rape of his sister, but it does not help Tamar. She is still an outcast. David still does not condemn the wrong Amnon has done. David weeps for Amnon, just as Tamar weeps for the crime against her, but David does not weep for Tamar. Her crime goes unacknowledged and yet another murder is committed in David's household.

† Dear God, help us not to keep silent in the face of wrong. Give us courage and the conviction of our faith. May we also learn to forgive those who have wronged us.

For further thought
• Rewrite the story through the eyes of Tamar.

Saturday 7 February
God brings the outcasts home

2 Samuel 14:1-14, 21-24

*Like water spilled on the ground, which cannot be recovered, so we must
die. But that is not what God desires; rather, he devises ways so that a
banished person does not remain banished from him.* (verse 14)

Today's text feels like history repeating itself. Once again David
makes a judgement about others that has repercussions on himself.
The wise woman spins the story as Nathan the prophet did, and
again David hears the cry of one in need, which turns out to be
a pronouncement on himself. Eventually, David decides to bring
Absalom back, with strict instructions that Absalom will not see the
king's face. Absalom is still excommunicated, living in exile within
the land.

As a prison chaplain I see many people who, after serving their
sentences, are treated as outcasts when they return to society.
I have known some families that would not forgive their son or
daughter for the crime they committed. The family has turned
its back on them. Without support, some ex-prisoners will never
become acceptable members of the community and others are
forced to reoffend, ending back again as outcasts in the prison
system. Society can be quick to judge and slow to forgive.

Like David, we may not want to accept ex-prisoners or even see
them, but God brings them home, God finds a way for them not
to remain estranged from him. I have seen how many in prison
receive hope, how they turn to God in their confinement and
their lives are turned around. Even though society continues to
excommunicate them, there are those that resist the pressure and
become useful citizens.

May we remember the words of John Bradford (1510–1555) as he
watched criminals being led to their execution: 'There, but for the
grace of God, go I.'

† Pray for those who are outcasts in society, that they may be accepted. Ask God to
 bring comfort to the victims of those in prison and also bring hope, forgiveness
 and peace to the prisoners.

For further thought
• Many prisoners do not have visitors. Have you ever thought
 about becoming a prison visitor? Check online to see how
 to apply.

Readings in 2 Samuel
3 The enemies of David

This week's notes are by **Nathan Eddy**

Nathan is editor of *Fresh from the Word*. His poetry and prose have appeared in magazines and scripture commentaries and he has worked as a journalist near Boston, USA and as a United Reformed Church minister and university chaplain in England. Nathan has spent a year living in monasteries in Ghana, Israel, Egypt, India, China and Japan, and he is an enthusiastic student of the Hebrew Bible, or Old Testament. He aspires to being the consummate breakfast cook for his wife Clare and two young daughters and is happiest getting lost on a bicycle.

Sunday 8 February
The Chosen One under threat

2 Samuel 15:1-14

Whenever anyone approached him to bow down before him, Absalom would reach out his hand, take hold of him and kiss him. (verse 5)

David has been called the first fully-formed character in world literature, and surely his story must be one of the greatest. The characters here in the story of Absalom's rebellion might at first seem pantomime in their vanity (Absalom) and piety (David). But a closer reading reveals political intrigue worthy of Shakespeare and a story of death and grief that (perhaps more than any other in scripture) has a force approaching the story of Jesus' death.

The smaller characters are surprisingly fully drawn: Ahithophel, who bargained everything and lost, and whom we meet today in verse 12, and Joab, the loyal general (or is he?). But it is David who enduringly fascinates. This Messiah King was a parent and a spouse (not always a model one) who, like Mary in the New Testament, knew the sword-like pain of losing a child. In David's brokenness and restoration I see Jesus' story, and all humanity's story, playing out in an often troubling world before an inscrutable but ultimately redemptive God.

The story begins with the kiss of betrayal by the rebel son as he curries favour with the people in the city gate. Shouldn't David be in the gate himself? Would Absalom be a better king after all?

† God of peace, in city gates and halls of power this week, respond to people in need.

Monday 9 February
On the run

2 Samuel 15:23-37

...let [God] do to me whatever seems good to him. (part of verse 26)

The image is cinematic in quality: their faces set towards the wilderness, the beloved city behind them; the priest Zadok and the Levites offer sacrifices by the ark of the covenant while the inhabitants stream out of the city gates, now refugees.

David, the anointed one, is one of the homeless. Once he led armies to victory from this city; now he leads a rag-tag band of followers without knowing even where he will spend the night. Jerusalem, the city of David, the city he conquered and built, the city in which God promised him and his descendants eternal rule, is behind him. Before him is only wilderness – the place of testing, where no one can make a home. The ark, the symbol of God's inviolable presence in the tabernacle, is on the run with them, borne by fragile human hands.

Wily David has met his match. Another canny survivor, Jacob, went on the run with his family and met his match in the wilderness at the Jabbok river (Genesis 32). David, too, is struggling with God. Will he survive? Will Israel? David's response is to send the ark back into the city, as if he doesn't need the protection. He is at God's mercy. But just when he is at his lowest ebb, climbing the Mount of Olives in tears, he finds his wits have not deserted him. A loyal follower, Hushai the Arkite, is standing on the summit, ready to serve. David sends him as a spy into Absalom's court to thwart Ahithophel's counsel. David offers a prayer to God. Will God listen?

† God of Jacob and David, Sarah and Hannah, give your blessing to those who struggle for it.

For further thought
• This is the first mention in the Bible of the Mount of Olives. What other Bible stories mention it?

Tuesday 10 February
Blessed and cursed

2 Samuel 16:1-14

Get out, get out, you murderer, you scoundrel! … You have come to ruin because you are a murderer! (part of verses 7 and 8)

In December 2013 the biggest tidal surge in 60 years overwhelmed the Norfolk and Suffolk coasts of England, near where I live. Overnight the coast was transformed. Dunes moved, grassy banks disappeared, beach parking lots and shelters were buried, and hundreds of people and businesses were flooded out by the powerful waters. In Lowestoft the basement of the only homeless shelter filled with water, destroying the only possessions of its residents.

David is at the centre of a storm of sorts. He is no longer in control – of people, of events, of the public, of his own kin. His defences have failed. Even a man watching the king flee Jerusalem can pelt him with stones and dirt and curse him and avoid punishment. We are a long way from the confident David who outwitted Saul or wrangled promises out of God after Nathan's revelation of God's unconditional love for him. It has taken David his whole life, and great crisis, to reach this point of humility, but he has reached it with a certain poise. It may be that God will restore his covenant blessing, David says graciously in verse 12.

David is strangely at peace at the centre of this storm. God chose David out of gratuitous love, not out of any hidden motive. Perhaps coming to the brink of losing everything has shown David this gift, at least, even though the landscape of his life has completely changed. Not even Shimei, or the chaotic power of the sea, can threaten that knowledge – although everything else, including his own children, may be taken away.

† God of life, hold back the waters that threaten so that your creation may pass through.

For further thought
• Why did God give David his covenant blessing in the first place? To remember happier times, have a look again at 2 Samuel 7 or 29 January.

Wednesday 11 February
Sex and the city

2 Samuel 16:15-23

So they pitched a tent for Absalom on the roof, and he slept with his father's concubines in the sight of all Israel. (verse 22)

One of the many quips attributed to British wit Oscar Wilde is 'Everything in the world is about sex except sex. Sex is about power.' Just ask David's palace women, who are the human face of Absalom's grab for control. Absalom and his court have entered David's city and occupied his house. Ahithophel shrewdly advises the ruthless next step, and Absalom obliges – showing Israel that Absalom now stands in David's role.

The story recounts Absalom's brute actions with little sentimentality. Do you think the storyteller takes the plight of women like these concubines as a matter of course? They are cynically invoked again by Joab, a man as ruthless as Absalom, in his confrontational rant at David after Absalom's death. Or does their wordless presence alone challenge the politics of Absalom and David before him? These women, and Shimei and Ahithophel, seem like nobodies in comparison to Absalom and David. But they offer another version of events – a personal story – that upsets the official royal story. We will watch this alternative story derail the official one in David's heart, too. Like the palace women, Jesus before Pilate was a wordless victim of political power games. Who is ultimately the more powerful, and how?

David's spy, Hushai the Arkite, has been accepted into Absalom's court. There are glimmers of hope in the advancing story, but Absalom and Ahithophel are consolidating power quickly, while David is wandering in the wilderness.

† God of the silent, speak your word of life in the place of death.

For further thought

- How has our world moved on in relation to sex and power since this story was written? Can you think of any contemporary versions of this story?

Thursday 12 February
The tide turns

2 Samuel 17:1-14

For the Lord *had determined to frustrate the good advice of Ahithophel in order to bring disaster on Absalom.* (part of verse 14)

In the first episode of the award-winning American dark comedy *Breaking Bad*, the main character, Walter, is given a cancer diagnosis: inoperable. Traumatised, his only response is to point out the mustard stain on the doctor's white lab coat. The way he responds to the crisis and remakes his life forms the central drama of the TV show.

Where is God in the haphazard messiness of life? We are told that God had determined to frustrate cunning Ahithophel's good advice. But why work in this way? Why not give Ahithophel bad advice in the first place instead of leaving David hanging in the balance? David's spy Hushai, by some lucky break, gives advice that is both attractive and completely wrong. Absalom goes for it – and events finally begin to turn David's way. Is God inept, or is God on the sidelines with us, as it were – watching, hoping, praying, guiding? Truly this king and all creation seem left (nearly) to their own devices. If this is the way God treats friends, one wonders how God treats enemies. Or perhaps God is not the problem-solver, the fixer-upper, that we desire.

When life falls apart, when the doctor utters what we most fear and the God we thought we knew so well turns out to be part fantasy, how will we respond? Will we wrestle a blessing out of the God of this brave new world? Walter the cancer patient decided to try. David will, too – but we'll have to wait to see how.

† God of Job, we know in our heads that our Redeemer lives; establish that knowledge, and that life itself, in our hearts.

For further thought

• Sometimes it's all we can do just to put one foot in front of the other. I know a former police officer who started going to church again in his 60s. 'Keep it moving,' he says, when the way forward isn't clear.

Friday 13 February
Beginning of the end

2 Samuel 17:15-29

[Ahithophel] saddled his donkey and set out for his house in his home town. He put his house in order and then hanged himself. (part of verse 23)

'Oh sit down, Oh sit down, Oh sit down, sit down next to me,' sings the pop group James. I dare you to sit down with Ahithophel in his little scene. His despair threatens to pull you under. It exerts a deathly tug on me, anyway. We first heard of Ahithophel on Sunday, when Absalom summons him from his hometown of Giloh. Today it's to that same home he returns. His advice rejected, he sees, correctly, the inevitable bloody end for Absalom and his court. He sees no options for his life, and he ends it, at home, alone.

In a sense, Ahithophel is a part of the collateral damage of Absalom's rebellion, just like the concubines who are to spend the rest of their lives locked away in a kind of death. Perhaps he had himself to blame, you'll say – he could have stayed loyal to David. I wonder how much choice he had when Absalom sent for him. At any rate he bargained, and lost. This tiny vignette is perhaps the closest the Bible gets to the awful inevitability of Greek or Shakespearean tragedy. I think of Judas in the New Testament, and shudder.

Did Ahithophel and Judas have a choice at the end after all? David started out as a nobody, a shepherd from the sticks. David was up against the odds time and time again, and prevailed. David had his options closed down but fought and prayed and pleaded, and came through. He was once where you were, Ahithophel. Ahithophel, O Ahithophel, there were options for you; there was life! There must have been another way. Rest in peace.

† God of the lost, show us a way home.

For further thought

- In 2 Samuel 23:34 a man named Ahithophel is listed as the father of Eliam, the father of Bathsheba (2 Samuel 11:3). Is it the same man? Is this David's past catching up with him?

Saturday 14 February
Behold the human being

2 Samuel 18:1-15

The king commanded Joab, Abishai and Ittai, 'Be gentle with the young man Absalom for my sake.' And all the troops heard the king giving orders concerning Absalom to each of the commanders. (**verse 5**)

David is once again the leader, rallying the troops and standing in the gate of the city as a king should. But the city is Manahaim, not Jerusalem, and it is beyond the Jordan, the boundary of Israel. This must be the end for David and his army if he faces defeat here.

But David the human being can no longer be hidden beneath the glossy coating of David the King. The personal story we glimpsed in the lives of the victims can no longer be silenced by the official story. Ignoring what would have been the better logic of war – the ruthlessness Absalom himself showed – David commands his soldiers to be gentle. 'I will do whatever seems best to you,' David says to his troops. What kind of king is this?

It takes Joab, that hardened person of war, to follow through on what David could not face: three javelins into the heart of the beloved son and erstwhile rebel, followed by abuse from Joab's henchmen. Absalom dies strung up in the tree. We seem a long way from the clarity we assume we have in the Bible. We are a long way from any kind of clarity at all in this nearly unbearable story. Instead we are sitting down with David at an awful moment in his broken life. And there is further to go with him yet. Will David the King rejoice in victory, or will David the father mourn his son and so protest harsh rule of the state?

† King of the universe, set our minds on the day when the wolf will lie down with the lamb, and make it our reality.

For further thought

• Was it right to kill Absalom? Share your views on our Facebook group today. facebook.com/freshfromtheword

Readings in 2 Samuel
4 David finally returns to Jerusalem

This week's notes are by **Nathan Eddy** (see page 41)

Sunday 15 February
Absalom, O Absalom!

2 Samuel 18:31 – 19:8

The king was shaken. He went up to the room over the gateway and wept.
(part of verse 33)

In 2013, my aunt died of cancer after a few years' illness, aged 60. Her death was a huge blow to her husband, her children, her sisters (including my mother) and her friends. My grandparents, too, both aged 90, had lost a daughter. I grew up hearing stories of my grandfather Roger dandling his middle daughter on his knee. Now she was gone for ever.

The Hebrew reflects David's moan of a cry at his son Absalom's death. It is almost animal-like. In a narrative with so much bloodshed, where women and children are often pawns between power-hungry men, let's pause at this portrait of a devoted, grieving parent. What's truly important in life? Is it really power and the throne?

We have all suffered and lost – perhaps those who have lost children more than most. In King David's moan I hear the cry of all who have suffered. I hear Mary weeping, and Martha and Mary mourning their dead brother Lazarus. I hear Jesus' cry, too. Jesus of Nazareth – Son of David, Son of Mary, Son of Man – is a king like David who understands human suffering, even the loss of a daughter.

† Risen Lord Jesus, show us the wounds in your hands and your side, and then share with us the life that can never be extinguished.

Monday 16 February
Returning home

2 Samuel 19:16-30

Should anyone be put to death in Israel today? Don't I know that today I am king over Israel? (verse 22)

Shimei's reconciliation with David closes an awful chapter in David's life. Shimei, remember, was the one who called David a murderer and heaped abuse on him. Here Shimei rushes to meet David – even crossing the Jordan to greet him. There is a measure of self-interest in Shimei's pleading, as David's return to the throne is clear. But David's response magnifies the graciousness he showed to Absalom. Shimei must live, even though he offended the Lord's anointed.

Sitting in Mahanaim, mourning his son, David was a broken king, barely holding it all together. Now David really and truly rises to the role of king, and human being – providing life, forgiving, and graciously receiving kindness. He is now a king who decisively chooses life for all he meets. Can we see Jesus' kingship in David's?

With Shimei come a thousand Benjaminites. What was once a weeping procession of refugees fleeing Jerusalem has become a royal procession of joy and reconciliation back to the city of peace. As I let this joyful procession play out in my mind's eye, I see another procession towards the city, with David at its head dancing wildly before the ark (2 Samuel 6). He was a much younger man then. Many years, great loss, and experiences of both joy and regret have intervened between then and now. His joints are stiffer now and his face bears a few more lines, but this mortal and fallible human being feels young again as he nears the Jordan and welcomes Shimei. He is once again God's anointed, the recipient of God's covenant blessing. He is going home.

† Lord Jesus, our lives are full of great joy and great loss, moments of redemption and regrets, too. Dance among us, O King! And lead us home.

For further thought
• Had Jesus lived a few more years on earth as David did, what would he have been like as an old man?

Tuesday 17 February
The kiss of life

2 Samuel 19:31-40

So all the people crossed the Jordan, and then the king crossed over. The king kissed Barzillai and bade him farewell, and Barzillai returned to his home. (verse 39)

Absalom cynically curried favour with the people with kisses; David here draws the story to a close with a kiss of life for Barzillai. His entry into his homeland is secure. He left a refugee but returns a gracious king, intent to provide for the least. It feels appropriate. Absalom's ruthless march to power ignored the weak and silenced the victims. David's joyful re-entry into Israel has been marked by his genuine listening to even the lowliest of his subjects. David shows that there is enough life and joy to go round. Barzillai returns to his home with a kiss of life from the king. Ahithophel returned to his home with the kiss of death.

Perhaps David's loss has opened his heart. His perspective has broadened and he is at ease with himself. He is a changed person, ready for a new chapter, ready for what God might have in store.

Reread the exchange between David and Barzillai. David invites Barzillai to 'cross over with me and stay with me' (verse 33); Barzillai declines, saying, in verse 35, 'Can I tell the difference between what is enjoyable and what is not? Can your servant taste what he eats and drinks?' The Old Testament, and King David in particular, focus our attention on the pleasure (and pain) of life here and now. So often in church we think about life after death; not so in David's company. So may you, too, hear David's invitation to enjoy to the full the years remaining to you. There is enough joy to go round with God's gracious king and God's people, who put the last first!

† Sovereign God, your kingdom come, your will be done, on earth as in heaven.

For further thought

• Imagine Jesus saying to you 'Stay with me in Jerusalem, and I will provide for you.' In your church, with people you love and who love you, savour the bread and wine that Jesus provides at his table.

Millennium goals

1 Eradicating extreme poverty and hunger

This week's notes are by **Malcolm Carroll**

 Malcolm works as an organiser for Greenpeace. He has a PhD in organisational studies. He's also a Baptist minister, having served in churches in Sheffield and Nottingham, and has been a hospital chaplain and a social responsibility officer in the Church of England. He lives in mid-Wales with his wife Becky, two children and other poultry. He enjoys outdoors stuff, classical music and is an Arsenal supporter. He has an organic allotment, which would be great but for the organic weeds.

Wednesday 18 February (Ash Wednesday)
Who is on the poor's side?

Matthew 25:31-45

Come, you who are blessed by my Father; take your inheritance, the kingdom prepared for you since the creation of the world. For I was hungry and you gave me something to eat, I was thirsty and you gave me something to drink. (part of verses 34-35)

One of the United Nations' Millennium goals is to eradicate extreme poverty and hunger. Huge challenges remain but we've gone some way towards this goal. But have we gone Jesus' way towards it?

I had arranged to meet the gypsies at their site to try to help prevent their eviction. I'd got to know these people and was burning with injustice on their behalf: a group of the most marginalised people I'd met. And half of them weren't there. They'd seen news of poverty elsewhere, had collected clothes and supplies and taken a lorry-load to Romania. One of the drivers came back without his shoes, he felt someone there had more need.

The poor and oppressed feature in every sort of literature in the Old Testament. From the outset, the God of righteousness and justice opposes poverty and oppression. Charity is not enough. It reinforces unjust structures and demeans the poor. Jesus' way is one of justice and compassion. He identifies himself as one of the poor. Church is a good place to find Jesus; taking sides with the poor and oppressed is another way. There's no better place to serve him.

† 'Make us worthy, Lord, to serve our fellow men throughout the world who live in poverty and hunger.' (Mother Teresa)

Thursday 19 February
The many faces of poverty

Lamentations 4:4-10

Because of thirst the infant's tongue sticks to the roof of its mouth; the children beg for bread, but no one gives it to them. Those who once ate delicacies are destitute in the streets. Those brought up in royal purple now lie on ash heaps. (verses 4-5)

I've been told by well-meaning folk that we'll never alleviate poverty, and even been told it's not our job – don't even try. And then they've quoted Jesus: 'the poor you will have always with you.' A cruel take on the fate of the poor, almost as bad as blaming them for their poverty. A cruel lack of theology.

The Old Testament is very honest about poverty and oppression. Quite often it doesn't use such general terms but tells stories, specific human examples. Poverty is suffered by real people in particular circumstances; they are oppressed and they hurt. 'Those killed by the sword are better off than those who die of famine' (part of verse 9). In Lamentations, you can feel the pain. And some folk think God tolerates this?

God made a covenant with his people and showered his blessing on them. One of the results of that covenant is a just community in which there is no poverty, no injustice (Deuteronomy 15:4-11). Jesus, speaking to a Jewish audience, tells them they will always have the poor among them because they never keep that covenant. His words were not about social policy but about sinful people and the need for a new covenant.

God emphatically does hear the cry of the needy. God is moved and angered by their plight. God works on their behalf and is their hope.

† Open my ears to the cry of the needy, and open my heart to be moved.

For further thought

• If I identify myself with the poor I cannot look for their praise, and it won't please the rich. So be it. In what way are you a source of hope to the poor?

Friday 20 February
Poor in the age of affluence

Genesis 41:46-49, 53-57

Joseph collected all the food produced in those seven years of abundance in Egypt and stored it in the cities … Joseph stored up huge quantities of grain, like the sand of the sea; it was so much that he stopped keeping records because it was beyond measure. (part of verses 48-49)

There you go. It can be done. Was done, by an Egyptian Pharaoh who appointed a slave from a nomadic tribe to be his Number Two: Joseph. It is being done in our time as, however falteringly, progress is made towards Millennium goals such as 'eradicating extreme poverty' and 'reducing child mortality' (halved since 1990). We have the means, the resources; the key variable is whether we have the will.

On the Caribbean island of Montserrat, I visited the library and found local records of slavery. Examples included the records of the sales of houses and their contents. In one case, a slave girl, listed in the section selling livestock, went for the price of a cow; a disabled slave went for much less. Exactly how much depended in each case on the state of the market.

The slavery of individuals and the indebtedness of whole regions remain drivers of extreme poverty and a powerful force for evil in the modern world. It's worth noting that only rarely in the Bible is poverty linked with idleness; usually it is linked with oppression. God continues with the poor and oppressed seeking their redemption. He continues to work, as with Joseph, through individual lives. God at work through Joseph the slave? Whatever next – a carpenter?

† In the age of affluence, where it is so easy to be rich in things and poor in soul, let the freedom and dignity of others be treasures to me.

For further thought
• If you can get online, check out the state of modern slavery and what to do about it.

Saturday 21 February
After the years the locusts have eaten

Joel 2:21-26a

You will have plenty to eat, until you are full, and you will praise the name of the LORD your God, who has worked wonders for you; never again will my people be shamed. (verse 26)

The scars on his arms were distinctive: crocodile attack. A number of children in his village had these marks, wounds suffered as the children performed the daily duty of trekking to the river to get water. The crocs were the biggest but not the only peril in the water. Some years later his village in Malawi had the opportunity to become part of a Fairtrade scheme, which guaranteed tea farmers like him sufficient income to enable them to invest in their community. The first result of this was a well. Fresh water, no germs, no crocs.

It doesn't have to be grinding poverty, slavery. After the years the locusts have eaten comes bounty that will take people – and the wild animals – by surprise. This is only a foretaste of what is to come: following this passage is Joel's prophecy of the Day of the Lord where God's Spirit is poured out on all people.

For me in the UK, how and where I shop today, as well as how I campaign, helps address extreme poverty. But how else can we form a relationship with the poor?

† Not in despair, but in hope, so help us be with the poor and oppressed, working for the good of all and respect for all.

For further thought
• Some Christians give thanks before eating; how about prayer before going shopping?

Millennium goals
2 Achieving universal primary education

This week's notes are by **Simon Goddard**

Simon Goddard is one of three Regional Ministers serving nearly 180 Baptist churches in the East of England. Having pioneered RE:NEW, a fresh expression of church in rural Cambridgeshire, he now enables and encourages other congregations in their mission and works ecumenically to plant congregations in new housing developments. He is co-author of Big Hearted: the gospel of simple words and a large heart and loves to talk about the awesome grace of God. Simon initially trained as a primary school teacher, and since ordination he has maintained an active interest in education, including serving as school governor.

Sunday 22 February
Thanking God for the gift of children

1 Samuel 1:20-28; 2:18-20

So in the course of time Hannah became pregnant and gave birth to a son. She named him Samuel, saying, 'Because I asked the LORD for him.' (verse 20)

Most Christian communities will mark the birth of a child with an act of thanksgiving. This isn't a private occasion but something that the whole congregation wants to celebrate and participate in. As one liturgy puts it: 'children are not the property of parents but, named before God, they are persons with whose welfare and nurture we are entrusted' (Christopher J. Ellis and Myra Blyth (eds) *Gathering for Worship: Patterns and Prayers for the Community of Disciples*, Baptist Union of Great Britain, 2005:52). All children are a gift from God and their well-being is our responsibility.

Hannah, as an act of thanksgiving, took her precious son Samuel to be educated by Eli, and we are told later that this schooling helped him 'to grow in stature and in favour with the Lord and with people' (verse 26). But Samuel's education subsequently proved to be good not only for him, but for the whole of his community. God chose this child to bring a fresh word to his people. This week we will be thinking about the Millennium Development Goal of achieving universal primary education, an endeavour that we can be sure will be a source of God's blessing to the world.

† Lord God, thank you for all that children bring to the life of our community, and for the benefits of our own education. Amen

Monday 23 February
The joy of learning

Luke 2:41-52

After three days they found him in the temple courts, sitting among the teachers, listening to them and asking them questions. Everyone who heard him was amazed at his understanding and his answers. (verses 46 and 47)

Sometimes people use this passage to illustrate the uniqueness of Jesus; how even as a child he was familiar with the ways of God. For me this account also tells us that Jesus was just like any other child – sharing that universal desire to understand the world in which we live. I used to be a primary school teacher, and there is nothing more satisfying than seeing the joy on children's faces when they've discovered something new. The challenge of teaching is not to get children interested in learning, but to nurture and direct their natural inquisitiveness. The task of teaching is not always to have the right answer, but rather to be asking the right questions that send children off on their own journey of discovery.

In 1999, when the Millennium Development Goals were set, there were more than 100 million primary-aged children who were being denied schooling. In 2011 that number had, thankfully, dropped to 57 million but this was still the equivalent of one in ten children in some parts of the world not having access to primary education. It is likely, therefore, that this goal will require further effort, beyond 2015, to ensure that it is fully achieved.

For Jesus, that journey to Jerusalem was one of discovery and understanding, one in which his parents, relatives and the community of faith were all involved. In a similar way, we too have a role and a responsibility to ensure every child has an opportunity to experience the joy of learning.

† Lord God, we pray today for those who do not have access to primary education. Show us ways to contribute to the organisations who are seeking to bring this situation to an end. Amen

For further thought

• Is there one teacher who sparked your interest in a particular subject? If you can, why not write to them and let them know.

Tuesday 24 February
Learning to love

Deuteronomy 6:4-9

These commandments ... Impress them on your children. Talk about them when you sit at home and when you walk along the road, when you lie down and when you get up. (part of verses 6-7)

At the very outset of their life together, God made the importance of education very clear to his people. God wanted them to be a learning community, a teaching community, a community that grew in understanding, and a community that passed this knowledge on to future generations. God wanted them to make use of every learning opportunity.

This passage from Deuteronomy contains the words (verse 5) that Jesus uses to begin his summary of what the Bible teaches: '"Love the Lord your God with all your heart and with all your soul and with all your strength and with all your mind"; and, "Love your neighbour as yourself"' (Luke 10:27). Love is both the context and the content of what God wants us to learn. Jesus teaches us to share God's love with the world, not only in words, but in actions too. That is why this particular Millennium Development Goal is so intricately linked with the others. Children will not fully reap the benefits of learning in a context of poverty, hunger, oppression, inequality and disease. Education is part of the answer – but the love of God urges us to do more to address these other global issues.

These verses also speak directly into the lives of our communities of faith. Children learn about God not only from what they are taught at church, but also through what they see and hear at home. Let us make sure we are practising what we preach!

† Lord God, help me share your love in practical ways whenever and wherever I can. Fill all that I do and say with your Spirit so that others will know of your awesome love. Amen

For further thought
Consider making a donation to a charity that tackles some of the issues raised, or perhaps sponsor a child overseas through a Christian charity.

Wednesday 25 February
Learning for all

Proverbs 31:10-31

She speaks with wisdom, and faithful instruction is on her tongue … Her children arise and call her blessed; her husband also, and he praises her. (verses 26 and 28)

The purpose of the book of Proverbs is to pass the wisdom and understanding of one generation onto the next. Written nearly 3000 years ago, Solomon outlines the benefits of learning, before offering a treasury full of his own 'pearls of wisdom'. His final chapter, which outlines the virtues of a wife with 'noble character', includes recognition of her wisdom, and praise for her commitment to education.

One of the obstacles in achieving the goal of universal primary education is the problem that girls are more likely to be denied access to schooling than boys. Without being able to learn basic skills as children, these girls grow up being unable to read or write. Globally there are about 75 million young women aged 15 to 24 years in this position, and we cannot allow future generations of girls to be held back in this way. In recent years this issue has been highlighted by the inspirational young campaigner Malala Yousafzai. The UN Girls' Education Initiative is also actively working with governments to help promote gender equality, particularly with regard to providing fairer access to education.

In the book of Proverbs wisdom is portrayed as a woman: 'Do not forsake wisdom, and she will protect you; love her and she will watch over you' (4:6). Isn't it regrettable, then, that being born a female should still be a barrier to gaining wisdom and understanding? Let this stir us in our prayers for children everywhere, boys and girls alike, to be able to enjoy the benefits of a primary education.

† Lord God, bless those seeking to provide girls with fair access to education, so that they too can grow in wisdom and understanding. Amen

For further thought

• See if you can buy or borrow the book *I Am Malala* (Weidenfeld & Nicolson, 2013) for insights into the stories of those children who cannot get an education.

Thursday 26 February
Lifelong learning

Acts 18:24-28

A Jew named Apollos ... was a learned man ... though he knew only the baptism of John. When Priscilla and Aquila heard him, they invited him to their home and explained to him the way of God more adequately. (part of verses 24 to 26)

Apollos had been taught well, for we are told that he had a 'thorough knowledge of the Scriptures' (verse 24). He was also passionate about what he had learned, and was now involved in the teaching of others too. What I really like about Apollos, however, is his ongoing desire to learn. At a certain point in their education some people become unteachable, thinking that they already know it all. Apollos, on the other hand, was humble enough to listen to what others had to say to him. For this reason he was able to grow in his understanding, and as a result he became 'a great help to those who by grace had believed' (verse 27).

Learning is like constructing a wall, and there is always room to build it higher. If this is to happen, however, it is vital that the foundations are solid. The skills learned during a good primary education, such as reading and writing, become the base upon which a life full of learning can be built. Those denied these basic abilities not only miss out on something that should be a right for every child, but they also have future learning opportunities stolen from them.

Think for a moment about all the books you have read recently, and all the new things you have learned since leaving school. In a response of gratitude I invite you to do two things. First, just like Apollos, always be open to learning something new. Second, continue to pray with me that no one would be denied the opportunity to learn.

† Lord God, thanking you for my own ongoing education, I bring to you all those who lack the skills necessary to learn new things. Amen

For further thought
• What new skill or area of knowledge would you like to develop? Why not begin to learn something new today!

Friday 27 February
Learning from the little ones

Matthew 11:25-30

At that time Jesus said, 'I praise you, Father,   of heaven and earth, because you have hidden these things from the wise and learned, and revealed them to little children.' (verse 25)

Yesterday we thought about our need to keep on learning, and to be willing to listen to what others have to say. Perhaps one place where we least expect to hear something new and insightful is from the mouths of infants, yet in my experience there is much that we can learn from the little ones.

If you've ever seen a child play then you will know the endless bounds of their creativity and imagination. Sometimes, as we teach children, we tend to smother this God-given gift, rather than nurturing it. A good education will enable children to express their ideas and their individuality, rather than fitting them into some predefined mould.

I think children also seem to be more keenly in tune with the heartbeat of God. I once saw an advert that underlined this point extremely well. 'There are lots of places … racism doesn't exist' the poster said, and the word 'Here' was written across the foreheads of six babies from different ethnic backgrounds. There are some things we can teach our children, such as prejudice and hatred, that they would do much better without.

As we come towards the end of this week focusing on the Millennium Development Goal of achieving primary education, let us remind ourselves of the potential of a good education. More than just being a place to learn lists of facts and figures, school can be a place where children are allowed to become the people God created them to be – and to fill the world with the love and joy God intended for it.

† Lord God, help me to seek after you, and to look for the truths you are revealing in the lives of children around me. Amen

For further thought

• What are some of the wrong attitudes that you have picked up over the years? Why not start to unlearn them today?

Saturday 28 February
Learning the things of God

Matthew 19:13-15

Then people brought little children to Jesus for him to place his hands on them and pray for them. But the disciples rebuked them. Jesus said, 'Let the little children come to me, and do not hinder them, for the kingdom of heaven belongs to such as these.' (verses 13-14)

This week we've looked at the reasons why we should be doing all we can to help every child have access to a primary education; and here is one more. Jesus tells us that children have an important role to play in the kingdom of God, and urges us to remove the obstacles that will stop them from coming into a relationship with God.

Teaching children to read opens God's word to them, and teaching children to write enables them to share that word with others. Teaching children to observe the expanse of the universe, and to explore the mechanics of the atom, causes them to wonder at God's world, and gaze in awe before the one who created it. Rather than stand idly by and face the rebuke of Jesus, Jesus urges us to do all we can to bring children into his presence.

So today we should thank God for those Christian agencies that have been so actively involved in addressing this Millennium Development Goal, and pray for their continued efforts. Let us also give thanks for the Christians who serve as teachers in schools across the world, praying with them that their lives would point towards Jesus, and encourage the children they teach to follow him, too. Pray particularly for those responsible for religious education in schools, as well as for the various school workers and children's ministries that seek to respond creatively to these words from Matthew. And let us, of course, pray for the children too: that as they learn they may come to know the amazing God of love.

† Lord God, thank you for the example of Jesus, who welcomed the children into his presence. We pray for all those who seek to help children find their place in the kingdom of heaven. Amen

For further thought

• As you go to church this week, why not think about how you could make your place of worship even more welcoming to children?

Millennium goals

3 Empowering women

This week's notes are by **Lynne Frith**

Lynne Frith is a writer, poet and Methodist presbyter in a central and inner city parish in Auckland, Aotearoa, New Zealand. Her pleasures in life include her adult children and her young grandchildren, listening to and playing music, going to movies and theatre, walking along the many beautiful beaches in the Auckland region. Lynne's creative inspiration comes from daily encounters with all kinds of people, time away from the city streets, and a lifelong passion for justice.

Sunday 1 March
The call to civil disobedience

Exodus 1:15-22

The midwives, however, feared God and did not do what the king of Egypt had told them to do; they let the boys live. (verse 17)

The midwives Shiprah and Puah, along with Zipporah who became Moses' wife, are the only women named in the first five chapters of Exodus. Other women appear in the story, but are identified only by their relationship to a man – as wife, daughter, mother, sister.

This suggests that these two women, midwives to the Hebrew women, were so out of the ordinary, so courageous and smart in their defiance of the king of Egypt's orders, that they were remembered by name.

Traditional interpretation of these biblical stories tends to focus on Moses and his path to leadership. Without the creative and subversive action of the women, their refusal to implement the edicts of oppression, the stories would have been very different. In their civil disobedience lie the seeds of Israel's freedom from oppression.

In one week's time, on 8 March, it is International Women's Day, on which we both honour the social, political and economic achievements of women and stand in solidarity with women who are struggling for freedom and justice.

The story of Puah and Shiprah is a fitting one with which to begin our reflections this week, in which we pay attention to some particular women in the biblical narratives.

† Pray for courage to speak and act against injustice.

Monday 2 March
Women are also good leaders

Judges 4:4-10

Now Deborah, a prophet, the wife of Lappidoth, was leading Israel at that time. She held court under the Palm of Deborah between Ramah and Bethel in the hill country of Ephraim, and the Israelites went up to her to have their disputes decided. (verses 4-5)

I don't remember learning in Sunday school about Deborah. I was nurtured in a denomination that, at the time, did not give many leadership positions to women outside of the women's organisations, so perhaps it's not so surprising.

Deborah appears almost out of nowhere, identified only as the wife of Lappidoth. There's no narrative establishing her credentials. She is one of four female prophets identified in the biblical record, was a judge, a military leader and strategist, a singer and poet, leading Israel in a time of oppressive foreign rule.

Deborah has a strategy to bring an end to this cruel regime, and summons Barak to act on the word of the God of Israel. Barak hesitates – perhaps because of self-doubt, or fear, or distrust of Deborah's leadership. 'If you go with me, I will go; but if you don't go with me, I won't go' (verse 8).

Deborah agrees to go with Barak, pointing out to him that there will be no honour for him, as 'the Lord will deliver Sisera into the hands of a woman' (verse 9). And the story unfolds.

Was it because Deborah was female that Barak hesitated, or because she was offering a different strategy?

In the Methodist Church of New Zealand we elect a president and a vice-president. While the first woman was elected vice-president in 1956 and the first woman elected president in 1985, never have two women been elected together, although it is not uncommon for two men to be elected.

How often are we, like Barak, uncomfortable with the leadership offered by women?

† Give thanks for the women you know of who have offered courageous leadership.

For further thought

• Are there barriers to female leadership in your church? In the community? What action could you take?

Tuesday 3 March
Radical hospitality

Ruth 2:8-9, 17-23

Naomi said to Ruth her daughter-in-law, 'It will be good for you, my daughter, to go with the women who work for him, because in someone else's fields you might be harmed.' **(verse 22)**

This story is most often read as being about hospitality, the practical outworking of hospitality codes like the one found in Leviticus 19:34: 'The foreigner residing among you must be treated as of your native-born. Love them as yourself, for you were foreigners in Egypt.'

It may also be read as a story about dependence and survival.

How fortunate for Ruth that Naomi's kinsman Boaz was as kind as his reputation. Ruth depended for her survival on the charity and compassion of a man who was a stranger to her. Not all migrant women are so fortunate.

Migrant women make up the bulk of low-paid workers in many countries. They are open to exploitation by employers and usually paid the minimum wage or less. A significant report recently released in my country highlighted the poor wages and working conditions for caregivers in residential facilities for the elderly. A minister of the government observed that such people did the work for love, as if that somehow justified low wages.

Like Ruth, stranded in an unfamiliar country but loyal to her new family ties, many migrant women struggle to support their families. They take what work they can in order to provide the basic necessities. Few find themselves the recipients of radical hospitality and protection such as Boaz offered to Ruth.

† Pray for just working conditions for migrant workers, and radical hospitality for refugees and asylum seekers.

For further thought

• What do you know about migrant workers in your community? How might you engage in the practice of radical hospitality?

Wednesday 4 March
A motherly God

Isaiah 49:13-18

Can a mother forget the baby at her breast and have no compassion on the child she has borne? Though she may forget, I will not forget you! (verse 15)

This is another text that I didn't hear about in Sunday school. The God I was taught about in childhood was unrelentingly male – a benevolent grandfatherly figure given to bouts of anger and vengeance.

It was not until I was training for ministry and reading feminist theology that a whole new way of understanding the divine nature was opened up to me. The imagery in Isaiah that depicts the motherhood of God allowed for patience, tenderness and compassion.

In today's reading, the love of God for the people is likened to the love of a mother for her children.

While a human mother's affection for her offspring might waver, God assures Zion 'I will not forget you.'

God's compassion will bring about the restoration of Israel, and in verse 18 the focus shifts towards mother Israel, whose family returns home.

A text such as this one opens up rich possibilities for our understanding of the divine nature but, just as not everyone has positive experiences of fathering, thus affecting the lens through which God is viewed, so it is for images of the maternal. Not everyone has positive experiences of mothering.

We are reminded that God has many facets, and that our imagining of the divine nature is limited by our human experience.

† May I be open to fresh revelations of the divine nature.

For further thought

• Search out and meditate upon other biblical texts that use feminine imagery to describe the divine nature.

Thursday 5 March
In the style of Lydia

Acts 16:11-15

On the Sabbath we went outside the city gate to the river, where we expected to find a place of prayer. We sat down and began to speak to the women who had gathered there. (verse 13)

Today I've been working with a group of women on a resource we're editing. We sat around the kitchen table, phones on silent, away from the demands of our respective ministries. To begin, we caught up over a coffee. Re-connected, we got to work, tossing ideas around, reflecting on the theological method that was used in the Hui (Maori word for gathering or assembly) that led to the resource, and reviewing the written contributions from the participants.

The Hui had brought together a diverse group of women, engaged in diverse ministries. One day of the Hui was devoted to creative workshops – and in the creative work, doing theology. As the women learned the art of Raranga (flax weaving), Siapo (prints on fabric), and weaving the Word, they talked and sang, and prayed, and kept silence.

In the Hui, and around my table, women gathered for a common purpose – to work together, participating in creation. Like the women with whom Lydia met, outside the city, by the river, we met away from the usual meeting places, taking and giving space for the creative spirit to do her work.

Like the midwives Puah and Shiprah whose story we read at the beginning of the week, Lydia was an independent woman, not defined by her relationship to a man. A successful businesswoman, she was also prayerful and community-focused. After she and her household were baptised, she offered hospitality to Paul and his companions, and prevailed upon them until they accepted.

Here we see once more a woman not bound by tradition and custom, who acts in ways she knows to be right, and good for the whole community.

† Give thanks for the work of your hands, and for those whose theology is expressed through creative media.

For further thought
• Visit a local art/craft gallery or exhibition and consider what spirituality might be revealed.

Friday 6 March
The new community

Galatians 3:26-29

There is neither Jew nor gentile, neither slave nor free, nor is there male and female, for you are all one in Christ Jesus. (verse 28)

I'm not sure when exactly I first rebelled against the notion that I could become a 'son' of God, as traditional Bible translations have it (verse 26). I was, and am, quite satisfied with being female.

Nor did I particularly cherish the thought that in following Christ, human beings in all their wonderful diversity became the same, as if they had been given a whirr in a kind of supernatural blender.

Carolyn Osiek reminds us that in Paul's day, while a daughter could inherit property, she could not, even if she was the firstborn, inherit the authority of the head of the household. She suggests that the best interpretation could be that all, female and male, in the sight of God, have the status legally afforded to the son. All through Christ inherit eternal life (*Women's Bible Commentary Expanded Version*, Westminster John Knox, 1998:424–425).

Like many biblical texts, these few verses from the letter to the Galatians may be used to support a range of possibilities. In my view the text hints strongly at freedom from the constraints of both privilege and servitude and points to a kind of equality to be found in the new community of Christ. In the new community, all have the same status in the sight of God. While this is undoubtedly good news for those who are excluded from leadership, or are not truly welcome, it may be a challenge to those who are accustomed to social status, privilege and power. If all are equally privileged, then the converse is also true – all are called equally to serve.

† Pray for those who are excluded for any reason – race, gender, sexuality, religious beliefs.

For further thought

• In your faith community are there some people who are never offered leadership roles or whose vocation is denied? Why? What might you do to encourage them?

Saturday 7 March
Courage, compassion, community

Romans 16:1-5

I commend to you our sister Phoebe ... I ask you to receive her in the Lord *in a way worthy of his people and to give her any help she may need from you, for she has been the benefactor of many people, including me. Greet Priscilla and Aquila, my fellow workers in Christ Jesus. They risked their lives for me.* (part of verses 1-3)

My grandmother was intelligent, forthright and compassionate, actively involved in church and community wherever she lived. I knew she was a supporter of the ordination of women, but it was not until 10 years after her death that I discovered by chance that she had been a trailblazer herself. I was visiting the church in the small town she had lived in during my childhood and spotted a photo in the porch, which had her among a group of men. When I enquired, I was told, 'Mrs Ericson was the first woman elected to the vestry in this parish.'

Forty years later, there would have been few remaining parishioners who knew my grandma. In that respect she's like countless other women whose gifts of leadership are forgotten but for a photo or brief reference in an anniversary booklet.

The women whom Paul commends must have been remarkable to even get a mention. First, there is Phoebe, 'a servant of the church'. The NIV downplays her role by describing her as a servant and one who helps others. The New Revised Standard Version, by contrast, describes Phoebe as a deacon and benefactor, which affords her some standing.

The next to be commended are Priscilla (or Prisca) and Aquila, co-workers with Paul, who risked their lives for him. We know little more about Phoebe and Priscilla than what the text says about them. What can be certain is that they stood out as leaders.

Let us reclaim and celebrate the lives and stories of those women in every generation who have stepped outside the customary roles to offer leadership.

† Remember with gratitude the women in church and community whose stories are seldom told.

For further thought

• Work with others to gather an archive of the stories of women who have offered leadership and ministry in your faith community.

Millennium goals
4 Improving infant and maternal health

This week's notes are by **Terry Lester**

Terry Lester serves as parish priest in the Cape Town suburb of Constantia. Over forty years ago his family was forcibly removed under the Group Areas Act from the very place he now serves. Despite this, past and current residents have continued worshipping together over these years. Terry has a heart in ministry for exploring together – as the body of Christ – forgiveness, reconciliation and reparation as we seek to become an authentic community of faith.

Sunday 8 March
The cry of the powerless

Genesis 21:14-19

God heard the boy crying, and the angel of God called to Hagar from heaven and said to her, 'What is the matter, Hagar? Do not be afraid; God has heard the boy crying as he lies there. Lift the boy up and take him by the hand, for I will make him into a great nation.' (verses 17-18)

Hearing a mother's passionate cry for her child is always heart-wrenching. As a hospital chaplain I have heard this cry in the neonatal unit and while comforting a mother whose HIV-infected little one was fighting for its life. It is this cry that reaches the ears of God, the cry of Hagar and Ishmael. As a slave, Hagar's and her son's futures were linked. Her rejection and that of her son move God to open a future for both, for God has a plan for the boy. The cry of the child is the cry of abandonment and being left to die. It echoes in the universal cry of a thirst for justice, a thirst for being seen and acknowledged.

For its time and context, scripture has surprisingly much to say about the place of women and children in God's plan for the world. That plan did not involve maintaining the status quo when it came to women and children. This week, new ways of seeing and embracing are explored and we are invited to trust God to lead into these new ways. Humble obedience will make us co-creators in not only rocking the world but also setting it right-side up!

† Lord, open our ears to the cry of powerless people. Help us to stretch out a hand to those who have fallen. Amen

Monday 9 March
Made in the very heart of God

Psalm 139:13-18

I praise you because I am fearfully and wonderfully made; your works are wonderful, I know that full well. (verse 14)

A mother once told me how she recoiled in horror at the sight of her newborn baby's deformed shape – she had no limbs, just a head and torso and with a little stump where a leg should have been. During pregnancy she was given the wonder drug thalidomide to counter debilitating morning sickness. The drug was later identified as the cause of shocking deformities in a number of children born all over the world. How does one live in full appreciation of being fearfully and wonderfully made when we have those who live with such birth defects and disfigurement? The daughter is now a grown woman and lives a fully integrated life. The writer of this psalm is sharing a secret that all should discover, whether you have birth defects, or were born with mental illness, or suffer disfigurements. Try as we might, we can't escape God's reach; we can only yield to the all-embracing reality that finds us in places we thought were well out of that reach. Turning to God is the only logical response to this reach of God, for our whole existence belongs to God. It is the journey to affirmation and leads us away from negation.

† Were I to flee to the vast plains of the Kalahari or ascend the cloudy peaks of the Ukhahlamba, even there you would find me! Wow! Amen

For further thought

• We are all wonderfully made by God. How will you appreciate today that all your fellow human beings are so wonderfully yet so differently made?

Tuesday 10 March
Crossing on dry land

1 Kings 17:7-23

For the jar of flour was not used up and the jug of oil did not run dry, in keeping with the word of the LORD *spoken by Elijah.* (verse 16)

Rivers and streams, rail tracks and roads were the dividing lines that kept people of different races apart when I was growing up. As physical barriers they were relatively easy to cross, needing no real effort. Yet very few would. Fear of what might happen to them if they defied the law kept people locked in the prison of separateness. Martin Luther King Jr said that the most segregated hour in America is Sunday morning at 11 am. It is much the same here, too! But people everywhere set boundaries to their empathy and imaginations that stop them from crossing over to the other side. As a prisoner gets used to the prison bars, so people get used to being separate and cut off from others. God liberates all from their prisons of fear: the Jewish prophet as well as the Gentile widow; the white, the black, the gay, the straight. Where is your Sidon? Which brook are you called to cross today? You may discover the power of God in ways you never thought possible, for freedom gives a whole new perspective on the stranger who, after all, is just someone you have not met before. The invitation is to enter into your promised land of flour and oil and resurrection life.

† God, reach out your hand and help us cross whatever keeps us from the undivided humanity of which you dream.

For further thought
• *Umuntu ungumuntu ngabantu* is an African proverb that says that a person becomes a person because of people; or, more personally put, I am because we are.

Wednesday 11 March
Lo! Children are a heritage

Luke 1:39-45

When Elizabeth heard Mary's greeting, the baby leaped in her womb, and Elizabeth was filled with the Holy Spirit. (verse 41)

A huge road sign announced, 'Children should be seen not hurt'. A society that hurts its children is on a fast track down a cul-de-sac. A society in which children are not heard is bound to hit a brick wall sooner or later. St Luke creates this familiar homely picture of two expectant mothers, yet there is a wonderful surprise waiting in the children who are to be born, who will rock the world, setting it back on its axis. The one will teach the teachers the art of living simply a life orientated to God without the many props people rely on. The other will teach lawyers the law of love and compassion as a way of obedience. It is wonderful that the world has had the privilege to encounter both and that both continue to be heard. Imagine how many millions of others would have leapt at the opportunity to teach our world to love and live, but died prematurely. Yet many continue to shout from the womb, grabbing our attention to care, to advocate and to do for them and their mothers what those in authority and power are failing to do.

† Today I remember, Lord, those who attend and work in clinics and neonatal units. I commit to work for the hastening of the day when women everywhere will have access to all they need. Amen

For further thought

• What are the gravest dangers threatening the health of infants and pregnant women in your community?

Thursday 12 March
'Get up, stand up, don't give up the fight'*

Luke 7:11-15

When the Lord saw her, his heart went out to her and he said, 'Don't cry.' Then he went up and touched the bier they were carrying him on, and the bearers stood still. He said, 'Young man, I say to you, get up!' (verses 13-14)

Why have we become so used to young men dying in their prime? Death has many faces and is seen most these days on the streets in the inner city housing estates where young men gather at all hours, aimlessly wandering with no prospects except the ever-present lure that will lead to their demise. Others are crammed into prisons filled to overflowing with other young men going nowhere fast. Still others are overwhelmed by parenthood when they themselves have known no nurturing or been shown much care and compassion. We walk wide berths around these types and warn our children to steer clear of them too. 'Don't engage, don't encourage, and don't touch!' Many have also built a ring around themselves as the absence of fathers in their lives has taught them not to trust any adult, whether a parent, police, teachers, social workers or religious workers. Mothers often are airbrushed out in this picture. They often bear the brunt and pick up the pieces, further compounding their pain and shame. Jesus sees and invites us to see the world through his eyes and touch the untouchable with his hands.

† Change my heart, O God. Make it soft to feel the pain and see the opportunities for gentleness and care.

For further thought
• Who are the untouchables in your community?

Friday 13 March
God's little ones

Mark 5:21-43

He took her by the hand and said to her, 'Talitha koum!' (which means 'Little girl, I say to you, get up!'). (verse 41)

Returning from a challenging but successful excursion to the region of Decapolis on the other side of the lake, Jesus is back among the familiar but not always easier people of Capernaum! The town, like all towns everywhere, consists of the seen and the unseen. Jairus, the highly regarded ruler of the synagogue, is clearly among the 'seen', but he risks this status when he makes known the dire state his very sick daughter is in. Sick women could place burdens on the devout, by putting the ritually pure at risk. Making public his daughter's illness, Jairus risked his place of importance at the synagogue – he risked all for her. The woman with the blood issue also risks but uses her own agency, taking control of her own future, maybe feeling empowered by others who risk. She reaches out to touch Jesus' garment. The men in the story do something that breaks a cycle, one in which victims are continually victimised. How do we show up when we most need to and, drawing on the strength flowing from Jesus, make a difference? Women bear the brunt and are most often the victims. Notwithstanding the powerful agency women have, men too have a different but vital role.

† Forgive me, Lord, for the times I have hurt the hurting and not stepped forward to protect the victimised.

For further thought

• What are the specific needs of little girls in your community, like the one Jesus took by the hand? How can your community nourish them?

Saturday 14 March
We are family

Galatians 4:4-7

But when the set time had fully come, God sent his Son, born of a woman, born under the law, to redeem those under the law, that we might receive adoption to sonship. (verses 4-5)

There was time when pregnant women were referred to as expectant mothers, and a father as an expectant father. As the months pass the expectancy grows until the moment the signs appear that the birth is imminent. The arrival will change the world of these parents for ever. St Paul draws on this image of the clock ticking to the birth of the child born to Mary who also, irrevocably, changes the status of every person past, present and future. All receive the full right as brother and sister of him who is born of Mary, touched by the Holy Spirit with God as Father. All were reborn in that moment, as the clock struck, into a new relationship with God and with each other. This God is not the abandoning type but one who desires that we know the love of the Father who embraces and cares for each. This is how we are viewed by our Father. Why, then, do we devise religious language or act in ways that treat some as though they are stepchildren in the family of God? Being born again is our Father's initiative in order for us to discover our connectedness with each other rather than make a show of our spiritual DNA.

† Help me to not compare myself to my brothers and sisters, Lord, but teach me to celebrate that, when the time had fully come, we were made your children. For this I thank you. Amen

For further thought

• Being 'born again' uses a feminine image for God. How might this image broaden our understanding of God's concern for the health of infants and mothers?

Millennium goals

5 Combating disease

This week's notes are by **Jennifer Smith**

 The Revd Dr Jennifer Smith is a Methodist minister in west London. She is from Boston, Massachusetts, and has lived in the UK since 1993. Before coming into the ministry she lectured in politics; she has taught mission in Nigeria and Sierra Leone regularly since 2001. Jennifer cares passionately about teaching as part of discipleship, so that faith is able to stand up to the hard questions of everyday life. She enjoys bluegrass music and is married to an Anglican priest with whom she has two adult step-daughters.

Sunday 15 March

Arguing with God: a righteous impatience

Psalm 6

Heal me, LORD, for my bones are in agony. My soul is in deep anguish. How long, LORD, how long? Turn, LORD, and deliver me; save me because of your unfailing love. Among the dead no one proclaims your name. Who praises you from his grave? (part of verses 2-5)

The sixth of the Millennium Development Goals speaks of combating HIV/AIDS, malaria, and other diseases. According to the UN fact sheet for 2013, the number newly infected with HIV has fallen by a third since 2001. Nearly 10 million people had anti-retroviral drugs in 2012; almost 300,000 fewer children were infected in 2012 than in 2001. Over a million deaths from malaria were 'averted' in the years since the Millennium Goals were adopted. Still, millions of people have died from HIV-related illness, malaria, and tuberculosis: millions suffer right now. What hope for any given individual, in the world of international politics and mass statistics? How long, O Lord, how long before each one is remembered in the counting?

The speaker in Psalm 6 argues with God: what good will it do you for me to die; no one praises you from the grave! The psalm gives us permission for a righteous impatience, and is as real about suffering as it is in the assurance of God's mercy. Here there is no brushing away of night sweats or pain in the telling of an international success story. Success is real, but God takes no rest until each one is remembered.

† God give me strength to hear the pain of the world. Stay close through the dark anxiety of night and bless me with healing. Amen

Monday 16 March
What we fear, what we believe

Psalm 77

Will the LORD reject for ever? Will he never show his favour again? Has his unfailing love vanished for ever? Has his promise failed for all time? Has God forgotten to be merciful? Has he in anger withheld his compassion?
(verses 7-9)

Part of the difficulty of living with disease, and combating it, is that disease stirs up some potent questions that go to the heart of our faith. If God is all-powerful and compassionate, why would any child die from malaria, or tuberculosis? Why would any adult die of HIV-related illness? Are people responsible for their disease, if they make poor choices like not sleeping under a mosquito net or having unprotected sex? Does it make a difference if they did not have money for a net, or were infected by a husband or wife?

These are the same questions we hear asked about God in today's psalm: 'Has God forgotten to be merciful? Has he in anger withheld his compassion?' (verse 9). Much as these questions are legitimate to ask, they are based on a misconception about God. The antidote to the fear that God is arbitrary and vengeful is to do exactly what the psalmist does in verses 13-20 and remember what we believe.

We believe that God works for healing and will recreate our whole global economy to get it, if that is what it takes. We do not believe that God punishes people by giving them disease; indeed we observe that the poor and powerless are far more likely to be brought low by the same condition for which the wealthy have treatment. We believe that God suffers with each person who suffers, and that God's compassion is endless.

† God of storm and wind, God of lightning and of trembling earth: claim me as a child of your flock. Show me the strength of your love and give me a gentle heart, that I may today show others your compassion. Amen

For further thought

• How has HIV/Aids affected your community, or not? How have you seen people of faith respond, or not? Join a discussion on our Facebook group today.

Tuesday 17 March
A big man learns to hear little voices

2 Kings 5:1-14

Elisha sent a messenger to say to him, 'Go, wash yourself seven times in the Jordan, and your flesh will be restored and you will be cleansed.'
(verse 10)

We see repeated in scripture what we know from life today: Millennium Goals aside, the wealthy and powerful are likely to get the best treatment for illness available. Part of the work of preventing disease has been bringing care into places with very little health infrastructure. But if I am able to afford it, I can travel all over the globe looking for the newest treatment, the most skilled surgeon, the best experimental drug. Just like Naaman, the wealthy can petition kings to get visas, buy aeroplane tickets, and take time off work to go anywhere for a treatment that might help.

However, there is a deep comedy that runs through the Hebrew scriptures. The tables are often turned on the powerful as wisdom comes from people (or animals: have a look at Balaam's donkey in Numbers 22:21-33) at the margins. In today's passage it happened twice: first the trafficked Israelite girl knew where to find healing, and then the servants saved the day when the 'treatment' did not conform to Naaman's expectations.

We need big, powerful, global initiatives like the Millennium Goals to spur the nations to address preventable disease. However, let us never forget that sometimes the global voice of the large institution can miss the local, sensible suggestion. Sometimes what is needed is not the parachuting in of extraordinary services, but listening in order to empower those who are most vulnerable on the ground.

In 2012, UNICEF worked with the Cambodian government to distribute over 13 million mosquito nets. Imagine one household who received a net; pray for their home and well-being today.

† God of healing, you desire fullness of life and health for all. We seek it too, for your sake.

For further thought

• What is your government doing about health care for the most vulnerable, who can't afford the care Namaan can?

Wednesday 18 March
See for yourself, the breadth of the river of God

Ezekiel 47:6b-12

Fruit trees of all kinds will grow on both banks of the river. Their leaves will not wither, nor will their fruit fail. Every month they will bear fruit, because the water from the sanctuary flows to them. Their fruit will serve for food and their leaves for healing. (verse 12)

Reading today's passage feels like the reverse of hearing a celebrity UN 'goodwill' ambassador report about a place of natural disaster or deprivation. Often their visits show the worst of drought or hunger, complete with pictures.

Talking about being guided along the river of life, Ezekiel related a dream that was as much better than normal life in affluent parts of west London as any overcrowded refugee camp is worse. 'You can't imagine how wide this river was – my guide took me 4000 cubits in before I could not pass – and the life on its banks: swarms of animals, fish and fruit trees!' It helps to hear the report of someone who has been to the place and seen the work. Then we can break down the statistics into manageable bits of experience. 'Son of man, do you see this?' asked Ezekiel's guide.

But maybe it is not all doom and gloom with the UN goodwill ambassadors. Celebrities draw the world's media to look at work that would not get attention on its own; without the presence of this or that movie star, it would be just another refugee camp, rural hospital, or HIV counselling clinic in a village market. Such visits walk a line between showcasing glimpses of progress, and exploiting tragedy. But, as with Ezekiel, the hope is that the authority of the prophet helps us hear news of extraordinary promise at the same time as it shocks us with the distance still to go.

† Gracious God, give us the strength to look today at the wonders of your creation as well as its suffering. Be our guide, our comforter, our redeemer, our healer. Amen

For further thought

• Sit and hear the question the guide asked Ezekiel: 'Son of man, do you see this?' What does God want to make sure you see today?

Thursday 19 March
Jesus, giver of full healing

Matthew 8:14-17

When Jesus came into Peter's house, he saw Peter's mother-in-law lying in bed with a fever. He touched her hand and the fever left her ... When evening came, many who were demon-possessed were brought to him, and he drove out the spirits with a word and healed all who were ill. (part of verses 14-16)

Scripture has many things to teach us about combating disease. Not least, it acknowledges that true healing will not be about just removing an illness, but restoring the person to full life and vitality. Peter's mother-in-law did not just become well when the fever left, but was restored to her place of power in the household: she got up and resumed her work. Twenty-first-century ears might wonder that she was healed 'to wait on him,' but we do well to remember that hers was an important place in the household. She was restored to her economic and moral role, her community and relationships with people.

I have visited a leprosy colony opened by the Methodist Church in Nigeria in the mid-1930s. It is a refuge for people whose disease had caused them to be driven out of their village or family for fear of infection. There, the first job has always been to address the disease and offer treatment to cure the leprosy. However, even a child knows that it will take more than that to restore someone to health. A home village will have to be visited and educated to understand the treatment and absence of threat. Church leaders will have to work against stigma. The person will need a means of supporting themselves and their household, and somewhere to live. Only then will someone long cured of leprosy be able to be healed of the full effects of the disease.

† Pray for all those who are making a new beginning today, especially leaving hospital or beginning treatment. May all find healing. Amen

For further thought

• Today investigate any of the charities that combat disease, such as The Leprosy Mission or Rotary International's campaign to end polio. Can you help in some way?

Friday 20 March
Called as ourselves, sent for the kingdom

Matthew 10:1-8

These are the names of the twelve apostles: first, Simon (who is called Peter) and his brother Andrew; James son of Zebedee, and his brother John; Philip and Bartholomew; Thomas and Matthew the tax collector; James son of Alphaeus, and Thaddeus; Simon the Zealot and Judas Iscariot, who betrayed him. (verses 2-4)

As we consider the Millennium Development Goals in relation to scripture it is easy to think only of the instructions Jesus gave here and elsewhere: 'Heal the sick, raise the dead, cleanse those who have leprosy, drive out demons' (verse 8). Today however, I want us to focus on who is called before we get to the 'for what purpose?'

The Gospel names the twelve in particular, with personal details about them. These are individual people, all with their own individual strengths and weaknesses, tempers and talents. Which one was good at administration? Which one always got people's backs up when they met? Who had a bad back, or struggled to keep awake after lunch? Jesus gave no general abstract orders but instructions to these specific people, with whom he had lived and travelled. He had confidence in them just as they were. It is important to me that the text says Jesus 'called the twelve disciples to him' (verse 1) before he sent them out. Like them, we are first called 'to' Jesus, to know the kingdom ourselves. We are not robots given instructions, but witnesses to the kingdom who then respond.

The macro-economic, global scope of the Millennium Development Goals is a good and necessary thing. But do not be overawed by the scale of the problems, or the progress reported: the work of healing is still given to particular people in particular places and times. You are big enough to take part just where you are.

† God of the strong and weak, the tired and awake, be near me today. Call me to you and say my name, that I may witness to your kingdom of heaven come near. Amen

For further thought

• Today take a moment to imagine Jesus calling you to him, before sending you out. What gifts does he see? What might he say?

81

Saturday 21 March
The necessity of companions, and prayer

James 5:13-16

Is anyone among you in trouble? Let them pray. Is anyone happy? Let them sing songs of praise. Is anyone among you ill? Let them call the elders of the church to pray over them and anoint them with oil in the name of the Lord. (verses 13-14)

At the end of a business meeting in any church committee there are often throwaway comments. These might formally be called 'any other business' but are actually the things the chair (especially if it is a minister) forgot to include earlier. They are sometimes the most important parts of the meeting, as they probably concern the actual things that are happening as opposed to the business that everyone will forget as soon as it is safely in the minutes. They are often obvious points that need reinforcement: are you in trouble? Pray. Are you happy? Give praise. Are you sick? Call the elders, and pray for each other with anointing in the name of the Lord.

Too often in the work of healing we miss the obvious easy tasks. Like Naaman in the reading for last Tuesday, we look for the big and flashy solution as opposed to the basic gifts of fellowship. As we close our consideration of the sixth Millennium Development Goal this week, let us remember those easy, obvious gifts we are given: prayer, praise, the companionship of people more experienced in faith than ourselves on whom we can lean. We have made significant progress towards the goal of 'getting to zero' – that is, no new HIV infections, no discrimination, and no HIV-related deaths. We have made significant progress towards ending deaths from malaria, TB and other diseases. This significant progress will be minuted and recorded, but do not forget the small advice that sustains us.

† O Lord, give us grace to pray when we need, to praise when blessed, and guidance from our companions on the way. Amen

For further thought

• How can we identify with the global scope of the Millennium Development Goals? Scripture helps open the personal stories behind statistics quoted in millions.

Millennium goals

6 Environmental sustainability and global development

This week's notes are by **Paul Nicholson**

Paul Nicholson SJ is a Roman Catholic priest of the Society of Jesus, known as the Jesuits. Until recently he was based in Birmingham, UK, responsible for the initial training (the novitiate) of candidates for the order from north-west Europe. He joined the Jesuits in 1978, after studying zoology at Durham University, and was ordained in 1988. He has since worked principally in the fields of spirituality and social justice. He edits the British Jesuit spirituality journal *The Way*, and is author of *Growing Into Silence* and *An Advent Pilgrimage*.

Sunday 22 March
God saw that it was good

Genesis 1:9-12

And God said, 'Let the water under the sky be gathered to one place, and let dry ground appear.' And it was so. God called the dry ground 'land', and the gathered waters he called 'seas'. And God saw that it was good. Then God said, 'Let the land produce vegetation'. (part of verses 9-11)

In this account of creation from Genesis, God does more than simply bring everything into being. As each thing is created, it is given its place. Thus by the end of the sixth day everything fits together in a harmonious and balanced whole, a cosmos. The original role of human beings is to tend and maintain this God-given order.

It is no mistake that the image for this creation is that of a garden. A well-tended garden shows something of this same balance and unity, whether it is a perfectly-manicured formal showpiece, or an artfully-crafted urban wilderness. And good gardeners aren't simply planning for an effective display this week or next. They will look months and years – perhaps even centuries in some cases – ahead.

God, in creating, likewise takes the long view. The created world is given the capability of growth and development. Human beings can appreciate this plan, and are called to work alongside God. Any fool can wreck a garden, but it takes both love and skill to cultivate it. The Millennium Goals speak of our desire to care for creation in just this fashion.

† Spend a few minutes looking prayerfully at some cultivated land – field, garden, or even a pot plant. Thank God for the work that lies behind it.

Monday 23 March
Unreaped fields and unpruned vineyards

Leviticus 25:1-7

When you enter the land I am going to give you, the land itself must observe a sabbath to the LORD. For six years sow your fields, and for six years prune your vineyards and gather their crops. But in the seventh year the land is to have a year of sabbath rest, a sabbath to the LORD. (part of verses 2-4)

Traditional agriculture allowed for periodic fallow times, during which some fields were left untouched, enabling the soil to build up again the nutrients drained by cultivation. Contemporary intensive farming, employing expensive artificial fertilisers, is tempted to do away with such unproductive times in order to maximise the return on its investment. Now we discover that, treated like this, over time soils inevitably lose their richness. As the scriptural writers knew, the land needs its sabbath.

God's promise is that, if treated well, the land will produce enough for human needs, even in the fallow times. It takes trust to observe a sabbath. Whether I am a farmer growing food, or an office worker processing paperwork, the pressure to produce can be overwhelming at times. Yet God offers an invitation to step back at regular intervals, allow for a change of pace, and rely on God's providence.

There can be sabbath places as well as sabbath times. Human development should not mean needing to encroach ever more widely on the entire land mass of our planet. It is good to have some areas that remain undeveloped, some land not subject to cultivation. In turn these lands can become the places in which I can be refreshed during my periods of sabbath rest.

The concept of sabbath, in time or in space, lends itself well to the goal of sustainable development. Those who take breaks from their work will ultimately achieve more than those who strive ceaselessly. Wild areas are needed for balanced ecosystems. The experience of those who first entered the Promised Land offers valuable lessons here.

† Lord Jesus, you reminded us that the sabbath was intended for our benefit. Help us to use this gift wisely, for the rest and recreation of ourselves and our planet, trusting in your providential care.

For further thought

• Where are your sabbath places? When are your sabbath times?

Tuesday 24 March

The land shall be a common treasury for all

Leviticus 25:13-24

The land must not be sold permanently, because the land is mine and you reside in my land as foreigners and strangers. Throughout the land that you hold as a possession, you must provide for the redemption of the land. (verses 23-24)

Often wealth is closely linked to land ownership. Those without title to their own land often become slum-dwellers, living in poverty on the edges of cities while struggling to find work. Each United Nations' Millennium Goal includes a series of targets, and the goal of environmental sustainability has a target of significantly improving the lives of at least 100 million slum-dwellers by 2020.

Leviticus recognises this problem of lack of land ownership and proposes a radical solution. All land, it suggests, belongs ultimately to God, and cannot be permanently appropriated by any human being. At most, someone might purchase the right to use a plot of land for a fixed number of years. After that, the original equal distribution made when the Chosen People entered the Promised Land must be restored. Inspired by texts such as these, the Diggers, a group of Protestant agrarian workers from the time of the English Civil War, declared, 'the land shall be a common treasury for all'.

In reading this, the aim is not simply to apply it literally, re-instituting the practice of the Jewish Jubilee Year. We are, rather, challenged to find equally radical solutions to the problems of our own day. The good news is that this is one target that the United Nations recognises has been met ahead of time. More than 200 million people gained access to improved facilities between 2000 and 2012, and at the same time the proportion of urban slum-dwellers in the developing world fell from 39 per cent to 33 per cent. We can, with God's help, bring about change for the better.

† Help me, Lord, to recognise that all I have and all that I am comes from, and belongs to, you. Help me to use it for the good of all, especially those most in need.

For further thought

• Try to find out who the biggest land-owners in your own neighbourhood are. How do they use the land they occupy?

Wednesday 25 March

Water, water everywhere, and not a drop to drink

Numbers 20:2-11

Now there was no water for the community, and the people gathered in opposition to Moses and Aaron. They quarrelled with Moses and said, 'If only we had died when our brothers fell dead before the Lord! [...] Why did you bring us up out of Egypt to this terrible place? (part of verses 2-3, 5)

It is estimated that it is possible to live for up to two months without food, but for less than a week without water. So the people of Israel here, wandering through the wilderness after leaving Egypt, have some cause to complain. Their situation is a dire one and truly offers a strong test of their faith in God. Yet God is constantly faithful and in the course of this passage abundantly provides them with the water they need.

Water isn't simply necessary for drinking, but also for basic sanitation. Another of the targets of the Millennium Goals is to halve the number of those without access to the water they need. This water must be safe to drink, and available sustainably. Meeting this target is a complex business. Irrigation schemes allowing successful agriculture in one area can so lower the water table as to make wells dry up downstream. Water is becoming an increasingly scarce resource, and thus a likely source of conflict.

By their trust in God, Moses and Aaron ensure that the people have enough water, not only for themselves but for their livestock too. It will be for the people themselves to work out how that water is to be shared and apportioned. We, too, are not called upon to create water but to ensure that no one is denied access to it according to their need.

† Jesus, you told the Samaritan woman that you were the source of living water; help us to make sure that all people have access to the water they need to live.

For further thought

• Notice today your use of water: for drinking, cooking, washing, cleaning and other sanitary needs. How much water do you think you use each day?

Thursday 26 March
No more debts and no more debtors

Deuteronomy 15:1-3

At the end of every seven years you must cancel debts. This is how it is to be done: every creditor shall cancel any loan they have made to a fellow Israelite. They shall not require payment from anyone among their own people, because the LORD's time for cancelling debts has been proclaimed. (verses 1-2)

The final Millennium Goal calls upon the nations of the world to develop a global partnership for development. Development isn't to be a task for the poorer nations alone, or for those that are well disposed or feel that they have resources to spare. Only by working together, rich and poor, north and south, can we hope to tackle genuinely global problems. And among the greatest obstacles to this co-operation are the debts poorer countries are said to owe to richer ones.

Part of the Old Testament Jubilee programme that we have been considering this week involves the periodic cancellation of debt. These debts are not simply reduced, or rescheduled. They are wholly written off, enabling a new start to be made. If this sounds like impractical dreaming, it is worth realising that it is a solution that has already been tried on occasion in our own times. For example, after much of its international debt was cancelled in 2002, Tanzania managed to double the proportion of its children in primary education.

The vision of this passage in Deuteronomy doesn't extend beyond cancelling debts between Israelites. Foreigners are still fair game here! The challenge today is to move beyond even this generous outlook and to recognise that in Christ all people become my fellow countrymen and women. Can we so arrange things that all people are freed from their debts, to live full and fully-human lives?

† Lord, you give us all that we have freely, without obligation. Help us to develop relationships between peoples and nations in ways that reflect this generosity in our dealings with each other.

For further thought

• See what you can discover about the Highly Indebted Poor Country (HIPC) and the Multilateral Debt Relief Initiatives (MDRI). You could start at www.one.org/international/issues/debt-cancellation

Friday 27 March
The poor you will always have with you

Deuteronomy 15:7-11

Give generously to [your fellow Israelites] and do so without a grudging heart; then because of this the LORD your God will bless you in all your work and in everything you put your hand to. There will always be poor people in the land. (part of verses 10-11)

Any assessment of progress towards achieving the Millennium Goals will show a mixed picture. Some targets have been met; others are still being moved towards. A few may by now have been shown to be impractical, or in need of amendment. New needs have arisen in the last decade, as new situations arise worldwide. No one pretends that global poverty will be finally eliminated by the 2015 deadline that these goals set. As Jesus remarked in another context, 'The poor you will always have with you' (Matthew 26:11).

The writer of Deuteronomy understands the continuing presence of the poor to be offering the better-off a never-ending opportunity of blessing. It is by responding with generosity to the needs of those around us that we open ourselves to receiving God's gifts. By contrast, God's judgement is reserved for those who are grudging towards their neighbours, or hope that they will find the relief that they need elsewhere. Thus, far from being an excuse to do nothing, the fact that there will always be poor people near at home and in far-off countries becomes an invitation to meet God by serving them.

In truth, if we cannot achieve environmental sustainability, we will all become increasingly poor and needy. Only global development in partnership will enable us to continue to enjoy the blessings of God's creation. If together we meet each other's needs, then together we will receive all that God has to offer.

† 'God loves a cheerful giver' – Lord, help me always to notice the needs of those around me, and to respond generously using the gifts that you have given me.

For further thought
• Take an opportunity to do something today that consciously responds to the needs of those you see around you.

A sure promise of life from God

Ezekiel 18:5-9

Suppose there is a righteous man who does what is just and right ... He follows my decrees and faithfully keeps my laws. That man is righteous; he will surely live, declares the Sovereign LORD. (verses 5 and 9)

This passage includes what might initially seem like an extraordinary mixture of 'righteous' practices: orthodoxy in religious ritual, sexual propriety, everyday morality, and a concern for social justice. You yourself might well, if asked to sum up the characteristics of a good person, offer a very different list. Admittedly, some things noted by Ezekiel have featured in our reflection this week on the Millennium Goals. We have considered the repayment of loans and the making of profit from the poor, for instance. But the main concern of today's reading is perhaps less to arrive at a full definition of moral rectitude. Rather, the Lord offers through his prophet a promise of life for those who commit themselves wholeheartedly to goodness.

Importantly, the life being promised here is not presented as an arbitrary reward offered by a capricious God to those who carry out his will. It is precisely by choosing to carry out these good actions rather than their wicked alternatives that we discover what it is to live the full life that God offers. It is indeed challenging to commit ourselves to the Millennium Goals, and to work towards the different targets that make them up. But the promise is that in doing that we will experience a quality of life, here in the present moment, that is better than we otherwise would – as well as beginning to live a life that can last eternally.

† Sovereign Lord, let me see clearly those actions in my own life that lead to its fullness; and give me the grace always to carry them out.

For further thought

- What more can you discover about how the targets that make up the Millennium Goals have been met?

Holy Week and Easter with John's Gospel
1 Holy Week with John (chs 12–13, 18–19)

This week's notes are by **Lori Sbordone Rizzo**

Lori Sbordone Rizzo is an itinerant teacher who works with adults and at-risk youth in the poorest communities of New York City. She studied biblical theology in preparation for a career in ministry although, by the grace of God, her classrooms continue to be outside the institutional church. She was stoked to be asked to write on her favourite New Testament text, and she welcomes *Fresh From the Word* readers to find her on social media to continue the discussion.

Sunday 29 March (Palm Sunday)
Worship the King

John 12:12-18

The great crowd ... took palm branches and went out to meet him, shouting, 'Hosanna!' 'Blessed is he who comes in the name of the Lord!' 'Blessed is the king of Israel!' Jesus found a young donkey and sat on it, as it is written: 'Do not be afraid, Daughter of Zion; see, your king is coming, seated on a donkey's colt.' (part of verses 12-15)

John's Gospel is full of unexpected encounters. Among my favourites is the meeting between Jesus and a woman who has become an outcast. She comes to the well in the heat of the day so she can draw water without being seen. Enter Jesus, a man who knows everything she has ever done yet does not define her by her failings. She has no idea how to handle the man, so she changes the subject and asks what mountain he worships on. Jesus responds with one of the great lines of this book: 'A time is coming when you will worship the Father neither on this mountain nor in Jerusalem ... a time is coming and has now come when the true worshippers will worship the Father in the Spirit and in truth, for they are the kind of worshippers the Father seeks' (part of 4:21-23).

Beloved, it is Holy Week. As in today's text, worshippers gather expecting to welcome a king, except this king is not riding an armoured chariot but a humble beast. Jesus makes his triumphal entry with his heart in his hands. True worship means coming into this conversation with our hearts in our hands as well.

† I'm afraid to ask what is required of the true worshipper, but I want to be in that number. I do. O dear God, protect the joyous!

Monday 30 March
A gift of scandal

John 12:1-11

Six days before the Passover ... a dinner was given in Jesus' honour...
Mary took about a litre of pure nard, an expensive perfume; she poured
it on Jesus' feet and wiped his feet with her hair. And the house was filled
with the fragrance of the perfume. (part of verses 1-3)

Six days before Passover, Jesus has just called a man back to life after four days in the tomb. Now the signs-and-wonders days are over. Jesus' next feat will be a display of powerlessness so terrible he can hardly grasp it. Whenever he tries to talk about it, his disciples shut him down. They can't deal with his negativity: 'You're the Messiah. What can go wrong? Have faith!' They're having dinner with Rabbi Jesus and Lazarus, the two hottest celebrities in Palestine. 'Don't bring down our high, dude!'

Only Mary has heard Jesus. The moment she grasps the awful truth, she is driven. Something precious has to break. Something costly needs to pour to the ground in pools and puddles causing others to exclaim in horror, 'What a waste!' The gift of this scandal assures Jesus that someone has heard him. Someone will live in the fear with him and help bear the impossible. Like Simon of Cyrene, she steps in and helps bear the cross.

Jesus' response in defence of Mary is one of the most quoted lines of scripture, invoked whenever churches feel the need to wash their hands. The older version, recorded in Mark, is not as popular, 'The poor you will always have with you, and you can help them any time you want' (Mark 14:7). God's children live in poverty, and we choose to accept this rather than change it. We spend money given to God on flowers for the altar rather than food for the hungry. I am not sure whom we are honouring with these choices.

† Help us, dear God, to honour you today by loving the ones you love, and listening to the ones with whom you grieve.

For further thought

• Do you ever wonder what the people who walk past your church pray about? How might your faith community respond if God asked you to love your neighbours with actions and in truth (1 John 3:18)?

Tuesday 31 March
A prayer for glory

John 12:20-36

Now my soul is troubled, and what shall I say? 'Father, save me from this hour'? No, it was for this very reason I came to this hour. Father, glorify your name!' Then a voice came from heaven, 'I have glorified it, and will glorify it again.' (verses 27-29)

Once, for love of God, I did something I knew would end badly. I brought my vocation to my church's gatekeepers and gave them permission to decide if it lived or died. As I drove to the appointments, the Spirit gave me these words, 'Father, glorify your name.' It's a terrifying prayer. It almost stops your heart to speak it. I was walking into the fight of my life, defenceless.

To this point in the Gospel, Jesus has been insisting that 'his hour' has not yet arrived. Then some Greeks call, and it all begins. I too met some 'Greeks' and in their own way they were saying, 'We would see Jesus.' Like the disciples, I ran to the Lord in panic, except Jesus flipped the script, saying, 'Lori, this is your hour.' I walked into the last meeting, and I was dead. They wanted nothing to do with me. In the end, all that remains is a ridiculous plea that God's goodness will be revealed in the mess. 'Father, glorify your name.'

I did a paper on this passage as a student, but it did not move me. Today I see the depth of love between Jesus and his Father, and I weep with them. Loving God will carry you to places you never knew you could handle and, at those thresholds, you hold open your hands and step forward not because you are strong or good but simply because you love God too much to let go. The seed falls to the ground and dies. Then, in the darkness: life.

† Father, glorify your name in my life today.

For further thought

- In John's Gospel 'glory' refers to the cross. Is this paradox true in your story? Can God be glorified in outcomes that feel like utter failure? I hope so!

Wednesday 1 April
Light at the break of night

John 13:21-32

As soon as Judas took the bread, Satan entered into him. So Jesus told him, 'What you are about to do, do quickly.' … As soon as Judas had taken the bread, he went out. And it was night. (verses 27 and 30)

I've been in a couple of 'revolutionary circles'. They start with something that is unbearably wrong; then there rises a vision of a much better way, followed by a suspicion that we might just be able to pull it off, and before you know it, you're an insider. Betrayals happen, but the motive is never money. The sin isn't greed, but fear or arrogance. The betrayer either feared for his own life or thought he knew better.

Maybe Judas turned because he feared they were all about to be arrested, so he cut a deal. Maybe he thought the arrest would force Jesus to get over himself and get back to the cause. Whatever his reasons, Judas comes to the meal with the plans in place, but he hasn't pulled the trigger. Knowing this, Jesus gives Judas the seat of honour at the dinner. It wasn't enough that Jesus washed his feet, now Judas must share a bowl of food with the man. Jesus is blitzing him with light in an all-out effort to win the brother back. It's a risk. My professor said, 'The same fire which hardens steel, melts wax.' Judas' heart did not melt.

'It was night' (verse 30). Darkness in the ancient world was total. There was no way to sneak up on Jesus without someone to lead them to him. The kiss at the end is cold. It's not going to sit well with his soul. Sometimes you can't love someone out of making a mistake. Betrayal is the unkindest cut because the wound goes deep, and the threat of infection is everywhere.

† Lord Jesus, you drank the poison and stayed the course. Help me to move forward in love.

For further thought

• They say, 'Keep your enemies close,' but can enemies be flipped? What can we learn about how God changes hearts that can mend relationships in our world?

Thursday 2 April (Maundy Thursday)
A truth that sets you free

John 13:1-17

Jesus knew that the Father had put all things under his power, and that he had come from God and was returning to God; so he got up from the meal, took off his outer clothing, and wrapped a towel round his waist. (verses 3-4)

Sovereign authority is a lock. Those who have it don't worry about crowns and castles; their authority resides not in what they have but who they are. Jesus is Lord of all. His authority comes from his Father; no one and nothing can change this. He has no doubt in him about who he is and whose he is, so he is free to do work that others would find humiliating. Shame cannot diminish him, neither can any fear or insecurity confuse his purpose. Jesus sheds his rabbinic vestments and begins our instruction on how God so loves the world.

Earlier in John, Jesus defended healing a paralytic by explaining, 'The Son can do nothing by himself; he can do only what he sees his Father doing' (5:19). Many people see 'god' as a supremely insecure being, constantly in need of praise to feel 'godlike'. Like the ancients, we fear that 'the universe' will swoop down and demand sacrifices as proof of our love. Jesus reveals a God who washes our feet. No tests. No stress. Just sit down and take off your shoes.

Tomorrow, Jesus will lay his body against the wood of the cross, open his hands and allow soldiers to drive nails into his wrists. God, naked and broken; but as sovereign as the day God spoke creation into existence. All is given so we can see who we are and whose we are. If we could grasp that truth, we would be free from the constant contest for approval. We could run after God's ways and proclaim the good news with abandon.

† God, give me grace this year to grasp who I am to you and who I am in you, so that I will be set free to love everyone as you do.

For further thought

• 'Now that you know these things, you will be blessed if you do them' (verse 17). How could knowing this truth about God change the way you do things?

Friday 3 April (Good Friday)
The heart of God

John 19:16-30

Jesus said, 'I am thirsty.' A jar of wine vinegar was there, so they soaked a sponge in it, put the sponge on a stalk of the hyssop plant, and lifted it to Jesus' lips. When he had received the drink, Jesus said, 'It is finished.' With that, he bowed his head and gave up his spirit. **(part of verses 28-30)**

Twice during his crucifixion, Jesus is offered something to drink. The first, wine mixed with gall, he refuses because it's a sedative and, even on the cross, Jesus has work to do. He hears the final confession of a thief, absolves his persecutors, and cares for his mother. Now he is thirsty – the one who claimed to have streams of living water at his command (4:10). He is God poured out.

When I'm arrested at political demonstrations, I never ask the guards for anything. If you admit a need to an enemy, you open yourself up to abuse. Jesus is the epitome of vulnerability. These soldiers have beaten him to the brink of mortality – 'just following orders'. Then they went off-book and viciously mocked him for claiming to be a king. Here they sit, laughing and cursing; casting lots for his clothes and calling him a dog. When I think of them that name we used for the police rises to my lips. We are all guilty of dehumanising our enemies. Yet here in our midst, Jesus is 'de-god-ifying' himself for us.

When Jesus cries, 'I thirst', he reminds the soldiers that he is no dog. When they respond, their souls are retrieved from hate. The 'vinegar' is in fact a sour-wine drink that the soldiers themselves have been drinking. Jesus has reached across the divide between God and humanity and met these men as men. Then, and only then: 'It is finished.' Need to see the heart of God? Look no further. Golgotha makes all of us equal, even God.

† Dear God, there is nothing you won't do for love. Honestly, that is both wonderful and terrifying to one who seeks to love as you do, but loving you leaves me no choice, so … forward.

For further thought

• If you make one step towards God today, he will walk across the universe to meet you.

Saturday 4 April
Love made perfect

John 19:38-42

Joseph of Arimathea asked Pilate for the body of Jesus. Now Joseph was a disciple of Jesus, but secretly because he feared the Jewish leaders … He was accompanied by Nicodemus, the man who earlier had visited Jesus at night. Nicodemus brought a mixture of myrrh and aloes, about thirty-five kilograms. Taking Jesus' body, the two of them wrapped it, with the spices, in strips of linen. (part of verses 38-40)

Joseph of Arimathea appears in all four Gospels. He was a rich man and prominent member of the council (Matthew 27:57, Mark 15:43) and may have been among those who voted to hand Jesus over to Pilate. He had heard the controversial rabbi, and quite possibly was moved by his preaching but, when a verdict was required, Joseph was silent in the face of the ultimate miscarriage of justice. To his credit, he did not hide as the sentence was carried out. He went to Golgotha and confronted the consequences of his actions.

Earlier in his Gospel, John reported about 'secret believers' among the leadership who failed to speak because they feared they would be banned from the synagogue. Among these was Nicodemus, who knew Jesus was a 'teacher sent from God' but was afraid to be seen with him in the daylight (3:2ff). John spares no punches in calling out these 'undercover brothers': 'they loved human praise more than praise from God' (12:43). In the end, John the beloved disciple and Joseph the cowardly committee-member are together. Standing beneath the cross, there is no fear. John will later proclaim, 'There is no fear in love. But perfect love drives out fear' (1 John 4:18). The cross of Christ reveals a love that finishes the work no matter the cost, and drives out all that is false. To hell with it! The love of God revealed in the life and death of Jesus is just too beautiful! There is no affirmation greater than the simple truth that God loves us perfectly. May our lives forever speak his praise.

† Perfect Love, reign in my heart today and for ever. Cast out fear and all that is false, and set me free to serve you.

For further thought
• When Perfect Love reigns, people who formerly lived in fear find themselves called out with linen and spices. Let us follow Joseph and Nicodemus and do likewise.

Holy Week and Easter with John's Gospel
2 Easter with John (chs 20–21)

This week's notes are by **Andrew Nagy-Benson**

Revd Andrew Nagy-Benson is the pastor of The Congregational Church (United Church of Christ) in Middlebury, Vermont, USA. A graduate of Yale Divinity School, Andy previously served churches in New Hampshire and Connecticut and taught as a lecturer of homiletics at Yale. He writes poetry and has contributed articles to the biblical commentary series *Feasting on the Word*. Andy and his wife, Gwen, and their three daughters live in Weybridge, Vermont, down the road from a sheep farm.

Sunday 5 April (Easter Day)
The empty tomb of Easter

John 20:1-9

So Peter and the other disciple started for the tomb. Both were running, but the other disciple outran Peter and reached the tomb first. He bent over and looked in at the strips of linen lying there but did not go in. Then Simon Peter came along behind him and went straight into the tomb.
(verses 3–5 and part of verse 6)

At the end of Wynton Marsalis's *The Majesty of Blues*, there is a three-part composition. The first part is called 'The Death of Jazz'. The second is 'Premature Autopsies'. And the last one is called 'Oh, But on the Third Day (Happy Feet Blues)'.

That last piece could be the soundtrack to this morning's Gospel lesson. The bass drum and snare drum begin beating like the disciples' hearts after they hear the news about the empty tomb. Then the double bass greets the clarinet and they're off. Like the disciples racing towards the tomb, the musicians never look back.

On that morning, the tune changes. Friday's dirge is replaced with a dance number. Hope has a pulse.

Sure, big questions remain. Not least: if Jesus is not in the tomb, then where is he? Still, even in the half-light of pre-dawn, the two winded disciples begin to see what the empty tomb means. If Jesus is not entombed, then the love of God could be on the loose. From now on, we will look for holy love in the land of the living.

† Gracious God, be gentle with us as we wonder. Rekindle our hope as we imagine your endless possibilities. Fill us with Easter joy. Amen

Is the gardener Jesus, or is Jesus the gardener?

John 20:10-18

He asked her, 'Woman, why are you crying? Who is it you are looking for?'

Thinking he was the gardener, she said, 'Sir, if you have carried him away, tell me where you have put him, and I will get him.'

Jesus said to her, 'Mary.' (verse 15 and part of 16)

Have you played the children's game called In Plain Sight? In Plain Sight is fine practice for an Easter people.

For those who don't know, here's how you play: you show your friends a common object, like a spoon. Your friends leave the room, and when they are out of sight you lay the spoon in the open – on the end table, on the arm of a chair. Then, your friends rush back into the room and they look everywhere at once. The spoon could be anywhere. It should be so simple to see it and, because it should be simple, it is not. The quick-eyed seekers race around the room, eyes flying past the spoon.

Then the moment comes: 'Oh, it's right there. Has it been there the whole time?'

Like that children's game, the story of Mary and the gardener and Jesus makes me wonder what I miss day to day. If Jesus can be here and there, then perhaps we'd all do well to look twice as we rush around.

Last year, in advance of an Easter service, I paid a visit to a class of young children at church. I read them John's Easter story. At one point I asked them, 'So, is the gardener Jesus, or is Jesus the gardener?'

One brave soul raised her hand and said: 'Yes.'

Indeed.

So, again, we look for holy love in the land of the living.

† God of love, will I find you today in the faces of the ones I meet? Let it be.

For further thought

• Read Mary Oliver's poem 'Mindful' from *Why I Wake Early* (Beacon, 2004) – a fine poem that explores the art of seeing.

Tuesday 7 April
The Holy Spirit of shared ministry

John 20:19-23

Again Jesus said, 'Peace be with you! As the Father has sent me, I am sending you.' And with that he breathed on them and said, 'Receive the Holy Spirit.' (verses 21-22)

In 2007 I participated in a public action to raise awareness about the threat of global warming. People gathered that day across the United States – from the levees of New Orleans to the melting glaciers atop Mt Rainer. There were 1400 different events with the same message to the US Congress: Reduce carbon by 80 per cent by the year 2050.

This event was inspired by seven people from Vermont. Seven people – one pew's worth of people – practised the art of collaboration to great effect.

The art of working together towards a common goal is nothing new. In fact, it is in play in this passage from John's Gospel.

On Easter evening, the disciples are locked up with fear. Do they fear for their own lives? Are they afraid that Jesus will come back to haunt them?

In the half-light of evening, Jesus is there – standing there – where they are. Mercifully, he does not ask them: 'Where were you on Friday?' He does not say, 'You let me down.'

He says twice, 'Peace be with you.'

Then Jesus does what exceptional leaders do: he shares his power. He needs someone to act on his behalf. He needs disciples to carry his light out of that room and into the world. He needs them to forgive as he forgives, to love as he loves.

So, he exhales power: *Here's my Spirit. My life.* With that, the locked room becomes a delivery room. The brainchild of shared ministry is born.

† These are the words we dimly hear: You, sent out beyond your recall, go to the limits of your longing. Embody me. (Rainer Rilke, *Book of Hours*, I:59)

For further thought

• According to the principles of community organising, there is a clear preference for 'power with' rather than 'power over' to bring about change. How might that relate to this scene of Easter evening?

Wednesday 8 April
Thomas and our need for evidence

John 20:24-31

So the other disciples told [Thomas], 'We have seen the Lord!'

But he said to them, 'Unless I see the nail marks in his hands and put my finger where the nails were, and put my hand into his side, I will not believe.' (verse 25)

'I'll believe it when I see it!'

As a child, I became familiar with that expression. It might have had something to do with my walking into the house with muddy sneakers for the billionth time. My mother would offer a well-earned corrective, I'd offer forecasts of better behaviour, and she'd say, 'I'll believe it when I see it.'

'I'll believe it when I see it' is a common and curious claim. It can mean 'I don't think this or that will happen.' It can mean, 'If what you say is true, then show me.' Either way, the expression does not convey much faith.

We could go further. Taken literally, the expression does not make much sense. If you are shown the improbable, what is there left to believe but your eyesight? In the Christian tradition, faith has to do with 'the conviction of things not seen'. *Not* seen. The appearance of resurrected Jesus comes to mind.

In the Gospel of John, Thomas declares that he will not believe that post-Easter Jesus is really alive until he can see and touch him. For this, we call him Doubting Thomas. It's an unfortunate nickname. Thomas is a human being with faith *and* doubt, knowledge *and* unknowable mystery, lodged in his heart and mind.

Like Thomas, I walk country roads with convictions and questions. I trust that God is with us, and I want to see evidence of heavenly love on earth.

† God of compassion, I believe; help my unbelief (Mark 9:24). Amen

For further thought

• Some say doubt is the opposite of faith, others say the opposite of faith is certainty. Which is closer to your understanding?

Thursday 9 April
Gone fishin'?

April

John 21:1-14

Early in the morning, Jesus stood on the shore, but the disciples did not realise that it was Jesus.

He called out to them, 'Friends, haven't you any fish?'

'No,' they answered. (verses 4-5)

The disciples are back home by the Galilean seaside. Apparently, Peter gets tired of sitting around and announces, 'I'm going fishing.' This is either the funniest or the saddest line in the Gospel. Here's someone who witnessed the bright light of the Transfiguration, who heard Jesus pray to 'Daddy' in the Garden of Gethsemane, who ran inside the empty tomb, who saw the risen Christ on Easter night. Now he's going fishing.

Peter and the disciples fish all night with nothing to show for it. The next morning, someone calls out from shore, 'Catch anything?' The fishermen shake their heads.

Then 'the someone' (who's starting to sound a lot like Jesus) offers some advice, 'Try throwing the nets on the right side of the boat.' The 'right' side of the boat – very funny. But they do it. Having worked on the salmon docks of Alaska, I would suggest that this is probably the first and only time in the history of fishing that a boat full of fish-less fisherman have heeded the advice of an onshore onlooker.

The fishermen throw the nets on the right side of the boat and the empty nets aren't empty any more: 153 fish later, the fishermen realise that the onlooker is Jesus, and Peter dives in to swim to his Lord.

Can you hear the echo of joyful laughter off the water? If you listen long enough, you might also hear the echo of the Gospel's prologue: 'Out of his fullness we have all received grace in place of grace already given' (John 1:16).

† God, surprise me today with the abundance of your love, that in receiving grace I may offer it to others. Amen

For further thought
• When unexpected good fortune finds us, do we perceive something at work beyond what we can explain?

Friday 10 April
Do you love me?

John 21:15-19

The third time he said to him, 'Simon son of John, do you love me?' Peter was hurt because Jesus asked him the third time, 'Do you love me?' He said, 'Lord you know all things; you know that I love you.' Jesus said, 'Feed my sheep.' (verse 17)

Earlier in John's Gospel, Jesus says to the disciples, '[The shepherd] calls his own sheep by name and leads them out. When he has brought out all his own, he goes on ahead of them, and his sheep follow him because they know his voice' (10:3-4). Any shepherd worth his crook can tell you Jesus is right.

I've been reading up on sheep for a while, and from what I've read, you don't herd sheep from the rear with shouts and prods. If you stand behind sheep and make noise, they'll run behind you. Sheep prefer to be led, and they will wait for the shepherd to show them the way.

Of course, we know that Jesus is not really talking about shepherds and sheep. He's talking about who he is and who the disciples are. Jesus is the one who leads, the disciples are the ones who follow.

And yet, as John's Gospel nears its end, Jesus calls Peter to be a deputy shepherd – one who will care for and lead the flock. Whatever authority Peter has to do this work comes not from a Genevan robe or clerical collar. Rather, his authority comes from a fierce determination to love the ones Jesus loves.

Likewise, our commitments to care for one another find their root in the Good Shepherd's final commandment: 'As I have loved you, so you must love one another' (John 13:34). Is there any other way to follow Jesus or to lead his flock?

† God, where there is hatred, let me sow love. Amen

(Commonly attributed to St Francis)

For further thought

• Some church members refer to themselves as 'followers of Jesus'. This implies confession of faith and adherence to Jesus's teachings. Might such a claim also resonate with Jesus' depiction of the sheep–shepherd relationship?

Saturday 11 April
Next witness, please

John 21:20-25

Jesus did many other things as well. If every one of them were written down, I suppose that even the whole world would not have room for the books that would be written. (verse 25)

Our youngest daughter is five years old. Each night, after some negotiation, she lies in bed and I read her stories. After the bedside light is turned off, I tell her she is loved and she tells me the same. She'll say something like, 'I love you, Daddy, from above the sky to below the dirt.' Our expressions of affection are genuine, if approximate. Is it possible to capture in words how much a parent loves his child, or how much a child loves her parent? There is always more to tell.

In that spirit, Johns's Gospel ends with a kind of disclaimer. After twenty chapters of Jesus' words and deeds, there is more to tell than anyone possibly could. In the author's words, 'the whole world would not have room for the books that would be written' about the life of Jesus.

Isn't that where we come in? If we take John's account of Easter and the days after Easter to heart, can't we expect to witness – and to hear others witness – to God's love on the loose?

There is no explicit assignment here, but there is an invitation for the church of every age to tell its stories, to share how the life and teachings of Jesus continue to stir minds and change hearts. So, we pick up where John's Gospel leaves off, because God is still speaking and there is something fresh about this Word.

† Still-speaking God, grant me the courage to listen and hear, to speak and tell of your everlasting goodness. Amen

For further thought

• Wisdom on full stops from comedian Gracie Allen: 'Never place a period where God has placed a comma.' (Last letter to George Burns, as quoted in Peter B Panagore, *Two Minutes for God: Quick Fixes for the Spirit,* 2007:73)

Moving into the future

1 The promise of the Spirit, the Counsellor

This week's notes are by **Alesana Fosi Pala'amo**

Alesana is a lecturer in practical theology at Malua Theological College in Samoa. Ordained as a minister of the Congregational Christian Church Samoa, his teaching and research interests include Christian ministry, youth and social ministries, pastoral theology, worship, and pastoral counselling. Presently Alesana is undertaking his PhD research in pastoral counselling through Massey University, New Zealand. Alesana is a counsellor to many people in the church, as well as several Pacific Islanders within the Auckland area.

Sunday 12 April
The place for counselling

John 14:1-4

My Father's house has many rooms; if that were not so, would I have told you that I am going there to prepare a place for you? (**verse 2**)

A house provides shelter and protection from the elements. It becomes a safe haven and provides privacy. A house can be subdivided into many rooms within the one overarching house, so that all rooms share the properties of a house. A traditional house of Samoa, called a *fale*, shares the properties of any house from Western and European contexts but with one major difference – it has no walls, doors, or windows. A Samoan fale is a structure of strategically placed poles between its roof and floor. Its openness means neighbouring houses share the problems and tribulations from each open house.

How wonderful is the house that Jesus has prepared for his faithful believers! His entire ministry has been about showing believers the properties of the Father's house. A house of many rooms, for all walks of life, all ages, that provides shelter and protection. It is a house of refuge, where one can feel safe. An open house to take our problems to, in knowing we will not be judged or treated differently. Our voices that are often brushed aside will be heard. It is a house that will remain through time and beyond time, remaining everlasting. A wonderful place to be counselled.

† Lord, help us to remember to come to your house, when our problems become too much. Amen

Monday 13 April
Show me the way

John 14:5-9

Thomas said to him, 'Lord, we don't know where you are going, so how can we know the way?' (verse 5)

Life has many challenges and, frequently, knowing where to get help is the first step towards addressing these challenges. Sometimes it becomes a case of poking aimlessly in the dark trying to find whatever it may be one is searching for. The Samoan proverb '*o le tele o sulu e maua ai figota*' can be translated as 'many torches gets the shellfish'. Commonly this Samoan saying is understood in the Samoan activity of reef fishing during the night. Traditionally the night sky lit up by a full moon provided enough lighting to perform this task. With the progression towards invented lighting from lanterns to kerosene lamps to battery-operated torches, the more torches, the easier it became to spot where the fish were. Its meaning: the more perspectives, the more lit up our paths become, and then we will know which path to take.

The disciples were searching for a way to follow. They had many questions but struggled for answers, and they were running out of time. Jesus showed them many signs along the way to light up their paths. Yet they were oblivious to the fact that right among them was the greatest light and pathway to the answers they were seeking. In times of distress and discomfort, of uncertainty and despair, we may overlook the way to God's blessings that are abundant among us. Jesus is the way to our Father God; Jesus is the way that we can be led along towards healing from our life problems and to everlasting peace; Jesus is the embodiment of God's grace and peace.

† Lord, show us the way to you so that your peace will give us comfort always. Amen

For further thought

- Do you feel at times you are always 'poking in the dark'? The answer is nearby. Faith in Christ will show you the way.

Tuesday 14 April
Like father like son

John 14:10-13

Believe me when I say that I am in the Father and the Father is in me...
(part of verse 11)

'The apple doesn't fall far from the tree' is a common saying that highlights the theme for today's reflection. The first time I heard this was when a fellow student at Protestant Theological University in the Netherlands shared this in reference to my then four-month-old son. Initially unaware of its meaning, the phrase soon taught me that in many ways my infant son and I shared several physical and personality similarities. Translating the meaning of this phrase to a tree familiar to Samoa helps me understand it. The coconut tree produces a fruit with many uses. The juice from the young coconut becomes a thirst-quenching treat. The cream from the mature coconut is used in many Samoan recipes. The husk and shell from the used coconut provides fuel for fire, and the leaves from the tree are woven for many purposes. Unlike the apple tree, one tries to remain a safe distance from under the coconut tree for the fear of falling mature coconuts that can result in serious injury and damage. Often the mature coconut that has fallen will, if left untouched over time, sprout a coconut shoot protruding from its husk – the signs and beginning of new life and re-growth.

Jesus gives us the purest example of all things God-like, for he is the Son of the Father. Jesus is love, so God is love. Jesus is life, so God is life. In fact, Jesus is the new life and re-growth that sprouts up from God our everlasting Father. Jesus is the perfect Son, from the perfect Father. Like Father, like Son.

† O Father, continue to teach us daily your ways through your Son and our Saviour Jesus Christ. Amen

For further thought

• Do you forget at times that we are just like our parents? Do you forget at times that children imitate what parents do?

Wednesday 15 April
The promise of the Wonderful Counsellor

Isaiah 9:6-7

For to us a child is born, to us a son is given, and the government will be on his shoulders. And he will be called Wonderful Counsellor, Mighty God, Everlasting Father, Prince of Peace. (verse 6)

How do you respond in honesty when your six-year-old pleads, 'but you promised'? This was a dilemma I faced while hosting a barbecue with my wife and sons, my sister and some family members one afternoon in Auckland. To attend to my son's plea of kicking his football around the backyard meant abruptly ending the conversations with my cousins mid-sentence; it also meant that some of the meats I was cooking on the barbecue would be left unattended for a few minutes. I did promise my son what he had asked, I just did not anticipate he would collect on my promise at that specific time. I kept my promise and kicked the ball around with my son.

The promise God made to his chosen people through the prophet Isaiah was precisely the hope that God's people were seeking. The best aspect of this promise is that God is known to be a promise-keeper. Jesus was born the Son of God with all authority of God the Father. Jesus has been predestined as the greatest and most wonderful counsellor for all people. Jesus' teachings of God's kingdom have authority over the natural and created world where all things are made possible; Jesus has healed the sick, touched the stubborn in heart, and has represented the oppressed and outcasts. Jesus even conquered death through his resurrection to eternal life. With Jesus as the Prince of Peace he brings peace for now with much more to come, in the eternal kingdom of God the Father, the King of Peace.

† O Christ our wonderful counsellor, remind us of the peace that you bring into our lives daily. Amen

For further thought

• Do you make promises you feel that you may not be able to keep? Promises made need to be realistic, simple, and – most important – kept.

Tell me what 'love in obedience' means to you

John 14:15-21

Whoever has my commands and keeps them is the one who loves me.
(part of verse 21)

A common practice of contemporary Samoan parenting is the 'do as I say because I know best' understanding between parent and child. Many Samoan young people whom I have ministered to and counselled would prefer a more open dialogue in the parenting they received. Yet they still obey the commands from their parents. When asked for reasons why, the common response was, 'because I had to'. Although this parenting practice may seem to demand passive obedience by Samoan young people, it actually echoes the underlying Samoan way or *fa'a Samoa*, the traditions and culture of Samoa. Respecting one's elders is a given for many Samoans; obeying parents' commands falls into the 'respecting elders' category. But understanding that at the heart of this type of parenting is an undeniable love of parents for their children makes it not that bad after all. Love comes before the command to obey. If parents didn't love their children, they wouldn't care about guiding or instructing them about life issues. Likewise, if children didn't love their parents, they wouldn't care about obeying or respecting their parents. To obey is to love.

Jesus taught his disciples of this 'love in obedience'. Because of the love of Jesus for his disciples and for humankind, these commandments are in place – because Jesus is love. Likewise, due to our love for Jesus and for God, we obey these commandments. To obey God is to love God. If we love God then we keep the commandments that he has left us. Love in obedience.

† O Lord, instil in us hearts that are obedient to you, our Father. Amen

For further thought

• Can you see the underlying love behind the instructions to obey? If not, what is clouding the love? It is awesome that someone truly cares!

Friday 17 April
Tell me what 'believing' looks like to you

John 14:22-24

Then Judas (not Judas Iscariot) said, 'But, Lord, why do you intend to show yourself to us and not to the world?' (**verse 22**)

When you witness an extraordinary event, even though you are seeing it, it does not always mean that you believe it. In fact the more unbelievable the event, the more difficult it is to grasp what you are seeing. In September 2009, several regions of Samoa were devastated by a tsunami considered as one of the worst natural disasters to have hit Samoa in recent times. I was on the west coast of Samoa when the tsunami struck the east and the earthquake that experts say read 8.3 on the Richter scale was hard to believe. It was only when our team arrived at the worst-hit areas of the island the day after with relief aid collected from Malua Theological College that the magnitude of the event sank in. Seeing does not always equal believing. Seeing can actually make the believing all that more difficult to sink in.

The disciples were privileged that Jesus revealed many signs to them so that they would understand God through what Jesus did. Yet many times the disciples did not understand the messages Jesus taught. For Christians today, believing means to not see and yet still believe. Faith is just this. God has revealed just enough through his Son Jesus Christ in order for the multitudes to believe back then, as well as now in the modern era. The beauty of it all is that there is still more to come. Believing in the love of God revealed and shown abundantly around us means to embrace God's peace. For when we believe, we find peace amongst the challenges that life may bring.

† Lord God, teach us to always believe in your love and grace. Help us to see the works of your love in our lives. Amen

For further thought
• Do we need to see to believe? Faith means trusting God wholeheartedly. We do not see God, however we see the many works of God's love.

Counselling God's peace

April

John 14:25-31

Peace I leave with you; my peace I give you. I do not give to you as the world gives. Do not let your hearts be troubled and do not be afraid. (verse 27)

An overarching goal of counselling in any setting, be it secular or from a Christian perspective, is to help the troubled person find alternatives that lead to peace. It is not simply a task of practitioners working to 'fix' the problem, but rather working alongside the troubled person to look at different ways that could help the situation. Together the person seeking help and the counsellor develop intervention care plans that will achieve the overall goal to any counselling encounter – finding peace. If peace leads to solutions to the problem, good. If peace leads to discovering ways of coping and healing for the troublesome situation, that is good too. Finding peace amid chaos and uncertainty is often the goal.

How amazing is our Lord Christ who brings this peace that many seek. Jesus departed from his disciples with the blessing of peace. The intervention care plan that God has done for humankind is the absolute display of love that cannot be repeated. Through the death and resurrection of our Lord we are saved. Our sinful ways are cleansed; our guilty conscience about ungodly behaviour has been sanctified through God's grace. What better intervention plan does one seek? God sent Christ into the world to intervene and to show us the pathway to God the Father. In parting from us, Christ has left behind his peace. God is peace, and through God we find peace among the many setbacks that may surface from time to time in our daily lives. In and through Christ we are given the joy of peace, to enjoy now and for evermore.

† Lord God, thank you for the peace you give us always. Help us to never lose sight of your peace. Amen

For further thought

• Sometimes sitting and praying without words brings our thoughts and emotions in sync with God's peace. Stop, and listen to God speak.

Moving into the future

2 The vine and the branches

This week's notes are by **Ian Fosten**

Ian Fosten is a director of a community theatre, a poet and leader of the ministry team for Norwich Area United Reformed Churches in the UK. He lives on the Suffolk coast with his wife and youngest children. He helped set up the St Cuthbert's Centre mission project on Holy Island (Lindisfarne) and has built and restored several wooden boats. He has a particular interest in connections between theology and landscape, and between scripture and the inevitable untidiness of everyday life. A collection of his poetry and writing is found on his blog 'Heaven in Ordinarie' at www.fosten.com.

Sunday 19 April

What appears on the bottom line?

Isaiah 5:1-7

The vineyard of the Lord *Almighty is the nation of Israel, and the people of Judah are the vines he delighted in. And he looked for justice, but saw bloodshed; for righteousness, but heard cries of distress.* (verse 7)

Whether it is in a vineyard, a business, a family or a relationship, how well we use the given ingredients of our life matters hugely to God.

A young man spoke well of himself. His experience was broad, likewise his competence. In fact, his past performance made him confident enough to offer advice generously to those around him. Time passed, appearances were good and if he was asked how work was progressing he would reply reassuringly that 'he was on it!' Time passed; some more; deadlines came and went. Promised work either failed to appear or was presented shoddily, late or incomplete. The atmosphere within the team turned chilly and sour. Then came a day of reckoning and the value to the enterprise of the time, money and trust invested in him was calculated. Sadly, the bottom line displayed a deficit, a loss, the emptying of all that promise for no useful gain.

The ultimate fruitfulness of a promising opportunity depends often enough upon factors beyond our reach but, within the life of God's kingdom, commitment and integrity still play a vital role.

† Today and every day, dear God, look carefully upon the work of my life and find my balance to be in credit. Amen

Monday 20 April
A worthwhile cost?

Psalm 80:8-11

You transplanted a vine from Egypt; you drove out the nations and planted it. ... it took root and filled the land. (verses 8 and 9b)

To read the Bible well we need open eyes, an open mind and an open heart. We also need to face the honest questions raised by the text if we want to hear God's word for today, and not merely have our pre-existing thoughts and prejudice rubber-stamped. So, in the midst of this song of national triumph, something jars; a phrase rears up that cannot be ignored or glossed over. Who were the people displaced by God's planting scheme? At what cost were they removed?

Western Europeans, mindful of a sometimes shady colonial past, hear only too clearly the resonance of such questions. The trampled cultures, the imposition of an alien way of knowing God, the abuse of trade and the reckless use of military technology are the questionable supports of exported civilisation and spiritual truth.

So what about this vine, uprooted from oppression in Egypt and planted by force on Canaan's fertile soil?

'Look to the fruit,' the Gardener explains. 'Taste and see the value of these vines; drink deeply and well from a vintage pressed out from grapes of love, justice, peace and joy. Hold up the glass to catch the luminescence of a true light to the nations, and a fragrance that lifts our spirits beyond the flavours of every day.'

The best way to read this victory song is to allow it to be illuminated by the servant Christ – taken, crushed and discarded in order to show the cost, power and all-invasive reach of love.

† Loving God, Living Word, help me to read the Bible honestly and well with open eyes, an open mind and an open heart.

For further thought

• Practise approaching the Bible with an attitude of listening before attempting to analyse or interpret.

Tuesday 21 April
Hard pruning: sweet fruiting

John 15:1-4

...while every branch that does bear fruit he prunes so that it will be even more fruitful. (verse 2b)

One April I walked part of the pilgrimage route to Santiago de Compostela in Spain. Beforehand I had joked that I was having a strolling retreat in the sunshine. The reality was very different. There was little obvious spiritual refreshment to be had, for the terrain was mountainous and the weather offered both blizzard and heavy rain with just a little sunshine. As we trudged through the famous Rioja wine region, cold, wet and footsore, I thought mostly of my journey's end and with it a hot bath and a bottle of the local produce. The vineyards we passed showed little sign of such promise – just row upon row of gnarled stumps beneath waist-high wires.

Within the plant world, grape vines present a paradox. I learned this from a gardening expert on a radio show. To a woman's question, 'how can I get sweet and tasty grapes on my vine?' he replied that, once the bunches had begun to form, she should reduce their number by as much as she dared, then she should cut back some more. She should go and have a cup of tea and then prune some more until she wept at the apparent loss. 'Then', he concluded, 'you will have yourself some sweet and tasty grapes!'

In choosing the vine as his analogy Jesus teaches us that it is out of the tough calls, the knock-backs, the weariness and the hard pruning of life's events that the sweetest wine of the kingdom is produced.

Bathed, rested and blessed in a truckers' motel outside Logrono, I toasted this marvellous truth.

† Help me, dear God, not to be precious or overly protective of myself but to trust my life to your pruning wisdom.

For further thought

• Consider what ordinary, mundane encounters in your life today might in truth be unlikely but real steps along your own pilgrim way.

Wednesday 22 April
Immersion rather than caution

John 15:5-8

If you remain in me and I in you, you will bear much fruit... (part of verse 5)

Holy Island, UK, also known as Lindisfarne, has been a focus for Christian mission for nearly 1,400 years. Today more than half a million visitors visit each year. In the 1990s I worked on the transformation of a redundant church building on the island into a contemporary place of welcome, hospitality, teaching and gentle evangelism. This exciting prospect came with a couple of problems. As it stood, the building offered neither comfort, heat nor a toilet. Second, the islanders were understandably wary of their home being turned into some kind of religious theme park by incomers like me.

Any thought that my time might be spent in quiet contemplation, prayer and writing was quickly dispelled by the practicality of living on a tidal island and the graft required to transform this inappropriate building into something fit for purpose. While liturgy and poetry did happen, they were overshadowed by digging service trenches, removing pews, laying floors, barrowing many tons of soil and setting out a welcoming garden.

After three years of immersing myself in building work, cautiously developing a ministry to visitors, and participating humbly in island life, I noticed two encouraging changes. First, the building was becoming alive as a focus of a worthwhile ministry and, second, we had earned enough respect to be accepted as a legitimate part of the local community.

Living in God's kingdom is rarely spectacular nor does it often bring instant rewards. It is, however, a way of living where prayer, love, commitment and holy graft are never wasted but are built carefully into healing hope and purpose for our broken world.

† This day and every day make of the work of my hands, the output of my mind and the offering of my love the sweet wine of your kingdom.

For further thought

- Do we sometimes limit our perception of the work of the kingdom to those activities that have the unhelpfully limited label, 'full-time Christian work'?

Caught up in a virtuous circle

John 15:9-12

My command is this: Love each other as I have loved you. (**verse 12**)

A vicious circle refers to a cycle of events or circumstances that revolves inevitably towards a destructive end. We see this played out in the replicating tragedies of abuse or poverty or violent solutions to violent problems. When the Bible speaks of sin it is just such a pattern that is in mind. The life, death and resurrection of Jesus demonstrate God's deep-hearted desire to break into the vicious circle of humanity's self-destruction and open up a better way to live.

A virtuous circle refers to a cycle of events and circumstances that build creatively and wholesomely upon each other. Jesus presents the initial elements of just such a virtuous circle – 'As the father has loved me, so I have loved you. Now remain in my love' (verse 9) – but then expands them to include any person willing to commit to this way of being. And whereas a vicious circle contracts into an ever tighter spiral of destruction, this virtuous circle of love is designed to expand and draw ever more people into it. So why is the virtuous circle of love not the preferred choice of humanity? Because, while falling into the vicious circle takes no effort, self-giving love requires us to make unconventional choices, take risks and take on the desires of our creator God rather than be guided solely by the voice of self-interest. To choose to join in the virtuous circle of God's love is not for the faint-hearted – but then, nothing in life of true and lasting value ever is!

† Since before the dawn of time, the Father loves; Long ago and far away, yet fully in the midst of life today, Jesus loves; Within my life's kaleidoscope of all that's broken or beautiful the Spirit shapes the possibilities of love; So encircle me, re-shape me, and use me for your loving purpose today.

For further thought

• Set aside a day for personal retreat and use this prayer as your focus.

Friday 24 April
Heroic love

John 15:13; Romans 5:6-8

Greater love has no one than this: to lay down one's life for one's friends.
(verse 13)

> *A soldier fulfils his duty*
> *loyally, professionally, courageously.*
> *If he is unlucky*
> *he will die in action and,*
> *rightly so,*
> *we will remember him;*
> *we will remember him.*
>
> *A carer sets aside*
> *the life she might have had,*
> *endures a loss of sleep and,*
> *perhaps, a loss of laughter, joy and peace;*
> *becomes a witnesses and companion to decline.*
> *She learns to balance on diminishing hope*
> *and sometimes falls –*
> *yet climbs on board again to give and give*
> *and give...*
>
> *will we remember her?*
> *will we remember her?*

Ian Fosten

† Mysterious Christ, who hangs upon a cross, for love's sake bless all who care heroically with your unfathomable peace. Amen

For further thought

• Who are the unacknowledged heroes in your community? How can you support them?

Saturday 25 April
Friends: what's in a name?

John 15:14-17

I no longer call you servants, because a servant does not know his master's business. Instead, I have called you friends, for everything that I learned from my Father I have made known to you. **(verse 15)**

It is said that to have at least one real friend in life is a joy, a privilege and an anchor for our sanity. To have more than six real friends is unsustainable. Whether or not that is true, real friendship is clearly no small idea and few people need more than one hand's worth of digits on which to number those who could be called upon at a time of deepest personal need.

With the burgeoning advent of social media the term 'friend' has tended to become synonymous with 'acquaintance'. Even that can be diluted still further to refer to the mere acquisition of someone's online contact details in order to add them to the trophy cabinet of 'virtual friends'.

When Jesus used the term 'friend' he invested it with the significance of an apprenticeship completed, a level of trust and reliability achieved. It was characterised by attributes such as mutuality, vulnerability, intimacy and risk. To be a friend of Jesus is to be rewarded with the mixed privilege of joy and obligation by which his own burden of work and ministry could be shared.

Perhaps the clearest sign of how deep and real a friendship is will be the extent to which you can be at home and wholly yourself in that person's company. This is the true quality of friendship that Jesus offers to all who truly would be his friends.

† Thank you, Lord Jesus, for trusting me enough to be counted among your friends.

For further thought
• Seek out opportunities to thank your closest friends for the trust and at-home-ness they give to you. Review your list of virtual friends and either take steps to make the friendship genuine or else weed out those who are included only to make up the numbers.

Moving into the future

3 Warnings of what lies ahead

This week's notes are by **Heather Tomlinson**

Heather is a freelance journalist with an interest in apologetics and helping the secular world to understand Christianity and its values. She has worked on *The Guardian* and *The Independent on Sunday*, and for *Christianity* magazine. She has also worked within the NHS for mental health services. She is passionate about social justice, especially in the world's poorest countries, and likes to chat in British Sign Language. She's active in her local Anglican church.

Sunday 26 April

Hatred for Jesus and his disciples

John 15:18-21

If the world hates you, keep in mind that it hated me first. If you belonged to the world, it would love you as its own. As it is, you do not belong to the world, but I have chosen you out of the world. That is why the world hates you. (verses 18-19)

I don't know many Christians who have been really persecuted for their faith, but that's because I live in the UK. In our culture, increasingly there are some who hate Christians, but they are thankfully rarely violent and are still a minority.

Once I wrote an article about former Muslims who had found faith in Christ, including an Iranian and Syrian and some British believers. I was struck by the sacrifices they make for Jesus. Some no longer talked to their family; others lived under different names for fear of violent retribution; some wanted to check who I was before they spoke to me. No one wanted to publish their real name. For many people in communist or oppressive Islamic countries, persecution is expected when they find faith in Christ.

In today's passage Jesus warns us this will happen. It's hard to understand, as he was a compassionate and humble healer – yet people hated him. And he says that, if we follow in his footsteps, we will be hated too. We can't become a Christian because we want to be liked. But as the previous passage reminds us, it is still our duty to love people who hate us.

† Dear Lord, help us to follow in your footsteps and really love those who persecute us, and support those who are hated for their beliefs. Amen

118

Monday 27 April
Speaking God's words without fear

Ezekiel 2:3-7

Do not be afraid, though briers and thorns are all around you and you live among scorpions. Do not be afraid of what they say or be terrified by them, though they are a rebellious people. You must speak my words to them, whether they listen or fail to listen, for they are rebellious. **(verses 6b-7)**

Once I was with a friend, and she seemed a little sad. I felt in my heart that God loved her very much, and was sad that she didn't know it. Then I heard a small voice: 'Tell her.'

I knew it was God. But, it took a good five minutes of feeling anxious and shifting in my seat before I could say the words. 'I know this sounds really strange … ahem,' I began, 'but I think God wants me to tell you that he loves you.'

She had always been uninterested in my faith, but she certainly listened to this. 'Well, it must be difficult to feel you have to say such things,' she said, perceptively. 'But perhaps…' she went on to tell me something very personal to her, which she thought might be the reason that God had wanted to communicate. And she seemed open for the first time to the idea that God existed and cared for her.

The reason I was anxious about telling her of God's love was because I didn't want to seem silly or odd. Our culture can be very dismissive of the spiritual, sometimes even hostile. Yet there are Christians all round the world who also obey God in telling people of his love, but who have much worse consequences to fear. If they evangelise, they can face violence, prison and even death. Think also of Martin Luther King, who continued to push for justice but also taught his followers to love and forgive their oppressors. His life was regularly threatened, and ultimately he gave it for this cause.

† Dear Lord, please help us to seek your voice and obey you in all things. Remove our fear. Strengthen those who are in danger for sharing their faith. Amen

For further thought

• Do you have a clear sense of what God wants you to say? What frightens you when you talk about God? How can you overcome this fear?

Tuesday 28 April
When kindness isn't returned

Psalm 35:11-14

They repay me evil for good and leave me like one bereaved. Yet when they were ill, I put on sackcloth and humbled myself with fasting. When my prayers returned to me unanswered, I went about mourning as though for my friend or brother. (verses 12-14a)

When I left journalism for a while, to work in acute mental health wards, I was full of enthusiasm. I wanted to do something compassionate to help people, rather than writing negative stories in the newspapers. So on my first day, I was full of positivity. I walked on to the ward, and a lady was sat in the corridor, glaring at me. '**** you!' she said loudly. It wasn't quite what I expected but it was a welcome reminder that our best intentions are not always understood or appreciated. I loved the quirky characters in my new job, but often their reasons for being ungrateful were very understandable, and they had much bigger issues on their plate.

If we are compassionate towards someone, our selfish human nature expects them to be grateful. And, unlike the people on hospital wards, not everyone has justifiable reasons to respond negatively. Still, we expect them to repay our kindness and make us feel better. But when that doesn't happen and we are repaid unkindness for our good deeds, it feels unjust. Missionaries have been killed because they went to love; aid workers are attacked.

Jesus showed true compassion. He knew he was opposed and hated but still he continued in his mission of healing, teaching and redeeming. He is the ultimate example of being paid evil for his kindness; he was tortured and killed on a cruel cross. His prayer for the suffering to pass was unanswered, and he felt that his Father had abandoned him. But still he loved.

† Dear Lord, thank you that you love us, even when we do not repay your goodness. Help us to follow you and continue to love those who treat us badly.

For further thought

- Have you ever been unjustly treated, and repaid evil for good? How do you feel about it now? How can you protect yourself while still loving that person?

Wednesday 29 April
Knowing the real Jesus

John 15:22-25

If I had not done among them the works no one else did, they would not be guilty of sin. As it is, they have seen, and yet they have hated both me and my Father. But this is to fulfil what is written in their Law: 'They hated me without reason.' (verses 24-25)

Sometimes the name 'Jesus' is one of the hardest names to say out loud. When we're asked about our faith, the easy way out is to talk about 'God' or being 'spiritual' or something else that might not offend many people. Jesus can be very offensive, and to say that he is God is very offensive. Why does he provoke such a reaction?

This passage suggests that hatred of Jesus is linked to hatred of his Father too. It's not possible to hate Jesus and love the Father, or love God. They are one and the same.

To those of us who know Jesus, hating him seems impossible. But it happens. But do those who hate him know what he did, how he lived his life on earth? Have they been given a true understanding of Jesus? Is the reason they hate him based on a false understanding?

Because of terrible things done in the name of Christ, some think that Jesus taught such behaviour. Others see the worst acts done by Christians and put the blame on Jesus. They do not yet know the true works of Jesus or his redemption. Can we show them the truth about Jesus' love for them, even if we take the risk that they will continue to hate?

† Dear Lord, thank you for the words you speak, the works you do and the salvation you provide. Help us to say your name freely and to represent you truthfully. May more people know your love for them. Amen

For further thought

• How might people pick up the wrong idea about who Jesus is? Have you ever misunderstood his works or his words? How can you help people to know Jesus?

Thursday 30 April
Serving God

John 15:26 – 16:4

All this I have told you so that you will not fall away. They will put you out of the synagogue; in fact, the time is coming when anyone who kills you will think they are offering a service to God. They will do such things because they have not known the Father or me. (verses 1-3)

When I first became a Christian, I was anxious about what people would say about it. I thought I could get teased, or even socially excluded. I knew some of my friends were not keen on Christianity. I have spoken to atheists who do truly seem as if they hate Christians, even if they're polite to me. They believe that religion is the root of all evil and that eradicating it will be a good thing.

To the most militant of atheists, it's become almost a mantra: religion causes wars, religion causes evil. The woes of political systems are ignored, and the perceived ills of Christianity are manifold. Hence, those who are Christian are actually doing wrong.

It is true that, through the ages, people have done evil in the name of God. They have tortured, maimed and killed. But in this passage, Jesus is clear: people who behave like this do not know Jesus or the Father. There may be many who claim that they are serving God by killing, but they are seriously mistaken.

There have been many Christians killed for their faith, by atheists and by people who think they are serving God. But when someone truly knows God, that person will not want to hate or hurt or kill. Jesus teaches us to love.

† Dear Lord, we pray for the people who think that they are offering a service to God by killing or doing evil. We pray that they would come to truly know you, so that they will find the path of love.

For further thought

• Is there anything in our own church culture that we think serves God, but isn't really doing so? How can we be sure of what service God wants? How can we help those who are misguided?

Friday 1 May
Conviction from the Holy Spirit

John 16:5-11

But very truly I tell you, it is for your good that I am going away. Unless I go away, the Advocate will not come to you; but if I go, I will send him to you. When he comes, he will prove the world to be in the wrong about sin and righteousness and judgment... (verses 7-8)

When I first started going to church, I was pleasantly surprised by how people behaved. They generally were polite, there weren't the bigots I'd been expecting, and there was a nice sense of community. In a word, it was – nice. I liked this idea of everyone always being nice to each other.

Then, when I found Jesus, I found real love, something much more profound. But with that came something else – conviction. The more I knew Jesus and his love, the more I realised how sinful I was. Even some things I did that I thought were 'nice' came from a bad heart. I wanted to change and, thankfully, Jesus was showing me a way to change. He showed me his grace both through forgiveness and the power to start changing my heart. As a result, I have much more love in my life than I ever would have had if I hadn't had this 'conviction' of sin.

In cultures that value self-esteem and dislike judgement we can ignore our 'bad side'. We can focus on our good aspects, and the good things we do. But if that's not balanced with an awareness of our faults, then we can't seek God's power to change.

Perhaps it's only when we know God's wonderful, amazing love for us, and have experienced his grace, that we have the courage to face up to our faults.

† Dear Lord, thank you for the gift of the Holy Spirit that you have sent to us. Thank you for both your love and goodness, and your conviction of sin. Help us to root out sin in our lives, and to seek your grace. Amen

For further thought

• What do the words, 'sin, righteousness and judgement' mean to you? Can you love more without being aware of what hinders that love?

Saturday 2 May
Guidance from the Spirit of truth

John 16:12-15

But when he, the Spirit of truth, comes, he will guide you into all the truth. He will not speak on his own; he will speak only what he hears, and he will tell you what is yet to come. He will glorify me because it is from me that he will receive what he will make known to you. (verses 13-14)

This week we have read some difficult passages from the Bible. We've looked at warnings of how the world will hate those who follow Christ, and we've looked at how the Spirit convicts people of sin and judgement. We've been told to expect suffering, opposition and a greater awareness of our faults.

What gets me through these challenges is God's presence. We are not on our own. God has sent his Holy Spirit, to guide us, to support us, and to comfort us. God's grace will keep us going – God's Spirit will guide us in the dark times – and God's truth will keep us from falling. Jesus and his love is worth all the trouble, and we will see great things as a result.

Sometimes, we see the wonderful results in this life. Sarah de Carvalho was a successful media executive and a Christian, but she felt the Spirit of God speaking to her to do something different. It persisted, and she obeyed. She moved to Brazil and started to reach out to the street children there, who had unspeakable horrors and dangers in their lives. She set up a charity to help nurture and love them. One day, she had a wonderful sense of God's presence, and heard the words, 'Thank you for obeying me'.

When we seek to hear the Spirit of God, he will guide us into truth, and we will see his kingdom advancing in the most needy and desperate parts of the world.

† Dear Lord, thank you for the guidance of your Spirit. Help us to hear you and to obey. Whatever happens in our lives, and whatever truths we discover about ourselves, may we know more of your comfort and grace.

For further thought

• Is there something God is wanting to say to you? What truth does the Spirit want to guide you into?

Moving into the future
4 In a little while...

This week's notes are by **Lesley George Anderson**

Lesley G Anderson is the former Superintendent of the North Trinidad Methodist Circuit in Trinidad, West Indies, a leader in the Caribbean Conference of Churches and a member of the ecumenical World Council of Churches' Pentecostal consultative group. He was President of the United Theological College of the West Indies, Jamaica; District President of the Panama, Costa Rica, Belize, and Honduras District Conferences of the Methodist Church; and a former Area Secretary of the British Methodist Church, serving the Americas, Caribbean and Europe.

Sunday 3 May
From death to life

John 16:16-18

Jesus went on to say, 'In a little while you will see me no more, and then after a little while you will see me.' (verse 16)

Jesus' disciples were utterly confused when he said the words above to them. They locked on to his words, 'in a little while'. What did Jesus mean? They possibly asked themselves, 'how long is "a little while"? When will Jesus depart and why?' When they believed who Jesus was they clearly understood he will die and rise from the dead to live again. Jesus assured them that he and the Father are one and will always be with them. The coming of the Holy Spirit will be a reality in their lives as their Comforter (see 14:16-17; 14:26).

My friend Revd Godfrey Elliott from Belize was diagnosed with a rare brain cancer. Hospitalised, he remained cheerful and spiritually confident. Hours before his death, he told us gathered at his bedside that, 'in a little while', he will die and rise with Christ. That day, just before midnight, he went peacefully into the arms of Jesus.

When 'in a little while' we must face sorrow, problems and difficulties, we too will have a Comforter. In this world we will face tribulations, but we can take heart that Jesus has overcome the world.

† Lord, in all our sorrows and tribulations, we thank you for being with us. Amen

From grief to joy

John 16:19-20

You will grieve, but your grief will turn to joy. (part of verse 20)

Jesus prepared his disciples for the role of the Holy Spirit in guiding them into all truth (verse 16). Jesus' focus is again centred on his unavoidable departure. He tells his disciples: 'In a little while you will see me no more.' Jesus assures his disciples that 'after a little while you will see me' (verse 19).

As Jesus assured his disciples he will not forsake them, so he assures us. He promises to send the Holy Spirit to comfort us in our times of trial, sorrow and suffering. He died to save us from sin and death. He now calls on us to live in the power of his resurrection. He lives and, because he lives, we will experience the abiding presence of the Holy Spirit with us. He will protect and enable us to overcome life's severe challenges.

Many of us have endured dark tunnels of grief, hardship and suffering for years. We feel the grip of an encircling, never-ending gloom. We have no peace. We have no sleep. We have been overcome by darkness of despair. In the midst of such darkness, Jesus rescues us. We are delivered!

When we keep steadfast faith in Jesus, who in his life, death and resurrection overcame the darkness of sin and death, we too shall overcome. We too shall rejoice and celebrate. His victory is our glorious hope! So, when we are engulfed with sorrow and we 'weep and mourn while the world rejoices,' let us never forget the words of Jesus: 'You will grieve, but your grief will turn to joy' (verse 20).

† Lord, give me strength to endure my grief and hope to experience joy. Amen

For further thought

• Read again verses19 and 20 and compare with Romans 8:38-39. What did you learn from the comparison? How can you live out what you have learned?

Tuesday 5 May
From suffering to deliverance

Isaiah 13:8; 21:3; 26:17

Terror will seize them, pain and anguish will grip them; they will writhe like a woman in labour. They will look aghast at each other, their faces aflame. (verse 8)

In these three verses Isaiah presents three powerful and dramatic images of a woman 'writhing in labour'. In these verses we are captivated by further images of 'terror', 'pain and anguish', 'look aghast', 'look of astonishment', 'look of bewilderment' and 'faces aflame'.

Isaiah brilliantly captures in words and symbols both the anguish and severity of pain that a pregnant woman experiences when she is about to give birth. Babylon, too, because of its cruelty and idolatry will face a very stressful and painful situation. Destruction by the Medes and Persians (as recounted in Isaiah 21:2-9) will be its fate.

These three verses in Isaiah indicate that deliverance from this period of suffering will be through the coming of the promised Messiah. The Messiah will come to liberate his people from their oppression and suffering. The Messiah is the good news of the gospel and Jesus Christ, the Messiah, is the content of the gospel. The Messiah is the hope for sinners. In and through belief in him, we will be delivered from our sin by his death on Calvary's cross.

The Messiah comes and he blesses. The Messiah comes and he judges. He calls us to repentance of our sins in order that we may live unto righteousness.

† When we 'writhe like a woman in labour' and are overwhelmed with tribulations, we thank you, Lord, for your sustaining grace and power to deliver us.

For further thought

• The Christian's life is not free from trials, troubles and challenges. While we are experiencing them, we are being rescued by Christ. Discuss, giving examples.

From temporary grief to permanent joy

John 16:21-22

Now is your time of grief, but I will see you again and you will rejoice, and no one will take away your joy. **(verse 22)**

Jesus applies the powerful childbirth images of Isaiah (in 13:8, 21:3, and 26:17) to his disciples. Jesus' intention is to illustrate how they will experience pain, sorrow and grief, at the time of his death. However, when through the power of the living God he is resurrected, they will rejoice. Jesus told them, 'I will see you again' (verse 22). This is not just a promise. It is Jesus' commitment to provide joy to his disciples. Certainly, the kind of joy that no one will take away from them!

A devoted wife ministered to her disabled and sickly husband faithfully for a whole year. Then suddenly she died. The family was devastated. I had just started my ministry in Colon City, Panama. In their agony, sorrow and despair, pastoral care was essential. Two months later, the husband died. This was an unbearable situation for the family. Their pain was intense. Their sorrow was overwhelming. Their cries were like that of a pregnant woman about to give birth. They questioned God about the two deaths coming in quick succession: 'Why?'

In their distress, the family shared a feeling of emptiness. The church reached out to fill that spiritual void. God the incarnate Christ spoke to their hearts. He died for their sin and was resurrected to assure them of eternal life. Learning that their loved ones were the heirs of eternal life, being believers in Christ turned the family's temporary grief into permanent joy.

† Lord Jesus, in the midst of our suffering, anxiety and misery, help us to experience your inexplicable joy and grace. Amen

For further thought

• Is it right to question God about the death of a loved one? Is it truly possible to experience permanent joy after temporary grief?

Thursday 7 May
From asking to receiving

John 16:23-24

Ask and you will receive, and your joy will be complete. (part of verse 24)

Revd Cynthia Clare, a Jamaican Methodist deacon and true saint of the church, was one of my tutors at Union Theological Seminary, Jamaica, West Indies. Coming from a Spanish environment, I struggled with English. When I asked for assistance, she willingly devoted herself without reserve to teaching me. I humbly sat at her feet and learned. In addition, she patiently taught me the scriptures and some basic spiritual insights.

First, she taught me that in life there are some painful experiences that are unavoidable. Sometimes we must struggle and suffer, before our 'joy will be complete' (verse 24). We must pray diligently and steadfastly in the name of Jesus.

Second, she showed me that, when we must go through periods of trial for the sake of sharing in the ministry of Jesus, we must take courage and stand firm in the faith to which we have been called. Do not be afraid to ask for anything in Jesus' name. Jesus tells us: 'Ask and you will receive' (verse 24).

I also learned from her that, in the power of the life, death and resurrection of Jesus, we must live in hope under the guidance of the Holy Spirit. The Holy Spirit will inspire us to keep faith and persevere in overcoming any or all adversity.

Prayer, perseverance, an excellent work ethic and the above formidable truths have helped me over the years to live in the victory of Christ's life, death, resurrection and ascension.

† Father, teach us how to keep on praying, asking and receiving in Jesus' precious name, in order that our joy may be fulfilled. Amen

For further thought

• Make your 'joy be complete' by committing yourself to help a needy person in your church or community this week. Challenge your peers to join you.

From obscurity to clarity

John 16:25-28

I came from the Father and entered the world; now I am leaving the world and going back to the Father. (verse 28)

Prayer is more than a private conversation between ourselves and God in which we raise only our own desires. We must also pray for others, reflecting Christ's all-embracing concern for all that marked his life and death. He loved his own to the end (John 13:1).

Ephraim Alphonse, a Methodist Minister from Panama and the first man to put into writing the Guaymi language of the indigenous peoples living on the Valiente Peninsula off the coast of Bocas del Toro, Panama, was a deeply spiritual man. I recalled him taking people into Wesley Methodist Church, Panama City, to pray in the darkness around the altar. Many testified of their conversion experience and of the miracle of healing. He prayed for others because, like Jesus, he loved and cared for people.

Jesus spoke to his disciples figuratively. Now he will no longer speak to them figuratively, but plainly and clearly. 'In that day' (verse 26) he will openly speak to them about his death, resurrection and the coming of the Holy Spirit. He will be the intermediary between the Father and his disciples. The Father loves the disciples because they loved Jesus and believed he came from God (verse 27).

In verse 28, Jesus summarises his deep relationship with the Father. 'I came from the Father' refers to the logos, the Incarnation; 'I entered the world' refers to Jesus' identification with humanity; 'I am leaving the world' refers to Jesus' death, resurrection and ascension; and 'I am going to the Father' refers to Jesus' eternal and intimate relationship with God.

† Lord, 'in that day' when we wrestle with pain and sorrow, lead us from obscurity to clarity of faith to pray boldly in your name.

For further thought

• By the resurrection and ascension power of Jesus, and the presence of the Holy Spirit in our lives, let us powerfully share God's word always.

May

Saturday 9 May
From tribulation to victory in Christ

John 16:29-33

In this world you will have trouble. But take heart! I have overcome the world. (part of verse 33)

Martin Luther King, Jr, the American Civil Rights leader and Nobel Peace Prize winner, went to Memphis, Tennessee, USA, in April 1968, to support the strike of the city's black garbage workers. The night before his assassination, in his memorable and unforgettable speech at the Mason Temple Church, he told his listeners: 'Like anybody, I would like to live a long life. Longevity has its place ... I've seen the Promised Land. I may not get there with you ... I'm happy tonight. I'm not worried about anything. I'm not fearing any man. Mine eyes have seen the glory of the coming of the Lord.'

King not only proclaimed with power and conviction his belief in Jesus Christ but demonstrated in his life that in the world we 'will have trouble' (verse 33). He was prepared to suffer with Christ for a better world. He recognised that Jesus has conquered evil in the world. Therefore, he was 'not worried about anything'. He was not worried about suffering, pain or death. He courageously faced them. He looked beyond himself to those positive expected changes that will benefit all others.

It was King's dream that all persons may live in the dignity of being truly human and experience peace and justice in this life. He, like the early disciples, believed that Jesus came from God. So he relentlessly fought in the power of God for all human beings. When we tend to become discouraged, let us remember the words of Jesus, 'Take heart! I have overcome the world' (verse 33). Jesus' victory on the cross is your victory!

† In a world of injustice and no peace, Lord, we are grateful that you are our justice and peace. Amen

For further thought

• In the world we will have trouble and face persecution. But don't worry! Jesus has overcome the world. Do you agree or disagree? Why?

Moving into the future
5 The time has come...

This week's notes are by **Catrin Harland**

Catrin is a Methodist minister and chaplain at the University of Sheffield, UK. She has a PhD in Biblical Studies and a passion for sharing the Bible with others. She spends much of her life putting the world to rights over a coffee with students, and trying to accompany people as they navigate the difficult transitions of student life. In her spare time, she enjoys reading, learning languages, playing the drums, watching sport and climbing, though she has rather more aptitude for some of these than for others!

Sunday 10 May
Glory to the Father, through the Son

John 17:1-5

After Jesus said this, he looked towards heaven and prayed: 'Father, the hour has come: glorify your Son, that your Son may glorify you. For you granted him authority over all people that he might give eternal life to all those you have given him.' (verses 1-2)

Jesus, facing the end of his earthly ministry, has been exhorting his disciples and sharing with them certain truths about himself and his mission. And here, at the close of that discourse, he prays for the fulfilment of all this. As we go through the week, and reflect on that prayer, we will find that that fulfilment is largely focused on the glorification of God, but not, perhaps, in the way we might expect.

The Father is to be glorified through the glorification of the Son but I wonder whether the disciples understood that such glorification must involve arrest, humiliation and a criminal's execution. Jesus' prayer also emphasises that the glorification has already begun, through his ministry of healing, preaching, compassion. And we will find that God is to be glorified through the work, the love, the unity and the simple identity of the disciples. Glory, in a godly sense, is not achieved through the grasping of power, but through acts of kindness, love, and a life lived for the sake of others.

This is the kind of glory to which the Church and the followers of Christ should aspire – the glory of God!

† Glorious God, may the life of Jesus be so perfectly reflected in the way we live that our lives tell out your glory.

Monday 11 May
Living in faith, as chosen ones of Christ

John 17:6-10

I am not praying for the world, but for those you have given me, for they are yours. All I have is yours, and all you have is mine. And glory has come to me through them. (verses 9-10)

Julia is a child with a special place in my life. She is not my daughter, nor my niece. In fact, she is not related to me by blood at all. She is my goddaughter. Her parents chose me as her godmother, and I chose to enter into that relationship. It is a unique relationship, in which we are bound together not by genetics, but faith – my faith and the faith in which she is being raised. As she grows older, I will hope to join her in wrestling with the big questions that will inevitably arise and, if she chooses for herself the faith that is central to our relationship, I will take pride in celebrating with her, in whatever way it is marked.

In praying for his disciples, Jesus now considers the relationship that he has with them. Our relationship with our Christ – just like that of the first disciples – is also one of faith and of choice. God has entrusted us to Jesus' care, and we can choose to keep God's word and to place our trust in Christ. The word translated 'believed', in verse 8, could equally mean 'have faith that' or 'trust', and that faith or trust characterises the three-way relationship. We are entrusted to Christ's care, and Christ accepts that as a sacred trust because we belong to God. And we trust in Christ, because he is sent by God. But what is most wonderful, is that Jesus also finds value in that relationship. In us, however fallible we may be, Christ is glorified!

† Pray for your godchild(ren), or all who look to you for an example in faith, that they may place their faith in Christ, to whose care they are entrusted, and who is glorified in them.

For further thought

• How does it make you feel to know that Christ is glorified in you? How will you show that glory in your life this week?

The flow of dew: a gentle mark of unity

Psalm 133

How good and pleasant it is when God's people live together in unity! It is like precious oil poured on the head… It is as if the dew of Hermon were falling on Mount Zion. For there the LORD bestows his blessing, even life forevermore. (part of verses 1-3)

This psalm constitutes a beautiful hymn to unity. The joy that comes from a life of unity is likened to the celebratory oil used to consecrate a priest, in the line of Aaron   also used to welcome a valued guest. And it is emphasised by the unimpeded passage of the dew that falls on mount Hermon, in the north, and flows down to the mountains of Zion, in the south; the unity of family mirrored in the unity of the nation.

The psalm is a song of pilgrimage, an occasion when people would come from all directions and be united in a shared aim and shared worship. The joy of which the pilgrims sing is not merely theoretical, but is lived out – however temporarily – in the act of pilgrimage.

And yet the very mountains mentioned, celebrating the unity of the Holy Land, cannot but remind us of the present-day reality there and in so many places. The joy of family and of nations living in unity sometimes feels like a tragically rare commodity. Yet the people of God are called to live together in unity and to celebrate that unity. For the unity of family and nation is a response to God's blessing. The dew flowing between Hermon and Zion is good especially because that is the place in which God's blessing is decreed. So, surely, wherever God pours out blessings, those blessings should unite us in shared pilgrimage, shared worship, shared purpose.

To live together in unity is good and pleasant – and it is God's will for us, the children of God.

† God of peace, we pray for Israel/Palestine, and for all places where neighbour is in conflict with neighbour, tribe with tribe, race with race, nation with nation. God of unity, let there be peace.

For further thought

• Jesus says, 'Blessed are the peacemakers, for they will be called children of God' (Matthew 5:9). How might you be a peacemaker, locally or globally?

Wednesday 13 May
One God, one love, one Church

John 17:11, 21-23

[T]hat they may be one, as we are one – I in them and you in me, so that they may be brought to complete unity. Then the world will know that you have sent me and have loved them even as you have loved me. (part of verses 22-23)

Foremost among the artistic masterpieces that have informed my taste over the years is one of the greatest romances in cinematic history. I refer, of course, to the unfailingly beautiful, often turbulent, always enthralling relationship between the Muppet characters Kermit and Miss Piggy. What makes the story of this ongoing love affair so captivating is their passion for one another despite their apparently complete unsuitability for one another – not only because one is a frog and the other a pig, but because of their radically different personalities, priorities and lifestyles.

Jesus prays for our oneness, with God and with one another, mirroring the profound unity that is to be found within the Trinity. We worship a God who is three and yet one, seen in different persons, yet held together in complete unity by perfect love. And we are called to live according to that deep, unifying love, as a witness to the love God has for us and for all people.

But unity is not the same as uniformity, and that can make it hard. The Church is a disparate, diverse collection of individuals, and sometimes we have to work at showing unity. It doesn't mean always agreeing, either; rather, Christian unity is surely about remaining focused on one another's humanity. It involves valuing, rather than being threatened by, diversity and difference. It means facing the challenges of disagreement and sometimes saying difficult things. Above all, it means keeping godly love at the centre of all our relationships, no matter how hard that may sometimes be!

† Holy God, help me when oneness and love are tough. Help me and your whole Church to see past difference of opinion, finding unity that is strengthened, not damaged, by difference of culture and gifting.

For further thought

• Whom do you find it especially hard to love? With whom do you never agree? Understanding is not always easy, but start by praying for them.

135

Thursday 14 May (Ascension Day)
One lost by the will of God?

John 17:12-13

While I was with them, I protected them and kept them safe by that name you gave me. None has been lost except the one doomed to destruction so that Scripture would be fulfilled. (verse 12)

Today is Ascension Day and, in his prayer, Jesus recognises that he is soon to be taken up into heaven, leaving his followers with the task of working together to understand all that his life on earth might mean.

I once cared pastorally for a young man who had experienced a significant bereavement, and been reminded of just that by well-meaning friends. They wanted to encourage him and build up his faith in the face of circumstances that they felt could only undermine it. And yet he had an amazingly deep faith in God's goodness, which carried him through the dark times. It was a faith they could not comprehend, which gave him the security to grieve and to be angry with God, and yet the confidence to declare that 'God is good!'

Today's section of Jesus' prayer raises profound and uncomfortable questions for me – questions to which I don't know the answer. If it is destiny that 'the one' should have been lost, does that mean that God willed it so? Does its fulfilment of scripture mean that there was no other way, or that it was God's plan? Was Judas simply a necessary piece of 'collateral damage' in the working out of God's plan of salvation? How do we hold together deep tragedy and a confidence in the goodness of God?

I don't know the answers to these questions but I do believe that, in wrestling with them, our faith is strengthened and deepened, and we become more able to say, in the face of what we don't understand, 'God is good!'

† Good God, give us a faith that can trust in your goodness, even through the pain of tragedy – a faith that is deepened by, and not afraid of, the questions that arise.

For further thought

• Which questions are a potential stumbling block for your faith? Is your faith strengthened by the wrestling, or challenged by the lack of answers?

Friday 15 May
Sent to where we do not belong

> **John 17:14-19**
>
> *They are not of the world, even as I am not of it. Sanctify them by the truth; your word is truth. As you sent me into the world, I have sent them into the world.* (**verses 16-18**)

I once spent a month in prison – as part of my training for ministry. It was a privilege and invaluable experience, but rarely have I felt more out of place! I was a young, middle-class, educated woman; the prisoners were, on average (though not invariably), rather less privileged, and a few had been in prison for longer than I had been alive. Some could share stories of deprivation and abuse beyond my imagining.

Yet the prison chaplains there were no better suited by background or culture. What they had, that I lacked, was a vocation. Prison chaplaincy is never easy but a chaplain, called and equipped by God precisely for ministry in that context, will feel far less out of place, because it is the place in which she is called to serve and to which she is called to commit. She belongs there.

Jesus speaks of his followers as not belonging to the world. This does not mean that we are required to detach ourselves from worldly concerns and live lives apart. On the contrary, we are commissioned by God, as those belonging to God's kingdom, and sent into the world to show God's love in the midst of its messier aspects.

It is surely significant that this prayer is spoken by Jesus – God living and working in the world, not detached from it, but loving it so much that he lived, died and loved, all in the midst of that world to which he did not belong.

And now we, the body of Christ, live out that ministry, day by day.

† Heavenly God, we thank you that you have called us, equipped us, and commissioned us. Help us to commit ourselves completely to the values of your kingdom and the needs of your world.

For further thought

• How do or might you live out the values of the kingdom, to which you belong, by your commitment to the world, to which you don't?

Saturday 16 May
Modelling the love of God

John 17:20, 24-26

My prayer is not for them alone. I pray also for those who will believe in me through their message ... I have made you known to them, and will continue to make you known in order that the love you have for me may be in them, and that I myself may be in them. (verses 20 and 26)

My children have inherited a number of things from me – my hair, my height, my temperament (and temper). Over time, we may discover whether my sporting ability (or lack thereof) is also evident in them. Other things may be not so much genetic as a reflection of the values that we, their parents, have demonstrated, for good or ill. Will they, for instance, share our literary or musical tastes, political perspectives or choice of football team?

Among all this, we aim to model for them a love of God and neighbour, aware that the example we set may be influential in their own development of their faith, and in the ways in which they choose to live it out.

† God, help me find the right words and actions with which to pass on your message, and so be glorified through me.

For further thought

• Take a moment to give thanks for those who raised you in Christian faith either as a child or as an adult, and for those whose lives you have touched with your faith.

Small is beautiful
1 God of small things

This week's notes are by **Catherine Williams**

Catherine Williams is an Anglican priest working as the National Adviser for Vocations for the Ministry Division of the Archbishops' Council, in the Church of England. Her role is to advise and lead the many vocation advisers around the UK who are encouraging and enabling Christians to discern God's call on their lives. Catherine lives in Gloucestershire and commutes to work in Westminster, London. Her husband Paul is also a priest and they have two adult children. Catherine enjoys singing, baking, cinema, and reading and writing poetry.

Sunday 17 May
Small creatures/big wisdom

Proverbs 30:24-28

Four things on earth are small, yet they are extremely wise. (verse 24)

Often our culture favours the biggest, wealthiest and most powerful: promoting this as the ideal. With God things are very different. God works through small and seemingly insignificant people and events. The least are of great importance in God's kingdom, and a small band of faithful Christians, filled with the Holy Spirit, can change the world.

Insects and small animals are often considered a nuisance – vermin – to be feared. But in Proverbs four small creatures are deemed 'wise'. Ants store away food when there is plenty so that their colonies can always be fed. Hyraxes – a type of small mammal – are able to make their homes in inhospitable places among the rocks. Locusts, though tiny, organise themselves into efficient and powerful armies that can change an entire landscape. Lizards can go anywhere, crossing social boundaries with ease and lodging in the most unexpected places.

For the Christian, prayer and worship feed and nourish when times are hard, and we can make a secure home in God our Rock. Individually we may seem insignificant, but together the Christian church is an incredible force: one family that transcends barriers of gender, race and social standing. Wisdom can be learnt from surprising sources.

† Lord, help me to honour and learn from your creation. Guide me in the ways of wisdom.

Monday 18 May
Youngest son/mighty king

1 Samuel 16:1, 6-13

Samuel asked Jesse, 'Are these all the sons you have?' 'There is still the youngest,' Jesse answered. 'He is tending the sheep.' (part of verse 11)

Samuel, obedient to the Lord, seeks out a new king for Israel. In ancient Near East culture a family's eldest son would be the natural choice for leadership. Samuel assumes that Jesse's eldest son, Eliab, must be the one he should anoint. But a surprise is in store. Eliab is not the one, nor any of his brothers presented to Samuel. Jesse's youngest son, David, is called in from the fields where he has been tending the sheep. The youngest son is called to be king. The irony is that, in Samuel's culture, the shepherd is a symbol of the king – the one who will lead and tend the flock. Everyone has overlooked David because he is the youngest yet his vocation is already being acted out in the fields. The Lord looks not at the outward appearance, but at the heart, and God continually calls the little and the least to step up into leadership.

In the Church of England we are working hard to encourage more under 30s to come forward for ordination and leadership. Too often our church culture has looked to older people for leadership, and assumed that young people aren't ready until they have sufficient maturity and life experience. God's calling of David reminds us that age and status should be no barrier to spiritual leadership. The God who calls also equips. God doesn't call those who are perfect. David's kingship is marked by mistakes – yet he is still God's choice for this role. God provides leaders for his people, sometimes in very unexpected ways.

† Lord, teach me to see as you see and to recognise and affirm the people you are calling to lead my community.

For further thought

• Who are the young people in your church or fellowship? What more could you be doing to encourage them?

Tuesday 19 May
Tiny seed/large tree

Matthew 13:31-32

The kingdom of heaven is like a mustard seed ... Though it is the smallest of all seeds, yet when it grows, it is the largest of garden plants and becomes a tree, so that the birds come and perch in its branches. (part of verses 31-32)

The country town I live in used to be famous for the production of mustard. 'Tewkesbury mustard' is mentioned in Shakespeare and so important was the product that it was wrapped in gold leaf and given to royalty. In medieval times its pungent flavour was valued in meat dishes, and its irritant properties used as a medicine to treat fever. Mustard grows from a very small seed and becomes a large plant, about 4 metres tall. Jesus uses this analogy to illustrate that, from tiny beginnings, substantial things can emerge. With poetic licence he suggests the seed grows into a large tree in which many birds find a resting place and a home. This is an echo from the Old Testament, where the tree is a symbol for a great empire.

For the small and newly emergent Christian movement this parable would have been an affirmation of their destiny. Surrounded by the mighty pagan Roman Empire, and existing in the shadow of the vast Jewish Temple of Jerusalem, the small band of followers of Christ may have felt, at times, vulnerable and insignificant. Jesus gives them a vision of how the kingdom will expand, flourish and open its doors to all comers.

If you are in a small fellowship today, do not lose heart. Hold on to this parable and believe that God can do incredible things with very little. As you remember the tiny mustard seed, also hold in your imagination the image of the sturdy tree, filled with life, vitality and birdsong, and have faith that God's kingdom will continue to grow and flourish.

† Lord God, bless the thousands of small Christian fellowships around the world. Keep them faithful to your vision of the kingdom.

For further thought

• Can a diverse range of people find a home in your church? What more could you do to make all feel welcome?

Wednesday 20 May
Little leaven/big bread

Matthew 13:33

The kingdom of heaven is like yeast that a woman took and mixed into about thirty kilograms of flour until it worked all through the dough.
(verse 33)

Making bread is a very satisfying activity. With an unpromising and dull pile of basic ingredients, some hard work and a lot of time and patience, the end product is delicious bread, which is the nourishing staple of many communities around the world. Yeast, which is a living organism, makes all the difference. It interacts with the other ingredients to enable the dough to expand and take shape. So successful is the process that people have been using it for thousands of years. Jesus uses this everyday analogy to demonstrate that even a handful of faithful followers can permeate and change a whole society. With just a tiny amount of yeast and a very large amount of flour – 30 kilos – the woman in the parable produces sufficient bread to feed over a hundred people. Jesus is reminding his listeners that it doesn't take much to make a real difference.

In Jesus' time, 'leaven' would have been used rather than yeast. Leaven is a small amount of mouldy bread that enables the process of fermentation to take place. This idea reminds us that God can use even rotten things to bring about his purposes and, by his working, they in turn are transformed into that which is good and wholesome. We cannot see the yeast or the leaven in the completed loaf but we know its effect and taste its results. So it is with the kingdom, which can be hidden, grows in secret but is constantly bringing new life to God's people.

† Lord, give us this day our daily bread. May it remind us of your kingdom and encourage us to serve you and others.

For further thought

• Make a list today of all the signs of God's kingdom at work in your community.

Thursday 21 May
Small door/eternal life

Luke 13:22-30

People will come from east and west and north and south, and will take their places at the feast in the kingdom of God. (verse 29)

Tewkesbury Abbey, where I worship, has enormous medieval wooden double doors. These are flung wide open to allow crowds in and out for special services, weddings and during the summer for the many tourists and pilgrims. Those of us who go in and out of the Abbey every day use a very ordinary small door, which is set into the big doors. It's only possible to pass through in single file and the door is so small that taller people have to stoop.

Our visions of the kingdom this week have been of a large tree where many birds perch, and an enormous loaf capable of feeding many people. The kingdom of God is vast and eternal and will be home to many nations. However, to get there, suggests Jesus, each person will need to enter through the narrow door – one by one. He also suggests that our entry requires some urgency since the door may be closed at any moment. He warns God's chosen people that, even though the prophets were their ancestors, it doesn't mean they have a right to be in the kingdom. Israel's enemies will come from all directions and will be welcome at God's feast.

Jesus is the door through which we enter into the kingdom. We cannot rely on another's faith, or push into the kingdom with the crowd. All are welcome at God's banquet; the invitation has been secured through Christ's death and resurrection. He is the way in and we must encounter him one by one, stooping low with humility as we acknowledge his sacrifice for the world.

† Lord Jesus, enable me to help many people through the door of your love into the kingdom. Teach me to enter your feast with humility.

For further thought

• When you next take Holy Communion, remember that people from east, west, north and south are welcome at the Lord's feast.

Little children/God's kingdom

Luke 18:15-17

Let the little children come to me, and do not hinder them, for the kingdom of God belongs to such as these. Truly I tell you, anyone who will not receive the kingdom of God like a little child will never enter it. (part of verses 16-17)

Whenever I prepare small children for admission to Holy Communion I am humbled and overawed by their faith and ability to articulate the profound mystery of God with simple, straightforward passion. Often their love for Jesus is overwhelming and challenges my own, sending me scurrying to my knees in repentance for my lack of trust and commitment. In our churches we are sometimes too quick to dismiss children as noisy, intrusive, or lacking sufficient knowledge to take a full part in our worship. The disciples were no different, shooing away those who were trying to bring children close to Jesus for his blessing. Jesus gives a sobering reminder to his followers and to us. We will never enter the kingdom of God unless we learn to receive it with childlike qualities.

Babies are utterly dependent on others for their needs. They have few worries and no responsibilities. Children naturally trust others and have the ability to love generously and easily. They have little status or wealth. They rarely own much, and sit light to time, living in the moment. Jesus remembered, perhaps with fondness, his own childhood and points us back to the simple qualities that make for good citizens of the kingdom. Striving in our own strength for membership leads nowhere. Trusting in God our parent and longing for the blessing of Jesus brings us close to the kingdom. We have much to learn from children, and they should have an equal and honoured place in our communities.

† Lord, thank you for children. Help me to rediscover from them the qualities that are needed for your kingdom. May I always trust in you.

For further thought

• Learn the names of the children in your church and pray for them. If there are no children in your church, pray that God will send some soon.

Saturday 23 May
Small lunch/big crowd

John 6:1-15

When they had all had enough to eat, Jesus said to his disciples, 'Gather the pieces that are left over. Let nothing be wasted.' So they gathered them and filled twelve baskets with the pieces of the five barley loaves left over by those who had eaten. (verses 12-13)

Many of our themes this week come together in today's familiar story of the feeding of the 5000. The faith and generosity of a child donating his packed lunch; small unsubstantial things becoming vastly significant; Jesus being the way into kingdom living; and the nations gathered and welcomed at the great messianic banquet. In this miracle, ordinary everyday things become extraordinary in the hands of Jesus and God is glorified. The people who experience it begin to get an inkling that something unusual and holy is going on. Transformation comes about when we trust God to provide, and believe that with God nothing is impossible.

What strikes me in this passage is that Jesus provided more than was required – there was a lot left over. Jesus is anxious that nothing should be wasted and he instructs the disciples to gather up the remains, presumably so that even more may be fed – those who aren't yet part of the crowd that is gathered. The abundance of God knows no bounds, and we too should be generous with everything we have, and especially with the love of God, reaching out further and further so that everyone can be fed and no one will be lost.

This passage is also an analogy of the Lord's Supper, where Jesus is the host and where his body and blood are taken, blessed, broken and given to feed his people. Just like those who experienced the miracle on the shore of Galilee, we come to the Eucharist with open empty hands and we receive back heavenly food in abundance.

† Lord, thank you for your vision of kingdom living, where all are welcome and nothing is impossible. Keep me faithfully seeking and searching for more people to be your citizens.

For further thought

- The next time you celebrate the Lord's Supper, remember there is always room at God's holy table for more hungry people. Invite them in.

Small is beautiful
2 Pentecost people

This week's notes are by **Tim Yau**

Tim spent 11 years in Christian youth ministry before training as a pioneer minister in the Church of England in Cambridge. He served as a 'rookie priest' in Peterborough, growing a church plant in a new housing development. He is now the Emerging Church Pioneer Minister for the Eastern Synod of the United Reformed Church. He spends most of his time in Ipswich establishing missional projects, and across East Anglia as a Fresh Expressions consultant. To his wife's dismay, he is a *Star Wars* geek and still dreams of being a superhero.

Sunday 24 May (Pentecost)
Feeling small?

Acts 1:1-14

They were looking intently up into the sky as he was going, when suddenly two men dressed in white stood beside them. 'Men of Galilee,' they said, 'why do you stand here looking into the sky?' (verses 10-11a)

It was a clear February night in 1986 when I heard about Halley's Comet returning to earth after its 76-year wandering through the depths of space. This was a once-in-a-lifetime opportunity to observe something truly wonderful. How could I miss it!

My hometown was dominated by the flame towers and smoke stacks of oil refineries and chemical factories. The night sky always glowed orange and the lit manufacturing plants were a constant reminder of the all-pervasive industry. To even have a chance of spotting the comet I had to get away from the light-polluted skies and find a dark spot.

Standing in a winter-silent field gazing at the immensity of the frosty Milky Way and considering Halley's lonely trail through the cosmos, I felt so small. I could hardly glance at the abyss above without feeling insignificant.

How much more must have the disciples felt staring into the clouds knowing that Jesus, the Son of God, had just left them on that lonely mountain, feeling small and incapable, not quite knowing what should happen next? This was how Pentecost began!

† Lord, help us to recognise that we are small, weak and ill equipped, so that we can begin to allow your Spirit to empower us.

Small acts of kindness

Acts 4:32-37

All the believers were one in heart and mind. No one claimed that any of their possessions was their own, but they shared everything they had. (verse 32)

I used to work for Youth for Christ. As a career move it was imprudent as the salary was low and finances were shaky but, as a step of faith, it was priceless because I was stretched and formed as a disciple. Money was always tight and at the end of the month we often prayed and thanked God for his provision, even though we were often faced with an empty bank balance. For this reason we were very grateful for small things and treasured little treats, things that today I can take for granted.

For my colleague Gill, one of her little treats was new clothes. She had managed to save up, find a bargain and bought herself a stylish jumper that she loved. That week we were setting up a music cafe in a marquee at a youth festival. The place was buzzing with activity, fun and laughter. Suddenly the cheerful atmosphere was punctuated with a shriek. Gill was aghast. Her new purchase was covered in bleach and the fading was already beginning to show. Gill's eyes began to fill with tears of frustration. We all knew what this little treat had meant to her.

One by one, without words, the team of volunteers began to step forward and place money in front of Gill. These were not rich people – they were mostly young students with little spare cash, but they knew what it meant to their friend. What started out as a frustrating accident turned into a festival of giving and by the end there was jubilant laughter and joyous tears all round that tent. Gill received more than a new jumper!

† Jesus commended the example of the poor widow who gave all she had. Let us, too, live lives of generosity, giving out of our smallness, and recognising our poverty. Amen

For further thought

• What do you and your faith community do when confronted with needs? What are the issues around you that small acts of kindness could transform?

Tuesday 26 May
The call to the small

Acts 6:1-7

They presented these men to the apostles, who prayed and laid their hands on them. **(verse 6)**

I was ordained in the historic Church of England. In this tradition, before you become a priest, you are first ordained as a deacon. The two roles have many similarities and the average person in the street wouldn't know the difference between them; however, the specific focus of the deacon's role is that of a servant. In the ceremony, the bishop proclaims that the candidates are called to 'serve as heralds of Christ's kingdom' and to 'serve the community in which they are set, bringing to the church the needs and hopes of all the people'. Then the bishop directly charges them to 'give yourself wholly to [God's] service' (from *Common Worship: Ordination Services*, Church House Publishing, 2007).

Sitting at the front of Ely cathedral, surrounded by a thousand well-wishers, sensing the gravity of monastic buildings that date back to AD 673 and the Abbess Etheldreda, and encircled by the pageantry of the institutional church, my feelings of inadequacy were palpable. Questioning myself I thought, 'Do they really know what I'm like? Can I really do this?'

Being a deacon is a lowly role; it's a call to the small, the marginalised, the weak, forgotten and overlooked. It's not glamorous work but it's a pivotal vocation. The apostles chose people who were known by the emerging Christian community to be 'full of the Spirit and wisdom' (verse 3). So, even though I was acutely aware of my own shortfalls, it was the gathered church that recognised the hand of God on me to serve. This call to the small is twofold: it's an orientation to the 'small' by those who identify themselves as 'small'.

† Lord God, you have entrusted us to serve the 'small'; help us to be worthy of that trust. Amen

For further thought
• Who are the 'small' people in your sphere of influence that are overlooked? How will you and your faith community seek to serve that group?

Small beginnings

Isaiah 51:1-8

Look to Abraham, your father, and to Sarah, who gave you birth. When I called him he was only one man, and I blessed him and made him many. (verse 2)

As a pioneer minister within the United Reformed Church (URC), I was invited to a national network meeting. The purpose of the gathering was to facilitate the cross-pollination of ideas and a greater understanding of viewpoints across the diverse interest groups within the denomination.

As part of the programme we were asked to imagine the URC as a human body and were tasked to place ourselves around the hall, positioned as corresponding parts of that physical frame. With lots of moving around, watching each other, and with good-natured chatter, we began to assemble. Who were the brains, the heart, and eyes of the organisation? But, more important for me, where did I fit as a pioneer?

So, I placed myself centrally and, when asked, announced that I was the penis. After a few raised eyebrows, nervous laughs and wry smiles, I explained that for something to live it needs reproductive organs and as an organisation we can ill afford to shy away from growth.

In the book of Genesis, God calls the 75-year-old, childless, city-dwelling Abraham and Sarah to leave the familiar home comforts of urban living and head out to the wilderness. God proclaims, 'I will make you into a great nation, and I will bless you' (Genesis 12:2a). After a further 25-year journey of longing, mishaps and adventures, Isaac is finally born.

Pioneering is journeying out in faith with God. If the church is to survive and prosper, we must, like Abraham and Sarah, expect that, by God's growth, one must become many.

† Lord God, though we may feel small, help us to work, pray and believe in growth, so that our small acts of faith are transformed into your great, world-changing vision. Amen

For further thought

• What is stopping you and your faith community from seeing growth? How can you keep the expectation of reproduction and growth central to your faith?

Thursday 28 May
Small wonder

Isaiah 60:19-22

They are the shoot I have planted, the work of my hands, for the display of my splendour. (verse 21b)

One sabbatical I spent a month in the south of France volunteering with A Rocha – an international Christian organisation that engages in scientific research, environmental education and community-based conservation projects.

With wellies in hand I headed for Les Tourades, their environmental study centre in the wetlands of Provence. On arrival I immediately realised I was woefully out of my depth: the centre was staffed by experienced environmentalists, scientific researchers and ecological theologians, yet I brought nothing to the table except my ignorance of all things green.

I was tasked to trawl the ditches and hedgerows of the Vallée des Beaux to catalogue wild flowers. The aim was to collect seeds from the various plants and to create a meadow of indigenous species. Every day I would cycle the back lanes to discover the hidden small wonders of God's creation. After two weeks I had over fifty markers dotting the countryside awaiting seed collection. Sadly, one day I was driving back to the centre and I got stuck behind a tractor that was mowing the roadside greenery. After a hurried conversation with the farmer, I realised that most of my findings were now gone: the project was decimated! Nevertheless, a few plants survived, seeds were harvested and the beginnings of a meadow were sown.

This wonderfully immersive experience of discovering the complexity of God's creation and humanity's impact on it helped me see the fragility of our world, as well as its often overlooked beauty. With vision, when we work with God, small wonders can become majestic.

† Lord God, though we may feel ill equipped for the task set before us and harassed by setbacks, give us your heavenly vision of the work fulfilled, so that we may persevere. Amen

For further thought

• In what areas of your life do you feel inadequate? How might God transform those inadequacies and turn them into small wonders?

Friday 29 May
The still, small voice

Luke 3:1-6

...the word of God came to John son of Zechariah in the wilderness.
(verse 2b)

Endless sand, excessive heat and the whispering silence of wind-licked dunes. The desert is a lonely place of extremes.

A few years ago I had the opportunity to experience the wilderness of the Arabian interior. The first thing that struck me was the huge distance we had to travel before we left all traces of humanity behind. Second, I was totally unprepared for the heat of the journey and the comparative cold once the sun had set. Finally, my idea of a desert safari was a sedate drive, furtively creeping up on the wildlife while taking a few holiday snaps: however, our driver and guide interpreted a safari as speeding as fast as you dare up and down the immense dunes. Great fun, but not a safari!

The desert is vacant, devoid of life and distractions. Once I got over the temperature and the quiet, it was the closest to nothingness I've experienced. The remoteness and isolation ultimately led me inwards, as there was little externally to consider. I spent only a while, alone with my thoughts, gazing at the setting sun in that dry and desolate place. It is uncomfortable having external control and securities stripped away – you become acutely aware of your vulnerabilities and your reliance on the other.

What must it have been like for John, living in the wilderness, existing on the margins of human society? It was in that place of weakness and exposure that God shaped him and spoke to him. When the noise of the world dissipates we can hear more clearly the still, small voice of God.

† Lord God, give us courage to forsake security and constant diversion, to find a place of solitude so that we may hear your still small voice and respond in faith, with confidence. Amen

For further thought

• What are the distractions around you that are stopping you from hearing God? How can you make space in your life to hear God?

Saturday 30 May
Small-group dynamics

Matthew 18:15-22

For where two or three gather in my name, there am I with them.
(verse 20)

Once, visiting a church service, I was confronted by a near-empty room. Sheepishly the leader turned to me and resignedly quoted the above piece of scripture. This saying of Jesus is frequently cited at Christian get-togethers to reassure attendees that Christ is present, even though attendance is low. I do agree that God faithfully dwells with his followers, no matter how small the gathering; but out of context this maxim is in danger of becoming a cliché.

Matthew's Gospel sandwiches Jesus' teaching here between the parables of the wandering sheep and the unmerciful servant. Both these stories deal with restoring relationships: the first ends in celebration; the second ends in punishment. At that time, Jewish rabbis taught that, 'if two sit together and words of the Law are between them, the Shekinah [God's presence] rests between them' (Mishnah, *Aboth* 3:2). Jesus' teaching goes further than the rabbis and re-interprets the 'divine presence' as himself. Consequently, gathering 'in my name' implies coming under Jesus' rule. Jesus' promise is a personal response to those who earnestly desire God's guidance in restoring broken relationships. As Christian communities, we don't need to rely solely on interpretation of the 'Law' but instead on our relationship with Jesus.

The former Anglican Archbishop Rowan Williams said, 'Church is what happens when people encounter the Risen Jesus and commit themselves to sustaining and deepening that encounter in their encounter with each other' (*Mission-shaped Church*, Church House Publishing, 2004:vii). Solo Christianity is a misnomer: no matter how small, we need the love and discipline of being in community to grow as disciples.

† Lord Jesus, you promised to be with us. Forgive us when we take that for granted and pursue self-interest. Give us confidence in the assurance of your presence to pursue the restoration of relationships. Amen

For further thought

• Which relationships create space for you to be in the presence of Jesus? What are the broken relationships you need Jesus to help you restore?

Readings in Mark (2)

1 Jesus sets out on his mission

This week's notes are by **Mark Woods**

Mark Woods is a Baptist minister and writer. He trained at Bristol Baptist College and had pastorates at Downend in Bristol and Alvechurch in Worcestershire before working for *The Baptist Times*, which he edited. He now has a writing ministry that includes serving as consulting editor of the *Methodist Recorder*. He is involved in leadership at Leckhampton Baptist Church in Cheltenham. His interests include literature, hymnology, theatre and film. He runs and swims to keep fit, neither very enthusiastically.

Sunday 31 May

Jesus takes on the forces of evil

Mark 5:1-13

When Jesus got out of the boat, a man with an impure spirit came from the tombs to meet him. This man lived in the tombs, and no one could bind him anymore, not even with a chain. For he had often been chained hand and foot, but he tore the chains apart and broke the irons on his feet. (part of verses 2-4)

This week's stories are about encounters with Jesus. Everywhere he went, he touched people's lives. Some he offended, some he healed or transformed. No one was indifferent.

This first story is about an exorcism – a troubling subject. Most people reading this might prefer to talk about mental illness. However, such stories in the Bible caution us against reducing everything strange to an imbalance of chemicals in the brain. Sometimes things are done that have a particular quality about them that could be described as demonic. A person, or a whole society, could be said to be in the grip of something bigger than themselves.

The use of the word 'Legion' is significant: for any Jew, the word would recall the Roman legions who had invaded the country. Jesus sending the 'legion' of demons into the pigs is poetic justice: the unclean invaders are sent into the unclean animals and destroyed.

So we have here a story of Jesus as the liberator, not just of the individual but of the society. He is not just a healer but a warrior victorious against the forces of evil.

† Lord, help me to discern right from wrong and good from evil. Teach me to trust in the victory of Christ over all the forces of darkness. Amen

Monday 1 June
Paying the price, counting the cost

Mark 5:14-20

When they came to Jesus, they saw the man who had been possessed by the legion of demons, sitting there, dressed and in his right mind; and they were afraid. Those who had seen it told the people what had happened to the demon-possessed man – and told about the pigs as well. (verses 15-17)

Two thousand drowned pigs represented a considerable loss to the wealth of the town. Perhaps it is not surprising that the people began to plead with Jesus to leave their region. Perhaps, too, it is not surprising that the man who had been healed wanted to come with him: life might not have been very comfortable for him if he had been held responsible for the loss.

It is more likely, though, that Mark intends us to see them as fearful not because of the economic costs of Jesus' visit (2000 pigs per demoniac was rather expensive) but because of what his actions revealed of the power of God. From being uncontrollably violent and destructive, the man was 'clothed and in his right mind'. He was no longer an outcast; he could take his place in society again.

However, the people had a point. God's Spirit is unpredictable and uncontrollable. Jesus broke the power of evil over the man, but he did so by breaking the status quo. Who knew what else he was capable of? Yes, a man had been restored to himself, but others had suffered loss. When we try to change the world for good, everything changes; revolutions are messy affairs.

Perhaps, then, when Jesus tells the man to go home to his family and tell them what God has done for him, he is saying: 'Show that you were worth this. Prove by your life that you were worth saving.'

That, it seems, is what he did: 'And all the people were amazed' (verse 20).

† Lord, your son Jesus paid a great price for me. Help me to respond with a great love for him and a great desire to serve. Amen

For further thought

- Restoration and healing are sometimes costly. How do we make them worth it?

Tuesday 2 June
Staying in touch with Jesus

Mark 5:21-34

At once Jesus realised that power had gone out from him. He turned round in the crowd and asked, 'Who touched my clothes?' 'You see the people crowding against you,' his disciples answered, 'and yet you can ask, "Who touched me?"' But Jesus kept looking around to see who had done it. (verses 30-32)

Two miracle stories are brought together in three Gospels: Matthew, Mark and Luke. A woman 'subject to bleeding' touches Jesus in the crowd as he is on the way to a sick girl. It was a common superstition that a holy man's touch brought healing but she is too shy, or too reverent, to approach him; her state of religious uncleanness would contaminate him and he could justifiably be angry.

When he feels power go out of him, Jesus stops and insists on identifying her. Though Mark tells us that she was made well, this was not enough for Jesus: this could not be an anonymous transaction. It had to be a real encounter, a personal relationship. He calls her 'daughter' and blesses her.

There is much in this story that speaks of grace. Jesus is hurrying to another appointment but he still has time for her. He does not care about religious contamination. He speaks kindly to her.

There is much that speaks of the depth of human need, too. The woman is socially and religiously isolated. Her husband may have divorced her. She was driven to approach Jesus because she had no other hope.

In the end, though, very little was required of her: not an eloquent statement of her case, or a learned affirmation of faith, or a commitment to service or discipleship. God's grace met her need when she touched the hem of Jesus' garment, as the old translations say.

We should be careful not to make grace too hard. Jesus made it easy.

† Lord, thank you for making yourself available to me, not according to my education or my background or my moral standing but according to my need. Help me to reach out to Jesus in faith that he will heal.

For further thought

- Do we make faith too complicated and give people the impression they have to jump through too many hoops to become Christians?

Wednesday 3 June
Believing in spite of the evidence

Mark 5:35-43

After he put them all out, he took the child's father and mother and the disciples who were with him, and went in where the child was. He took her by the hand and said to her, 'Talitha koum!' (which means 'Little girl, I say to you, get up!'). **(part of verses 40-41)**

If grace was easy for the woman who was healed of the flow of blood, it was almost impossibly difficult for Jairus, the father of the sick girl. Jesus had stopped on his way to see her. By the time he started again she was dead. Jesus, though, simply urges him not to be afraid, but to believe.

He says that the little girl is only sleeping, but this is meant to be read as a miracle story. The Aramaic words 'Talitha koum' are preserved in the Greek of the Gospels, a powerful indication of a memory transmitted by one who was there.

In the face of the evidence – a dead body, wailing friends and relations, a heartbroken father – Jesus says, 'Don't grieve too soon.'

This is a very human temptation. We are too often faced with sadness and loss, and imagine that they are irredeemable. Sometimes they are. People do die, and there are other deaths too: marriages die, friendships die, glittering careers run into the sand. God does not guarantee success at anything, and sadness is the price we pay for being alive.

However: Jesus sometimes says, 'Don't grieve too soon' – and there is a miracle. Against all the evidence, something wonderful happens. Not all deaths, it seems, are terminal – we are given permission to believe in resurrection.

Sometimes we need to pray for the strength to bear deep sadness. Sometimes – and just as hard – we are called to have the faith to hope.

† Lord, help me to believe when believing is hard. Help me not to doubt, in the darkness, what you have shown me in the light, and always to trust in your goodness and mercy.

For further thought

• Are there times in our lives when we have grieved too soon and missed God's blessing of resurrection?

June

156

Thursday 4 June
Ideas above his station

Mark 6:1-13

'Where did this man get these things?' they asked. 'What's this wisdom that has been given him? What are these remarkable miracles he is performing? Isn't this the carpenter? Isn't this Mary's son and the brother of James, Joseph, Judas and Simon? Aren't his sisters here with us?' (part of verses 2-3)

'Who do you think you are?'

We ask the question of someone who we think is putting on airs and graces, claiming a position that doesn't belong to them.

It seems to have been asked of Jesus. The local boy returns to his hometown and starts teaching his elders and betters what to think and how to behave. That was how they saw it, at least, and they didn't like it. Mark tells us, shockingly, that Jesus 'could not do any miracles there', except heal a few people; their lack of faith in him had reduced his ability to express his power.

When someone challenges us to justify our claims to pre-eminence, we have two options: we can argue with them and demonstrate our superiority, or we can admit defeat and slink away quietly. Jesus chose a third way. He demonstrated his authority without claiming it. He sent his followers out not to be quartered on people like Roman troops but to be received into their houses as guests; and if they were not welcome, so be it.

This acceptance of rejection was his own attitude, and it was to be the model for his followers. But rejection is not met with a stoical indifference: it has consequences. It is those who will not be hospitable who are the losers, as they do not share in the blessings of the kingdom.

Christ always offers us a free choice. He does not impose himself on us; we should not seek to impose him on others.

† Lord, help me to respect other people's right to reject my insights and beliefs, and to leave them in your hands. Give me the grace to cope with rejection without losing my ability to care.

For further thought

- Have Christians been too willing to try to impose their views on people rather than just offering them?

Friday 5 June
Disturbing the comfortable: Jesus and John

Mark 6:14-29

Herodias nursed a grudge against John and wanted to kill him. But she was not able to, because Herod feared John and protected him, knowing him to be a righteous and holy man. When Herod heard John, he was greatly puzzled; yet he liked to listen to him. (verses 19-20)

This is a story that is full of colour – particularly the colour of blood. It is the subject of paintings and grand opera; everyone knows about John the Baptist, Herodias and Salome.

What we sometimes miss, though, is that it is also a story about Jesus. Herod, the ruler of Galilee – the 'King' is a courtesy title – had imprisoned John from fear of his influence. However, he knew him to be a 'righteous and holy man'; he was puzzled by him, but 'liked to listen to him'. A rash promise shamefully kept led to John's death. Now, though, it seemed he was back.

The story has three things to say to us. It speaks of the demands of goodness. John could not stay silent in the face of wickedness; he had to speak. Religion is not just about being nice to people. Second, it speaks of the cost of goodness. The ancient Jewish historian Josephus says that John was imprisoned in the terrible desert fortress of Machaerus. He would pay with his life for offending Herod's family. Jesus and his disciples faced exactly the same risk. Third, though, it speaks of the attractiveness of goodness. Herod could not lock John up and forget him; neither would he willingly have executed him. He was drawn to his conversation and his teaching even while he rejected it.

Jesus, too, had a quality that unsettled and worried people. He could be rejected – he could even be crucified – but he could never be ignored. Goodness is like that.

† Lord, help me to be courageous when it is costly to do the right thing. Help me not to be overawed by other people's power, but to remember that I serve the King of kings.

For further thought

• Do we live lives different enough to disturb people, and are we confident enough not to mind if they don't like us because of it?

Saturday 6 June
Enough and to spare

Mark 6:30-44

By this time it was late in the day, so his disciples came to him. 'This is a remote place,' they said, 'and it's already very late. Send the people away so that they can go to the surrounding countryside and villages and buy themselves something to eat.' (verses 35-37)

Amid the speculations about what 'really happened' on the green grass of the Palestinian hills – what a camera might have recorded – we sometimes miss the core of the story. What is being presented to us is at one level a revisiting of Old Testament stories about miraculous multiplications of food: Elijah in 1 Kings 17, Elisha in 2 Kings 4. Jesus is the heir to these great men. At another level, it is a profound exploration of the collaborative nature of the continuing work of Christ. He tells his disciples, faced with the hungry crowds, 'You give them something to eat.' They are, of course, unable to do so; the task is beyond any human power. When Jesus multiplies the loaves and fishes, though, instead of handing them round himself, he gives them to his disciples to serve. They are commanded to give, and then they are given the resources to give. The nourishment they are enabled to provide is inexhaustible because its source is God himself.

So this story is very challenging. Jesus did not feed the 5000; instead, he made it possible for his disciples to do so. It is the same today: Christ has no hands but ours.

It is also very comforting, because it speaks of God's everlasting mercy. It is enough for each of us; we have no need that he cannot meet. It is enough for all of us. No matter how much the world changes, knowledge expands and ideas evolve, Jesus still has more to give.

† Lord, I reach the end of my own resources very quickly. Thank you that I never reach the end of yours, and that there is enough to spare for every need.

For further thought
• Are we discouraged because of the size of the task ahead? Is it because we think it's up to us, not up to Jesus?

Readings in Mark (2)

2 The kingdom of God comes near

This week's notes are by **Dafne Plou**

Dafne is a journalist and social communicator who works on technology for development in an international organisation. She's a member of the Methodist Church in Argentina and participates in the Ecumenical Committee in her local town to promote dialogue, organise Bible studies and prayer circles with the participation of people from different Christian churches. In her local church, in Buenos Aires' suburbs, she is in charge of 'Community building and fellowship'. She's also a women's rights activist and participates in the women's movement in her country.

Sunday 7 June

Take courage! It is I. Don't be afraid!

Mark 6:45-56

Immediately he spoke to them and said, 'Take courage! It is I. Don't be afraid.' Then he climbed into the boat with them, and the wind died down. They were completely amazed. (part of verses 50-51)

They ran to the basement when they heard the tornado siren – thirty children and their church leaders, all caught in the storm. As lights went off, they could only hear the storm growing. Some of the children cried, others kept silent, very afraid. 'Let's take courage!' said one of the leaders. 'We're all together, in a safe place, and we know Jesus looks after us.' A few minutes later, they were singing the usual camp songs, encouraging each other to leave fear aside. Trust was back.

Many times we need to take courage to face difficult situations in life. Unlike the children at the camp, we think there's no safe place to go to and no one to share our concerns and fears. Modern society seems to tell us that we should be able to solve everything on our own. That's the rule! Why trust anyone else? But as Christian we know that's not the way to go. We are not alone. We belong to a community where people care for each other, where we find sisters and brothers we can rely on, where fear is defeated by faith in Jesus Christ.

† Dear Jesus, help us to open our faith community to others; to announce your immense care and love for all.

June

160

Monday 8 June
Truth and open hearts, no to judgement

Mark 7:1-13

So the Pharisees and teachers of the law asked Jesus, 'Why don't your disciples live according to the tradition of the elders instead of eating their food with defiled hands?' He replied, 'Isaiah was right when he prophesied about you hypocrites...' (part of verses 5-6)

I rang the bell at the parsonage. Surely the minister was back from the cemetery. Such a sad event. A young member of one of the church's founding families had died in the capital city, after some sickness. The boy used to attend services when he came home for Mothers' Day or Christmas. I remembered his Sunday school days. A cheerful, intelligent lad, who loved reciting Bible verses by heart.

The minister opened the door and looked at me in distress. I saw pain in her eyes. 'He died of AIDS and his parents never told us he was sick,' she muttered. 'His mother said to me, "It was not because of you, pastor, believe me. But we didn't want to arouse people's judgement."' I sighed. It was hurtful and hard to understand. What about us, their church community? Did the parents think we were like the Pharisees: harsh, judging, bitter with our words, unforgiving? Would we have rejected the boy and his family, accusing them of having 'defiled hands'?

Traditions of the elders have gone. People make mistakes and take the wrong turn. Are we ready to nourish a community of hope and confidence that leaves judgement aside and assures those in distress that we have learned from Jesus to understand, love and forgive? We need to build such communities, as signs of a new realm where no one feels excluded.

† Jesus, we know we can hurt others badly with our words and attitudes. Help us to accept others as they are, and share with them that a new life is possible if they let you embrace them. Amen

For further thought

• Plan how to get involved in community organisations that help those in difficulties. Is your church ready to open its doors without prejudices and judgement?

Overcoming prejudices and contempt

Mark 7:14-23

Nothing outside a person can defile them by going into them. Rather, it is what comes out of a person that defiles them. (verses 15-16)

I arrived at the Methodist Centre in the shanty town. It was time for the weekly Bible study with the women's guild. I saw a teenage girl talking to the pastor. There was something about that girl that caught my attention. Then, I realised, she was not a girl, she was transgender! What's she doing in church? Blonde hair, make-up, expensive breast surgery. Such a young girl! Where did she get all that money from? I felt uncomfortable, almost angry at her disruptive presence.

The pastor approached me. Surely she saw a grimace on my face. I felt ashamed, but still I found the situation disturbing. 'In truth, this is Sebastian,' the pastor told me. 'He ran away from home some months ago and now he's back, all changed, and wants to be called Lucy. She's waiting for her mom and says she'll stay for the Bible study.' Was my discomfort showing? Would my prejudices contaminate this gathering?

Other women arrived. Some of them were teenage mothers, others house helpers, most of them street vendors. They took Bibles and sat in a circle. Lucy also took one. Women greeted her and no one seemed surprised by her looks. The mother arrived and they sat together, holding hands.

And then, suddenly, my uneasiness was gone. Lucy was enjoying the peaceful gathering. There were no shouts, no mocking, no insults, no abuse. There was acceptance and care. I could see clearly now. It was Jesus the disruptive one challenging me to overcome prejudices that contaminated me and threaten to contaminate others. I was now ready to enter the circle.

† Dear Jesus, help us to eradicate the prejudices that keep us trapped and open our communities to those who need you, no matter how disturbing they might look.

For further thought

• Do you believe Jesus can change your life? In what ways? Talk with your church group and friends about it.

Wednesday 10 June
Keep talking about it

Mark 7:24-37

They begged Jesus to place his hand on him. (part of verse 32)

Don Pablo has played musical instruments in church since he was very young. He started playing the piano at Sunday school when he was fifteen. Children call him 'Mr Piano' and clap loudly when he starts to play. He can play all sorts of music, and he's even better when playing tangos and milongas with his accordion in social gatherings. One can feel his joy when leading others to sing, not only hymns, but popular songs and new rhythms.

But in his 60s, Don Pablo's sight started to fail. Doctors diagnosed his disease would get worse and surgery would not solve it. Every Sunday and in prayer circles the congregation begged for Don Pablo´s sight. He had to accept early retirement from his job but decided to volunteer as pianist in charity activities, nursing homes and church services whenever he was invited. There was always someone there to drive him along when needed. He could not see well, but there were many eyes looking after him.

At 88 Don Pablo was the first one to play the new electronic organ in church. New medicines had helped him to maintain his sight. He saw very little, but enough to pass on his enthusiasm and joy when he started to play the organ that morning. We could all tell that Jesus' hand had always been on him. We couldn't stop talking about it.

† Thank you, Jesus, for answering our prayers in very concrete ways. Let us keep our faith and trust firm. Amen

For further thought

• Have you ever thought of volunteering to help in community or church services? Are you ready for that? Talk about it with your friends or church group. Don't hesitate. There's always lots to do for those in need!

Thursday 11 June
Bring and share!

Mark 8: 1-10

He told the crowd to sit down on the ground. When he had taken the seven loaves and given thanks, he broke them and gave them to his disciples to distribute to the people, and they did so. (verse 6)

December 2001 is a month no one will ever forget in Argentina. The economic crisis struck the country in a hurtful manner. Banks shut down, people lost their savings, and there was no money available for anyone. Hundreds from the poor areas invaded supermarkets and sacked them. On TV news one could see families running away, carrying packets of sugar, noodles, cookies, cereals, the usual things they could easily have bought a fortnight before. Looting was the rule.

We went to the Methodist Centre in the shanty town to meet with neighbourhood leaders and our lay people there. Families were hungry and they needed help. At least, we could still pay for the electricity, and the centre's kitchen was ready to be used. But where could we get food for all those people? We didn't have money either!

'Let's ask people to bring whatever they can share to cook a meal!' said someone. We did and the miracle happened. Little by little neighbours came by and brought whatever they had at hand: a few onions and potatoes, half a packet of noodles, flour to bake bread; the list grew and grew. It was such a blessing! That day around eighty people had their first decent meal after days of trouble. Families took home the leftovers and there were enough goods to cook for the next day.

For almost a year, as many donations came in, this soup kitchen at the church centre served a daily meal to dozens of families. Every day they prayed and gave thanks for the wondrous miracle they were witnessing.

† Thanks, Jesus, for showing us that miracles are possible if we are open to be in solidarity with those in need. Amen

For further thought

• What about Jesus' compassion? We live in a society that seems to have lost those sorts of feelings. Instead of compassion, blame and fear take the lead. Reflect on what the Gospel is telling us about this.

Friday 12 June
Signs from heaven

> **Mark 8:11-26**
>
> *The Pharisees came and began to question Jesus. To test him, they asked him for a sign from heaven. He sighed deeply and said, 'Why does this generation ask for a sign?'* (part of verses 11 and 12)

How many times have we heard people saying 'Do you believe in God? Then, why is it that he does nothing to stop wars, nor to protect little children from dying of hunger, nor to stop the destruction of our planet?' In anger, they demand 'signs from heaven' but never think of involving themselves to find solutions to the problems they describe.

There was a boundary dispute in the southern mountains between Chile and Argentina in the early 1980s. Some politicians and the military started to talk about possible attacks and invasion of territories by 'enemy' armies. Were Chileans our enemies? They were just the people next door, on the other side of the Andes. Couldn't this be solved peacefully? One could feel the danger as the army started to send soldiers to the conflict area.

Human rights organisations, social movements, churches and many individuals committed themselves to stop the confrontation. Simultaneously, people gathered in all sorts of places to pray for peace. There was a spontaneous ecumenism that brought Christians together at that difficult time. Finally, both governments decided to call for an international mediation to help them solve the dispute. Could we say this decision was a 'sign from heaven'? Or what kind of sign did we expect? Clouds in fire? Dropping stars? Earth trembling? Do we need that kind of sign in order to believe?

If we're ready to have open eyes and ears, we'll surely see many signs from heaven in our world today. But no signs will show unless we commit ourselves to make them real.

† You blessed the peacemakers, Jesus. Let us see signs of your kingdom in all efforts for peace, at all levels; and in families, neighbourhoods and the world. Amen

For further thought

• Read the newspaper today, on paper or on the internet, and look for positive news. Can you see there any signs of God's goodwill for all of us? Take a moment to reflect and pray.

Saturday 13 June
Was Jesus a 'celebrity'?

Mark 8:27 – 9:1

Jesus and his disciples went on to the villages around Caesarea Philippi. On the way he asked them, 'Who do people say I am?' They replied, 'Some say John the Baptist; others say Elijah; and still others, one of the prophets.' (verses 27-28)

When we read this week's readings in Mark, we cannot but wonder at all the travelling Jesus did in a few days. He crossed the lake twice, visited many villages and towns, even in foreign regions, and was also in the main city, Jerusalem, debating with the Pharisees. His disciples were not the only ones to accompany him: there was always a crowd around. And it was a faithful crowd ready to listen to his teachings (they stayed with him for 3 days in the middle of nowhere!), to pay attention to the debates with other religious experts, to wait for miracles and to comment on the great things that were taking place.

Was Jesus a 'celebrity'? People would wait for him at the seashore, or carry the sick on mats to wherever they heard he was. The marketplace, the town centre – many of his miracles and teachings took place in popular gathering places. People surely admired him and thought he was mighty and powerful.

Didn't Jesus know all this? Surely, but he needed to hear what his own disciples had to say, to know if they were understanding his message. Being recognised as 'the Messiah' meant they expected a winner, not someone ready to sacrifice himself for humanity's sake. But Jesus did away with the 'celebrity's pattern'. His commitment, courage and immense love sustained him as he walked the way to the cross.

† Help us, Jesus, to understand your teachings fully and respond to your call with true dedication. Amen

For further thought

• Are we ready to make any sacrifices today? Reflect on what modern society 'preaches' today and what it means to follow Jesus now.

Duties of government
1 Good and bad government

This week's notes are by **Malcolm Carroll** (see page 51)

Sunday 14 June
Big stories in small lives

Genesis 41:25-36

*And now let Pharaoh look for a discerning and wise man and put him
in charge of the land of Egypt. Let Pharaoh appoint commissioners over
the land to take a fifth of the harvest of Egypt during the seven years of
abundance.* (verses 33–34)

Here's a wise Pharaoh, who accepts the challenge that's coming,
looks for the right leader – 'one in whom is the spirit of God'
(Genesis 41:38) – and appoints the Hebrew slave, Joseph. Joseph
and his family end up honoured in Egypt. Then along comes a dumb
Pharaoh, and the Hebrews are forced into slavery once again.

Slavery, the story of brothers, riches and famine all mingle in the
Joseph story. So do strategic thinking and redemption. Joseph's
plans reach beyond Egypt to include bringing his father and
brothers to safety in Egypt.

There's another, greater, strategist at work. From the Joseph story
comes the story of redemption from slavery and the first appearance
of the people of God as a nation and the gift of the covenant –
which paves the way for the Jesus story and the redemption of
all humankind.

It is amazing, humbling, that the cosmic story of salvation can be
read from the stories of individuals. The story of a slave becomes
the story of the redemption of a people. God's mightiest works
have been achieved through the humblest of means.

† Whether in times of feast or famine, let me always serve your redemptive
  purpose.

June

The leader, authority, and putting things right

Leviticus 4:22-26

When a leader sins unintentionally and does what is forbidden in any of the commands of the Lord his God, when he realises his guilt, and the sin he has committed becomes known, he must bring as his offering a male goat without defect. (verses 22-23)

He was an undercover cop, and kept that part of his life under cover well. To many of us, Mark Kennedy was a friend, a fellow activist, to one a lover. After the Kennedy scandal broke, we were invited to appeal our criminal convictions handed down for a peaceful protest on a coal train bound for a power station. Our protest had been about climate change. The Kennedy case is about justice.

Here was a policeman who had acted beyond his authority. But it was murkier. The prosecution had known of such things but not made that known to our defence. And further, this wasn't the first time – it was systemic.

Good news is that it was the justice system through the Director of Public Prosecutions who invited us to appeal. Far better to have a system whereby sometimes the guilty may go free than a flawed system where the innocent may be convicted.

We can think of places where leaders will commit sins intentionally and let their people or staff suffer for it. Most of us can think of systems that, even if systems can't act sinfully, they sure can act stupidly. It's hard though to imagine a place where, as in this passage, even the unintentional sin has to be put right by making the perfect sacrifice. Bad leaders will sacrifice their own people to hang on to power. What sort of leader is prepared to be sacrificed for his or her people?

† Often we don't get things right; rarely do we admit it. But you, Lord, are our perfect sacrifice.

For further thought

• Good leaders from time to time may look to their people for forgiveness. When last did a leading politician do this? When last did I?

Tuesday 16 June

The gift of distinguishing between right and wrong

1 Kings 3:5-14

Your servant is here among the people you have chosen, a great people, too numerous to count or number. So give your servant a discerning heart to govern your people and to distinguish between right and wrong. (verses 8-9)

The people wait expectantly. In walks the ruler, wearing yellow, including a matching handbag. I was one of those expectant people: the Queen had come to visit a Church Urban Fund scheme in Hyson Green, Nottingham. Yes, I remember it well. It was Friday 8 June 1990. Remarkably, she looked rather like my mum. And I remember her perceptive observations and questions, also her willingness to listen. It would be unfair to hold her up as a perfect model of monarchy but how good it is when rulers listen, when leaders ask questions. Solomon asked the right question, asking for wisdom in administering justice.

A ruler or leader, especially in God's way of doing things, administers justice by drawing down on God's wisdom – big-picture justice, a picture that is a mix of God's vision, the teaching through law and prophets, the covenant with his people; most of all, the saving love and justice revealed in Jesus.

Solomon asked for wisdom. God granted his wish. He also got what he hadn't asked for: a long life, honour, riches. Riches enough to buy a nice yellow outfit.

† We pray for leaders who seek to serve their people: grant them wisdom. We pray for people oppressed by their leaders: grant them freedom.

For further thought

• We take Jesus as our model for private life. Is he our model for public life and leadership too?

Wednesday 17 June
Putting the people first

Nehemiah 5:14-19

But the earlier governors – those preceding me – placed a heavy burden on the people and took forty shekels of silver from them in addition to food and wine. Their assistants also lorded it over the people. But out of reverence for God I did not act like that. (verse 15)

A friend was in Paris, wandering around a museum. He came across a senior policeman who was walking cadets through an exhibition on the Holocaust, which – sad to say – showed some of their predecessors' complicity in it. He asked the senior policeman why the cadets were there. 'They are learning today's lesson: there are orders that must never be obeyed.'

Putting people, all people, first: a great guide for the would-be ruler, leader, manager. But how hard, when power comes whispering in your ear. How hard to put people first.

It was the end of another weary election campaign and, in the UK, we'd just exchanged one broadly right of centre party for another. I was exasperated; my friend was full of admiration. Exasperated, as I could see little chance of progressive policies. My friend's admiration, he came from elsewhere in the world: 'Power has changed hands and not a single life has been lost.'

What is the test of a good government, a good leader? Putting the people first. If I have authority over others, what should I have about me to help me be a good leader? If I have to accept authority, how I can I help those who lead do those things that make for good?

† If I must make decisions affecting others let me serve them also.

For further thought
• In my circumstances, are there orders that I must never obey?

Thursday 18 June
Promoting justice

Jeremiah 22:1-5, 13-17

This is what the LORD says: 'Go down to the palace of the king of Judah and proclaim this message there: "Hear the word of the LORD to you, king of Judah, you who sit on David's throne – you, your officials and your people who come through these gates. This is what the LORD says: Do what is just and right..."' (part of verses 1-3)

It was the greatest challenge to Greenpeace in the last 30 years. The crew and climbers had their briefings and knew the risk of the penalties they could face under international law and Russian law for protesting against the Prirazlomnaya oil rig and against exploiting the Arctic. No one expected the authorities to react outside the law, bring bizarre charges of piracy and hold the protestors in custody so long. I suspect it's taken Greenpeace to a new place.

Sure, we'd always done the peaceful direct action that you see with Gandhi and Martin Luther King. But now has come the disproportionate suffering that highlights the injustice that shows the world where bad power lies. As well as drawing on Gandhi and MLK, we also borrow Quaker terms, describing our actions as 'bearing witness' and 'speaking truth to power'. On Gazprom's Prirazlomnaya, thirty of my friends were speaking truth to a global power.

Jeremiah had to declare God's message. Yes, that's what prophets do. But look where he had to deliver the message – in the seat of power, face to face with the king, surrounded by the king's weapons of state: speaking truth to power.

It is a tale of two epitaphs: a ruler who is remembered as 'right and just'; and the one eye-to-eye with Jeremiah, who will be remembered, if at all, as having had the burial of a donkey.

If I'd been Jeremiah I'd have started an on-line petition and stayed well out of the king's palace. But speaking truth to power is more than being vocal. It's about being visible and vulnerable.

† By your grace, take my social witness to a new place, visible and vulnerable.

For further thought
• In what ways, in my time, is it given to me to speak truth to power?

Friday 19 June
Abusing power

Exodus 5:1-18

This is what the LORD, the God of Israel says: 'Let my people go, so that they may hold a festival to me in the wilderness.' Pharaoh said, 'Who is the LORD, that I should obey him and let Israel go? I do not know the LORD and I will not let Israel go.' (part of verses 1-2)

It's next to the prison, the right place for it when you think about it: Nelson Mandela Park in Leicester, UK, where the park sign carries his name and the words 'The March to Freedom is Irreversible'. 'March' is figurative, as much of his own journey was spent in jail. A convicted terrorist with a passion for the freedom of his people. His time came, and so did the time when South Africa gave a model to the world with a nationwide drive for reconciliation. Truth and reconciliation: to call those who had abused power to account; then to move on.

Power here is power over people. Pharaoh will not let go of power so won't let go of the people. He overworks them, requiring them to do the impossible – make bricks without straw – to keep their minds off things such as freedom. It's a sign of corrupt bosses that they overwork their people. Here, work is the opiate of the people, administered by force.

This Pharaoh isn't just his own boss: like many leaders he's also his own god. However, the time comes when God will call him to account. Power must be held to account. The scene is being set for the Exodus, which will be the beginnings of the covenanted people of God. And the end of this Pharaoh.

Who am I to challenge today's bad Pharaohs? On the far side of Nelson Mandela Park, the sign again has his name and this time these words: 'There is no easy walk to freedom anywhere'.

† Lord walk with me, for my freedom is walking in your way.

For further thought

• Power without accountability is like bricks without straw: it doesn't work, the house will fall. Where do I see power that must be challenged?

Saturday 20 June
When they refuse to listen

1 Samuel 8:10-22

But the people refused to listen to Samuel. 'No!' they said. 'We want a king over us. Then we shall be like all the other nations, with a king to lead us and to go out before us and fight our battles.' (verses 19-20)

I walked, we walked, maybe 2 million of us. An almost overwhelming experience, to be stood, waiting to move, watching thousands and then tens of thousands file through London, calling on Prime Minister Blair not to support the US in a second war against Iraq. So you want a leader, just like everyone else, one who will lead you into battle? What if it's the wrong battle?

To be fair to Blair, maybe he was right; he's on record as saying he holds himself as being accountable to God for that decision. I can now put myself on record as saying: Fine, Tony, but you were also supposed to be accountable to us, the people. The biggest peacetime march of UK citizens since who knows when, yet we went to war. I felt that the 2 million of us had failed, and got told off by a professor of politics. No, we didn't stop that war, but may have stopped the next one. So it came to pass that in 2013 the UK did not support a US push for military action against Syria.

The people want a king. Yes, those who were freed from being slaves now want to be subjects. In the development of the kingship idea, God comes across as distinctly unkeen on the idea. But it happens, and the work of the prophet gets harder and riskier.

Having chosen a king, the time will come when once again the people make a choice of ruler. Rather than have king Jesus they choose a notorious prisoner called Barabbas.

† 'Christ of the upward way, my guide divine; where you have put your feet may I place mine' (Walter John Mathams).

For further thought
- Stand up for the powerless and the powerful will move against you.

Duties of government
2 Our response

This week's notes are by **Liz Clutterbuck**

Liz Clutterbuck is a curate in the Church of England, having been ordained in 2014. She trained at St Mellitus College, combining a theology degree with three years on the leadership team of a central London church. Prior to ordination training, she was a researcher for the British Methodist Church, researching the 'missing generation' (those aged 25–40 years) within the church. She is passionate about blogging, Twitter, mission, baking, travel and handbags – and loves it when she manages to combine as many of her passions as possible!

Sunday 21 June
Rejecting wise advice

1 Kings 12:1-15

But Rehoboam rejected the advice the elders gave him and consulted the young men who had grown up with him and were serving him. (verse 8)

We all know what it feels like to face a dilemma, and to seek the advice of those we trust or look up to. Ideally, everyone we ask will offer the same advice and thus we'll know exactly what to do. However, it's likely that the advice will differ according to people's experience and wisdom – which is exactly what Rehoboam discovered when faced with the question of whether or not he would lighten the load of his father's servants, in order that they might serve him too.

Within a few verses, we discover the results of Rehoboam's decision to ignore the advice of his father's elders and instead take his contemporaries' counsel – the Israelites refused to recognise him as king. Most of the dilemmas we face will not have such far-reaching consequences, but it's a valuable lesson. Recognising whose advice is the wisest is a difficult but valuable skill, but one that God can assist with. Perhaps if Rehoboam had asked God to reveal the right course of action, the conflict could have been avoided.

† Lord, help us recognise wise counsel when we need it. Enable us to trust that you will lead us in the right direction through our dilemmas.

Monday 22 June
Refusing to take responsibility

Matthew 27:11-26

When Pilate saw that he was getting nowhere, but that instead an uproar was starting, he took water and washed his hands in front of the crowd. 'I am innocent of this man's blood,' he said. 'It is your responsibility!'
(verse 24)

'I wash my hands of this!' I wonder how many people who utter this phrase on a regular basis realise its origin. Pilate's washing of hands after relinquishing the responsibility of Jesus' crucifixion has become a modern metaphor for getting out of a difficult situation. Refusing to take responsibility for a difficult situation is always tempting, especially if we don't think it's really our business to deal with it.

For the last three years, I've been training for ordination, learning all the things a church leader is meant to know. As an ordinand in a church placement, I've had some responsibility but always with the safety net of two ordained people who would take ultimate responsibility for my actions. It was a safe place to try new things, take chances and grow. Now I'm a curate, I'm a little higher up the chain of command, but officially I'm still in training and my incumbent is in charge. But, before too long, the ultimate responsibility of leading a church will rest upon my shoulders. I won't be able to pass the buck or wash my hands of tricky situations – and that's a good thing!

We grow into responsibility, and a sign of maturity is the ability to accept responsibility where it's appropriate. It's challenging, and that is when the knowledge that we share this responsibility with God is important to remember!

† God, let us never forget that we share all our responsibilities with you and that you provide us with the strength and wisdom to see them fulfilled.

For further thought

- Spend some time thinking about your various responsibilities and those who support you with them. Pray for each area and all those involved.

Tuesday 23 June
'Not so with you'

Matthew 20:20-28

Whoever wants to become great among you must be your servant, and whoever wants to be first must be your slave. (part of verses 26-27)

In the kingdom of heaven, the rules followed on earth are turned back to front. The first shall be last and the last shall be first.

It's a natural human instinct to want to be first – to be top of the class, winner of the race, to reach the highest echelons of society – but Jesus shocked his contemporaries with the news that this attitude found no favour with God. Instead, greatness comes through serving, just as Christ served us.

How easy is it to do that? To put aside everything that society tells us we should be aspiring to, and serve instead? In all probability, not easy at all!

It's interesting that in the church – the very place where people ought to understand this concept – it can be difficult to overcome the pursuit of power and influence. Congregations look up to their leaders, putting them on a pedestal, when in fact clergy have been called to serve, not to have power over others. It's one of the reasons why clergy are paid a stipend instead of wage – it's an allowance to enable them to serve their congregation or parish, without needing a job to support them. I'm not sure that they would go as far as to say that they were 'slaves', but they're certainly servants!

† Lord, help me to put aside my earthly desires for power and influence. Give me a humble spirit that enables me to serve my brothers and sisters.

For further thought

- Find an opportunity to serve rather than to be served today. Reflect upon how serving made you feel, and look for more opportunities to do so.

Wednesday 24 June
'Do not put your trust in princes'

Psalm 146:1-10

Do not put your trust in princes, In human beings, who cannot save.
(verse 3)

When was the last time you put your trust in a prince? For most of us, that will probably be 'never'! (Unless you've been privileged to meet a member of a royal family and were trusting them not to be late.)

Once upon a time, it was those with royal lineage that we trusted to lead our nations wisely, but today governments made up of 'ordinary' people hold that role. In Britain, the Queen may be the head of state, but the day-to-day running of the country rests with parliament.

But that's not really the point that the psalmist is making here. Instead it's the fact that we shouldn't be trusting mere mortals over and above God. We should rest our hope in the God who created the world and who sent his son to die for our sins.

In classic fairy tales, the princess is rescued by her prince (preferably on horseback) and it's very tempting, even today, to hope that someone will rescue us in times of trial. For example, many single people believe that 'everything will be OK' once they're married and have someone to depend upon. But that ignores the role that God plays in our lives. The God who frees, heals, protects and loves – surely that's better than any earthly prince?

† Lord, release us from a belief that a human can fulfil the roles that are God's alone. May we trust in you with all our heart, mind and soul.

For further thought

• Think of an area of your life that you need to entrust to God. Write it down and, over the course of the day, read it over again and lift it up in prayer.

June

'Submit to authorities'

Romans 13:1-7

Give to everyone what you owe them: if you owe taxes, pay taxes; if revenue, then revenue; if respect, then respect; if honour, then honour. (verse 7)

Here, Paul is echoing Jesus' teaching in the Gospels about giving back to Caesar what is Caesar's. We have a responsibility to uphold the government God has appointed, by providing the resources it needs to run the country, provide society's infrastructure and support those in need. Paying taxes becomes a form of social responsibility – which is why we often see public outcry when it's revealed that large firms are avoiding paying it.

In the West, we may complain about having to pay taxes; the choices governments make in spending them; and those who try to avoid them; but we are usually fortunate not to have to worry about corruption. Around the world, resources are taken away from areas that need it most – such as education and health care – by corrupt officials and politicians, fed instead into their own pockets or military provision.

We submit to the authorities in giving up our wages, trusting that they will be used for good purposes. Similarly, we honour the churches we belong to by sharing our wealth with them, again trusting that it will be used for good. We are responsible for our giving just as those we give to are responsible for using it wisely.

† Lord, we pray for those with the responsibility of spending our taxes and our offerings to the church. May they be used wisely, and without corruption.

For further thought

• Investigate the latest anti-corruption or anti-tax evasion campaigns and pray for the contexts in which this is an action.

Friday 26 June
Civil disobedience?

Acts 5:17-29, 41-2

The apostles left the Sanhedrin, rejoicing because they had been counted worthy of suffering disgrace for the Name. Day after day, in the temple courts and from house to house, they never stopped teaching and proclaiming the good news that Jesus is the Messiah. (verses 41-42)

I wish I had been a fly on the wall that morning, to see the looks on the faces of the Sanhedrin when they realised that their prisoners had got out without anyone knowing! It's a passage of scripture that's almost cartoon-like in its plot, with the apostles bearing an uncanny resemblance to the Scooby-Doo gang in their ability to escape!

The apostles are stirring up society, continuing Jesus' ministry by sharing news of the new life that was open to all. What I find incredible is not so much the angel coming to set them free as their response to the punishment they received from the Sanhedrin: 'The apostles left the Sanhedrin, rejoicing because they had been counted worthy of suffering disgrace for the Name' (verse 42).

When was the last time you rejoiced that you had suffered? More to the point, when was the last time you suffered disgrace in the name of God?

All over the world, Christians are under attack for their faith – in 2013 over eighty people were killed when a church in Peshawar, Pakistan, was attacked after the Sunday morning service. Similar atrocities occur over and over again across the globe. For many of us, following the Christian faith will never be an act of civil disobedience, but would we be willing to break the law if it came to it? And, most important, will we stand alongside those who feel they must, in solidarity?

† Thank you, Lord, that we are able to worship you freely, without fear of persecution. We pray for those who suffer disgrace in your name and ask that you would continue to bless and encourage them.

For further thought

• Research what it's like to be a Christian in a hostile environment, and commit to holding those people in prayer.

Pray for all in authority

1 Timothy 2:1-7

I urge, then, first of all, that petitions, prayers, intercession and thanksgiving be made for all people – for kings and all those in authority, that we may live peaceful and quiet lives in all godliness and holiness. (verses 1-2)

In the fraught world of earthly politics, it's very easy to forget about the role that God has in it all! How many times have you yelled at the TV or radio when you've heard a politician say something you strongly disagreed with? How many times have you criticised a party's policies over a drink with friends, embroiled in political debate? When was the last time you prayed before you voted?

Prayers for those in authority are included in the liturgy of most Christian denominations and, week in and week out, congregations say the words or utter an 'Amen' in response to them. But how often do we really think about what we're praying? Are we only praying for those politicians who do things we're in support of? Do we ever pray for a political leader we didn't vote for?

Even if the party in power is one we'd never vote for, it's important to cover them in prayer so that God equips them to do the best job possible. Isn't it bad enough that the party you support lost, without leaving government without the support of prayer?

I'd like to challenge you to spend time each week looking at the issues facing politicians – what policies they're debating or voting on; what events they're having to deal with; and what challenges they may be facing. Pray into the details. Put aside your political affiliations and pray that God might rule over all governments and authorities.

† Lord, we lift to you all those in positions of authority – in our local communities, our national governments, and international bodies. May they know that they rule under your governance.

For further thought

• Take up the challenge described above and resolve to pray for politicians in more depth.

Building peace

1 Making the effort

This week's notes are by **James Pritchard**

James is a Methodist minister currently serving as Free Church chaplain at Keele University, based in the thriving Keele Chapel. He is interested in discipleship, particularly in relationship to how faith impacts on our everyday life. Concerns for peace, justice and the care of creation come as a natural response to his faith. James is married with young children; he enjoys walking, singing, photography, and geocaching. He is interested in social media's ability to connect people across boundaries and as a tool for campaigning and mission.

Sunday 28 June
Walking in the way of peace

Isaiah 2:2-5

Come, let us go up to the mountain of the Lord, to the temple of the God of Jacob. He will teach us his ways, so that we may walk in his paths. (part of verse 3)

Today begins two weeks of notes focused on peace: God's peace and, therefore, being people of peace. God's peace is a wonderful gift of the Spirit; these notes, however, offer us an opportunity to reflect on God's desire for peace in the world, leading us to consider our place as peacemakers.

Many of the passages that deal with peace come from the wisdom and prophetic books of the Bible, recognition perhaps that true peace is often beyond where the world currently is, which is as true of biblical times as it is of today! The world is not at true peace but God desires it to be. Prophetic passages like today's offer an insight and vision into what might, or indeed, will be.

Isaiah's image of the 'mountain of the Lord' is used symbolically to reflect where God's presence is experienced and known. Those who have gone to the mountaintop come back transformed and ready to walk in God's light and peace. The passage encourages us to meet with God, and to draw near to God, but be warned: in doing so we are changed and our vision of the world is transformed.

† God of peace, draw us to the mountaintop to meet with you. Give us a vision of the world as you would have it. Amen

Transforming weapons into tools!

Micah 4:1-4

He will judge between many peoples and will settle disputes for strong nations far and wide. They will beat their swords into ploughshares and their spears into pruning hooks. Nation will not take up sword against nation, nor will they train for war any more. (verse 3)

Today may feel a bit like 'déjà vu', for much of the passage reflects the words contained in yesterday's passage from Isaiah. In scripture I am always struck by things that are repeated, for they suggest they are words that demand our attention (although things that are not repeated are obviously still important!).

So here we have words repeated, of swords being turned into tools and nations not taking up arms against another. The image of a sword being turned into a ploughshare or a spear to a pruning hook is a powerful message. In wartime Britain, railings and other metal objects were melted down to be turned into weapons and tools of war. Here in scripture is a vision of the opposite transformation. I sometimes wonder what kind of world it would be if the energy and finance that are put into training and equipping for war were instead put into agricultural development in the world.

Another repeated phrase is focused on 'the mountain top'. Martin Luther King Jr's final speech spoke of having been to the mountain top and seen how things will one day be. He recognised he might not see its fruition in his life but it didn't stop him doing all he could to bring the day nearer. We may not see true peace in our world but that doesn't mean we should stop working towards it.

† Transforming God, who turns weapons into tools, transform me that my life might reflect your desire for the world. May I be a tool to bring about your peace. Amen

For further thought

• If you could have God change or transform one thing in your life what might it be? What tools do you have to work for peace?

Tuesday 30 June
...as the waters cover the sea

Isaiah 11:6-9

The infant will play near the cobra's den, the young child will put its hand into the viper's nest. They will neither harm nor destroy on all my holy mountain, for the earth will be filled with the knowledge of the Lord *as the waters cover the sea.* (verses 8-9)

Back in 1963, Martin Luther King Jr stood at the Lincoln Memorial and declared, 'I have a dream'. His dream was both political and spiritual. His dream was rooted in what he desired and longed for; it was aspirational – not in a personal sense of seeking what was good for him as an individual but in imagining God's will for the world. His dream was not like the fleeting fantasies of our sleeping dreams but rather reflected the hopes and dreams we hold within our hearts.

Isaiah's prophecy, on the other hand, has the hallmarks of a fantastical dream, a vision of other-worldliness where wolf and lamb are friends, where a child is safe in a cobra's den. This fantastical dream or vision is important, though, because it gives insight into God's heart, into the very depths of God's will. In this vision is true peace, demonstrated by a vision of harmony. It echoes the harmony of Martin Luther King's dream; where black and white, slave and free are at one with each other. It is a vision based not on power over another but on equality and peace.

This strange ecological vision will not be fulfilled until the earth is filled with the knowledge of God; it will be possible only when everyone and everything is wrapped up in God's ways. Martin Luther King's dream may have seemed a distant hope; and indeed it is still to find true fruition.

Isaiah's vision isn't yet true, the whole earth isn't aware of all of God's ways... but one day...

† Vision giving, peace-maker God, may we live at peace with one another. May we seek the day when your glory fills the earth. May your vision inspire and guide us in our living.

For further thought

• How in harmony with your fellow human beings are you? How in harmony with God's world are you? What could you change?

June

Wednesday 1 July
Blood on our hands?

1 Chronicles 22:7-9

My son, I had it in my heart to build a house for the Name of the LORD my God. But this word of the LORD came to me: 'You have shed much blood and have fought many wars. You are not to build a house for my Name...' (part of verses 7 and 8)

In this strange passage David is having a heart-to-heart with Solomon; he is confessing to his son. David had desired to build a great temple to glorify God but he clearly heard God's disapproval of his grand plan. God is so not willing to overlook many of the things David has done and in particular the blood that has been shed for which David has been responsible. The wars and bloodshed are something God very clearly disapproves of, so much so that he won't accept the desire of David to build a temple.

It is a challenging message; one that leads me to wonder how God might look at us and our lives. Is our worship to be acceptable or is it marred by the way we have chosen to live, or by the blood that is metaphorically on our hands? What in our lives is not glorifying of God but reflects opposition to God's ways? Have we created barriers to true worship – not just the worship that happens in 'the house of God' (churches and buildings set aside for worship) but in the world God has lovingly created? Are our hands clean or, are they like David's, stained? This passage does, however, contain hope: Solomon will build this temple, Solomon will be a man of peace – things can be different, and things will be different! We believe in a God of transformation. Even if we feel our hands are stained, we can trust that God can transform them.

† Merciful God, forgiving one, mend my life and ways. May all I am and do bring you glory.

For further thought

• What might be the barriers to true, 'whole life' worship of God? What in your life might need changing? (Don't dwell on guilt; seek forgiveness!)

Thursday 2 July
Seek peace and pursue it

Psalm 34:11-14

Whoever of you loves life and desires to see many good days, keep your tongue from evil and your lips from telling lies. Turn from evil and do good; seek peace and pursue it. (verses 12-14)

This psalm calls us to be people who seek peace – people who take seriously living in God's ways. The psalm calls us beyond superficial 'niceness' to godly living, seeking to live positive lives directed towards God's ways. To be people whose tongues are not used for evil but good, people rooted and grounded in God, seeking to do good and seeking peace...

The psalm says 'seek peace and pursue it'. It's a very active phrase. To pursue something involves making an effort to achieve it, to strive in order to accomplish something. Driven business leaders have a clear idea of what they want to achieve and they set out a clear method in order to achieve their aim – to pursue their goal.

This passage encourages us to pursue peace in a similarly purposeful way. It challenges us to be active in the process, not simply to be praying or longing for peace, but working for it.

But how might we do that? World peace may be beyond our individual reach, but we can make a start. We can pursue peace in our own life and in our relationships, seeking to keep our tongues from evil and speaking truth, not lies. Why not work out an action plan – things that are achievable – in order to be working towards peace in your life? Maybe it's as simple as the words we use of others or our response to those who are very different from ourselves. Consider how you might pursue peace and work towards it.

† Help me to keep my tongue from evil and my life rooted in you. Help me to be a worker for peace, not simply seeking peace but pursuing it.

For further thought

• How can you not just seek peace but pursue it? What could you change in your life, community, or the wider world to pursue peace?

Peace and prosperity for all

Psalm 122:6-9

Pray for the peace of Jerusalem... For the sake of my family and friends, I will say, 'Peace be within you.' For the sake of the house of the Lord *our God, I will seek your prosperity.* (part of verses 6, 8 and 9)

Today's ancient words from the psalms sadly have immediate relevance and resonance. Jerusalem continues to be a place not of true peace but of conflict and division. Jerusalem is a place where neighbours are divided and where true peace is but a hope, or a dream.

To say 'peace be within you' is to wish people well. To seek their prosperity is to desire the best for them. To say 'peace be within you' in Jerusalem is to pray for understanding, tolerance and respect between Jew, Muslim and Christian. Peace suggests far more than the absence of war; it begins with the personal working towards being at peace with another individual. Full peace must reflect not just interpersonal relationships but positive international relationships too, for peace is also about equality and justice. In Jerusalem it is hard to see true peace but, as always, there is hope. Friendships are forged by neighbours on different sides of political or religious boundaries, and there are those so committed to peace that they will stand up for others' rights or endanger themselves for another's freedom. These are people who live as peacemakers, those who seek to embody peace in all they do or say. Peace among people can only ever really be true peace if people are able to receive and live with it within themselves. The greatest peacemakers in the world are those who begin with themselves. Mother Teresa famously said 'If you judge people, you have no time to love them.' If we spend our time and energy judging and dividing ourselves from others, where will peace be born?

† Peace-giving God, may I know your peace; may I seek your peace; may I share your peace; may I live out your peace.

For further thought

• Pray for a place of conflict; pray for true peace with justice. Consider how you might seek others' prosperity. What might that mean for you?

Saturday 4 July
Shalom – God's peace in the world

Jeremiah 29:4-14

Build houses and settle down; plant gardens and eat what they produce ... Also, seek the peace and prosperity of the city to which I have carried you into exile. Pray to the LORD for it, because if it prospers, you too will prosper. (verses 5 and 7)

There are certain places where we may feel at peace: maybe a special spot by water, or a garden or a park. Personal peace can be encouraged by music or silence and by space simply to be. For some, however, the experience of personal peace is hard. For some life is not 'peaceful', maybe because of extreme poverty, warfare or ill health. It is not always easy to feel 'at peace'. Here in the passage from Jeremiah we have God's people being encouraged to be at peace in an uncomfortable place, to be at peace in a foreign, alien land – in exile.

The encouragement of this passage is to seek peace, but it isn't simply to be at peace personally but to seek peace for others – specifically 'to seek the peace and prosperity of the city' where they are in exile. The Hebrew meaning of peace found in this passage is an idea of peace that is greater than an individual's feeling of being 'at peace'. Here peace is rooted in 'shalom', a broader, more holistic, peace. To seek shalom is to seek the welfare and wellbeing of others, including the physical place itself.

I believe God's will is for shalom in the world; for us to be at peace with one another and with creation. This passage encourages us to move towards that vision, even if we find ourselves in hard places, or in experiences that are far from peaceful. The challenge is to remember God's plans and to work towards their fruition, working for true 'shalom' in the world.

† God of peace, may I remember your plans. Help me not simply to seek what is good for myself but to pray and work for peace and shalom in the world. Amen

For further thought

• What might it mean to seek the peace and prosperity of where you are? Remember those for whom shalom/peace is a distant hope.

Building peace

2 He is our peace

This week's notes are by **Aileen Khoo**

 Aileen grew up in the Methodist Church, from attending Sunday school through youth fellowship and finally Trinity Theological College, Singapore. On graduating she became a diaconal minister, working as Director of Christian Education for 35 years. Now retired, Aileen continues to spend her time leading Bible studies and training Bible study leaders (especially experimenting in participatory Bible study methods) besides doing what she always enjoys – teaching and playing the cello. Among the institutions of higher learning she has taught in are Seminari Theoloji Malaysia, Malaysia Bible Seminary, and Te Deum, where she taught Christian Education and Church Music.

Sunday 5 July

Peacemakers

Matthew 5:9

Blessed are the peacemakers, for they will be called children of God.
(verse 9)

This sermon of Jesus describes the kingdom of God, what his disciples must do. It is not addressed to individuals, but to the community of faith. What is promised here is not reward for being good or for meeting requirements but God's gracious response to the human condition as it is, especially that of the disciples.

Jesus in the Beatitudes is actually saying 'Work for peace'. Disciples are not just 'to be'. They are called 'to do', to be engaged in working for peace. Jesus expected the disciples to do the same things he had been doing, which the God of peace is doing. In this time of war and terrorism we are called to be peacemakers. The world says blessed are those who are competitive, aggressive; but Jesus, the Prince of Peace, says blessed are those who are peacemakers.

The community that is blessed does not just sit passively, waiting for and then enjoying God's blessings. Rather, we live as if the rule of God is present in all its fullness. By the way we live, we translate these words into reality. If you want to be called a child of God, be sure you are a peacemaker!

† I will listen to what God the Lord says: he promises peace to his people, his faithful servants – but let them not turn to folly. (Psalm 85:8)

Monday 6 July
Instrument of peace

Romans 14:10-23

Let us therefore make every effort to do what leads to peace and to mutual edification. (verse 19)

As the culmination of the ethical exhortation of this letter, Paul writes an extended discussion on the relationship among groups with varying, even conflicting, religious practices and ethnic divisions. Paul emphasises the joy of fellowship and love. Don't judge or be a stumbling block. Rather, welcome one another. God indeed is holding out God's welcoming hand all the time. To welcome one another is to seek actively to know and to understand another's reasoning and judgements.

Like Jesus, we love and accept each other, and try to build each other up rather than tear one another down because of the ways in which we differ. God is at work creating a new heaven and a new earth where the entire cosmos will live in peace. Shalom is harmony between God and us, between us and nature and in the relationship between human beings. It is not in competing and 'winning', but in helping others win their way to peace.

Reconciliation begins when all are able to acknowledge with Paul that all people belong to God. The love that marks Christian relationships is itself a powerful testimony to Christ's presence. The church, filled with Christ's Spirit, is the instrument for building the unity of all humanity.

† I seek you with all my heart; do not let me stray from your commands. I have hidden your word in my heart that I might not sin against you. (Psalm 119:10 11)

For further thought
- Instead of judging, what should occupy our energy? What do you need to do to promote unity in diversity?

July

Channels of peace

Ephesians 2:11-22

For he himself is our peace, who has made the two groups one and has destroyed the barrier, the dividing wall of hostility. (verse 14)

The language of hostility and reconciliation in this letter implies that all is not well with the congregation and that some threat from outside the church demands the protection afforded by this apostolic letter. How in the world can God bring people together, given a world made up of diverse peoples at enmity with one another? It is by the blood of Christ! Jesus on the cross puts 'to death' hostility between people. In Malaysia, as well as in other parts of the world, our society is made up of religious intolerance, sectarianism, prejudice, discrimination and racism.

Now, in Christ, the gap has been closed. Enmity between races, barriers between classes, misunderstanding between sexes have been bridged. Jesus has made peace. From hostile elements God has made 'one body'. By being reconciled to God, we are at the same time reconciled to one another. If we choose sides, creating division, we are doing the devil's work; if we unite, we are doing God's work. We are called to help in the breaking down of walls of hostility like the Berlin Wall; and in the unification of Vietnam and Korea, and of our own communities.

We are the people who in Christ are now a part of the true Temple with Abraham, with the prophets and the apostles, with Jesus Christ as the cornerstone. As the Temple held Judaism together, so the Church will hold the new humanity together.

Differences in culture are not valid grounds for disunity. If we are at peace with others through the blood of Christ, let us live that peace. In Christ, the barriers that separate are down.

† Love and faithfulness meet together; righteousness and peace kiss each other. Faithfulness springs forth from the earth, and righteousness looks down from heaven. (Psalm 85:10-11)

For further thought

• Unity is God's purpose. What can we do to help bring people together? Write a letter to someone within your church, urging forgiveness and reconciliation.

Models of peace

1 Thessalonians 5:12-22

May God himself, the God of peace, sanctify you through and through. May your whole spirit, soul and body be kept blameless at the coming of our Lord Jesus Christ. (verse 23)

We lack peace with ourselves and others. What causes you to blow up? The first Thessalonian letter helps us see the quality of relationships appropriate to the family of God. Paul called us to be at peace among ourselves.

In scripture peace and justice go together. They are inseparably linked in God's mind and action. Justice in Hebrew is rooted in the idea of the rock-like stability and unchanging purpose of God. God is steadfastly and unflinchingly dedicated to establishing on earth what is in heaven. No wonder Jesus taught his disciples to pray 'Thy kingdom come'.

Real peace is the well-being of harmony within community. This can be achieved only with justice, and it is God's justice that peace shall reign on earth. If peace and justice are integrally related then the call to act for peace is a call from God to do justice. Living as a citizen of heaven's kingdom involves abandoning the ways of the world and adopting a different set of values.

What is truly important is the way our values are expressed in our actions to reflect the ethic of compassion. We need inner purification and peace before we can work for peace. Holy people have an 'inner' mark of character and an 'outer' mark of compassion. We can expect God to act now and work out God's will in you and me!

July

† If I have repaid my ally with evil or without cause have robbed my foe – then let my enemy pursue and overtake me; let him trample my life to the ground and make me sleep in the dust. (Psalm 7:4-5)

For further thought

- Is there a peace or justice issue that threatens to bring social conflict in your community? What can your group do to redress the underlying injustice?

Harbinger of peace

Hebrews 12:14-15

Make every effort to live in peace with everyone and to be holy; without holiness no one will see the Lord. (verse 14)

Make peace your aim. In our world, the way a conflict is solved is by killing the enemy. By abolishing the conflicting part we think we will achieve peace. Peace achieved by this kind of violence will lead the world only into greater oppression. We need to shun revenge and embrace reconciliation. Peace is not freedom from all trouble but a right relationship between people, where hatred is banished, where everyone seeks nothing but their neighbour's good.

The entire universe is yearning for the peace that characterised creation on the seventh day but was destroyed by the disobedience of humankind. Peace through Christ and his indwelling Spirit gives assurance to every Christian that all is well. In that peace we know we are never alone, never defeated. We have the assurance that God will care for us and guide our ways.

We rely on the compassionate God who weeps with us in the midst of any cruel destruction of life, not a God who rescues the good people and punishes the bad, but one who reconciles and would want his children to stop fighting. A coerced or enforced peace would be an artificial peace based on like-mindedness or homogeneity.

It is easy to lose heart, grow weary, become discouraged, give up. To strive means making an effort. We anticipate the final kingdom and participate now in the realm of God ushered in by Jesus Christ by putting others first and self last. This is peace for the future and not just our time. It is the kind of peace that we agree to work for together!

† My heart is not proud, Lord, my eyes are not haughty; I do not concern myself with great matters or things too wonderful for me. But I have calmed and quietened myself. (Psalm 131:1-2a)

For further thought

• In failed relationships, is it because one or both parties didn't try hard enough?

Friday 10 July
Peace the only victory

Revelation 12:7-12

They triumphed over him by the blood of the Lamb and by the word of their testimony. (part of verse 11)

Here is a description of war in heaven between evil and Michael and the angels. But Satan is hard to get rid of. The enemies of God create strife, war, trouble. He is the trouble-maker desiring his own way rather than the ways of God. He is the deceiver, whom Jesus called the 'father of lies', who continues to ravage the earth, even though he has been conquered 'by the blood of the Lamb' and by people's testimony. Notice that the faithful witness of the church will help defeat Satan!

The war continues. The dragon, who could not win in heaven, continues to deceive the faithful on earth. The demonic powers know they are losing the battle, but they struggle on, harder than ever. The final victory is certain, but the earthly struggle continues. We live in the heat of the battle.

We are participating in a drama much larger than our own life story. We are not merely observers; we are actively engaged in a vast spiritual war. God and countless people are involved. Everything is at stake; a battle is being waged for the hearts and souls of human beings.

It is peace, not war that will triumph in the end. The saints are praying for this continually; their prayers rise like incense. How might you become a more powerful person of prayer?

† Rise up, O God, judge the earth, for all the nations are your inheritance. (Psalm 82:8)

For further thought

• Are you doing anything in your community to eliminate violence in public media or to eliminate war toys for children?

July

Saturday 11 July
Pursue peace

1 Peter 3:8-12

They must seek peace and pursue it. (part of verse 11)

Misunderstanding and miscommunication surround us. This madness and greed for material possessions divides human communities and finally destroys our fragile earth. We produce missiles costing millions, nuclear bombs and chemical weapons to keep peace without justice. Divisions, apartheid, genocide and devaluation of human life characterise our society. But God does not abandon us in our despair. God calls us to speak the language of liberation, connection and unification; the language of peace, calling us to be workers for a new creation.

Martin Luther King and Mahatma Gandhi, together with people like them, acted in the unshakable knowledge that we do not arrive at the truth by violence, nor justice by hate, nor peace by hostility. In a world of hate, terror and tactical cunning, they placed their faith in the power of the spirit and the superior strength of goodness, gentleness and complete truthfulness.

Most people believe that using force is the surest way of getting what you want. But there has been a radical opposition to the logic of violence since the time of Jesus Christ. Violence unleashes violence in return. We are called to make peace, even when the way to peace is through struggle. To 'seek' implies that peace is difficult to get, but worth everything we've got.

Jesus suffered unjustly, bearing the insults and pain. So Christians respond with love rather than react in anger. Whoever would love life and see good days must 'seek peace and pursue it'. This is among the things that make people righteous.

† In peace I will lie down and sleep, for you alone, Lord, make me dwell in safety. (Psalm 4:8)

For further thought
- Choose one difficult relationship you are experiencing. How can you bring about peace in it?

Readings in Mark (3)

1 Towards Jerusalem: encounters

This week's notes are by **Erice Fairbrother**

Erice Fairbrother is an Anglican priest who lives as a Benedictine Solitary in the Wellington Diocese in New Zealand. During 2013 she left parish ministry to focus on her poetry and develop her ministry as poet theologian and teacher. Using the genre of poetry, her poems are able to explore theological themes in metaphor, imagery and voice that are often beyond the constraints of prose. As a solitary, Erice continues as a teacher in formation, and she offers retreats, writing seminars, spiritual counsel and pastoral supervision.

Sunday 12 July
Brief encounters: glimpses of the divine

Mark 9:2-13

After six days Jesus took Peter, James and John with him and led them up a high mountain, where they were all alone. There he was transfigured before them ... and a voice came from the cloud: 'This is my Son, whom I love. Listen to him!' (verse 2 and part of verse 7)

It can happen anywhere. For a friend of mine it is over the frozen foods in the supermarket. Those moments of ordinary encounter. Moments when we notice something about the person next to us, something that transforms him or her from stranger to someone with whom we are drawn to speak. Sometimes it's sharing a smile, or noticing signs of stress and responding. Whatever these encounters are, for a moment Christ is present as we share and encourage. They are literally moments, but in them something has changed, something indefinable yet life giving.

Peter, James and John had often climbed the countryside with Jesus. It was an ordinary day, perhaps, when they suddenly encountered Jesus as never before. A moment when the man they knew was revealed as one in whom God was made present. They wanted to hold that moment. Don't we, when amazing things happen to us? Yet these moments of glimpsing Christ, of letting Christ be glimpsed in us, can be only moments, briefly encountered. To see, to speak and to let go of them takes faith! Faith that even the briefest of encounters can offer transfiguring glimpses of the divine, changing everything!

† Christ, you let others see who you really were. Give me courage to let others glimpse something of your life in and through me.

Meeting the dark with the light of faith

Mark 9:14-29

After Jesus had gone indoors, his disciples asked him privately, 'Why couldn't we drive it out?' He replied, 'This kind can come out only by prayer.' (verses 28-29)

Sometimes we really do have to take our faith seriously! Families can find this when someone they love is destroying his own life and the lives of all around him by drug and alcohol addiction. Often the first response is to pour out love – unconditionally. And then we learn that this too is used and manipulated. So we pour out resources, hoping that with helping to provide shelter and support things will change. But these too disappear into the bottomless pit of addictive wastage. And then the day comes when we realise that the most loving thing to do is to let go entirely. Not to stop loving but to hold that love ready, all the while waiting for the genuine search for loving healthy relationship to be restored. However, in reality, that time of holding can feel like a very long and endless night.

The words of Jesus become so real when we are faced with the limitations of what we can do for another. It challenges our faith as the question becomes 'Do I trust God enough, to trust myself enough, to let go and just pray, pray by holding faithfully the light of love?' It is not easy, for then we encounter the doubt that asks 'Is prayer enough?' It is the ongoing temptation. Yet to resist it is to find the resilience, the strength, to continue to hold on to the light, when ones we love cannot yet hold that light for themselves. Truly, some things can be changed by prayer.

† Christ, light and hope of my life, may I learn more and more to trust that you hear the prayers of my heart, and may I be glad in that.

For further thought

• How hard do we find it to trust God with what seem to be the impossible situations we encounter in our lives?

Recognising Christ:
encounters with young people

Mark 9:30-37

Jesus took a little child whom he placed among [the twelve]. Taking the child in his arms, he said to them, 'Whoever welcomes one of these little children in my name welcomes me.' (part of verses 36-37)

Living with young people the second time round is a challenge! I found this out recently when, having retired from parish ministry, I returned to my home city and began boarding with my daughter, and two teenage granddaughters. Their welcome was unconditional. For me, I have had to rediscover that unconditional part in myself, in the daily encounters with my granddaughters and their friends. It is a different way of sharing my life – I have found cartoons competing with my favourite, more 'worthy', programmes, alongside having meals at odd times according to teenage schedules. I had seen a parish struggle to have children in the forefront of worship and now I too am faced with having teenagers in the forefront of my life again. It's meant learning about honour and respect being about mutuality; shared lives about letting the young set the pace, too; about experiencing the humility of them leading me.

It is so easy to settle into retirement with a sense of entitlement. That somehow we've earned something, that building the kingdom is left to others now. Jesus suggests otherwise – that there is no place of entitlement in the kingdom. It's lifelong, never to be outgrown. Building the faith is the work of all – from the very young to the old – and when Jesus holds a child close we are given a powerful metaphor for where God's values lie. The mission of the Church is not an age-related activity! In Christ there is no room for entitlement, only for love's greater inclusivity and Christ-centred humility.

† God of community and grace, grant that may I have the humility to recognise your voice and your love in the lives of those around me and choose always to learn, wherever I may be.

For further thought

• When do you find it easier to look for recognition rather than recognising where Christ is in the ordinary encounters of your daily life?

Wednesday 15 July
Encountering God in the unexpected

Mark 9:38-50

Truly I tell you, anyone who gives you a cup of water in my name because you belong to the Messiah will certainly not lose their reward. (**verse 41**)

In a different city, rushed to a strange hospital without friends or family, my friend found herself in a very lonely place. To have arrived for a conference healthy, only to experience a stroke was a very fearful place to find herself. In the ward, in the night, a sense of being far from God's presence grew larger, threatening her faith, shaking her soul. The chaplain, she was told, was on call for emergencies only. Yet her need for faith's reassurance felt like an emergency, and despair began to overwhelm her.

At this point a doctor on duty popped in on unexpected impulse. Soon the two women were talking into the night. The doctor, a Muslim woman of faith, recognised my friend as a Christian woman of faith. One was seeking the presence of God, the other bringing that presence with love, and with respect for the faith of the seeker. My friend has never forgotten that ministry. The act of remembering continues to honour the faithfulness of the one who ministered to her that night.

To hold the cup of water out to another helps us cross all kinds of barriers, prejudices and beliefs. To fill the hands of another with hope is to offer the cup of living water. To receive that cup from an unexpected other is to experience the great compassion of Christ. In such encounters God's presence is recognised in mutuality and love.

† God of all, give us humble hearts to recognise you even in the most unlikely moments, so that overcoming all barriers, we may build your peace on earth with mutuality and respect.

For further thought

• Take time to recall moments when you have seen the hand of God in the most unexpected places, and give thanks for that memory.

Thursday 16 July
Encountering life's hard questions

Mark 10:1-12

Jesus then left that place and went into the region of Judea and across the Jordan. Again crowds of people came to him, and as was his custom, he taught them. (verse 1)

Life can throw us some pretty hard questions. Questions that arise, for instance, in the face of tragedy, in times of having to relocate, times of change or times of redundancy – and most often there are no easy answers. I remember a Christian couple whose sacred vows had held them faithfully together in sickness and in health, for 60 years. However, a sudden decline in health meant that he could no longer look after his wife. After a hard struggle they were forced to be separated, with her going into 24-hour care, and him into the role of hospital visitor. 'Until death do us part' became a question – how to do this when they had vowed never to part? Understanding illness as a form of death was not a help. A promise had been made, and he was terribly saddened by his inability to care for her in this final 'sickness'.

Sometimes it seems we can only live with the questions. Keeping to the letter of the law is not always helpful, and the right answer may not ultimately be the most life-giving or the most loving. Sometimes, when life questions us, we have to find answers we never thought we would contemplate. Jesus often showed that he knew the answers the law demanded of his society but the readings over this week show that he was able to counter legal rigidity with the embracing law of love – balancing what may be the right thing with what may be the most loving response.

† Keep me open, O Christ, always to look to your way of love when life leads to shifts and changes I could never anticipate.

For further thought

- Is it possible to let the hard questions we face become an opening into a deepening sense of God's grace and protection in our lives?

Whose kingdom is it?

Mark 10:13-16

When Jesus saw this, he was indignant. He said to them, 'Let the little children come to me, and do not hinder them, for the kingdom of God belongs to such as these.' (verse 14)

As Missioner in an impoverished part of New Zealand I found myself leading Sunday services in a large hall with a congregation of no more than twelve. They longed for children and a Sunday school. So we prayed for children. For many weeks we prayed. Then late one Sunday three young kids appeared. They sat uncomfortably on the large chairs, and the youngest ran about alarmingly! At the cuppa afterwards they asked for milo and drank most of it! The chocolate biscuits were all rapidly consumed. That week when we prayed for children, it was suggested that our prayers had already been answered. Even though they had come because they were hungry and even though they had eaten and drunk all our Sunday best, it seemed we had prayed and God sent these kids. We wondered and continued to pray.

Then one day one of the group during prayers thanked God for 'those three hungry kids'. And to our wonder, the very next Sunday they appeared – still late, still wanting food rather than God. And so they began to teach us: that the suffering Christ still comes to us as a vulnerable child who needs shelter, food and love. They taught us about making contact with families with nothing; they taught us about God's love being about sharing our lives beyond Sundays. They taught us about being Christ in the world. And, most important perhaps, they showed us to whom the kingdom really belongs and opened our eyes to see it.

† Give me a heart that is open to receive your answers to my prayers, and eyes that can see you in the suffering ones, the hungry and the unloved.

For further thought

• Do I see groups and organisations that help children in need as co-builders of the kingdom of God here on earth?

Saturday 18 July
Crossroads: choosing to travel lightly

Mark 10:17-22

Jesus looked at him and loved him. 'One thing you lack,' he said, 'Go, sell everything you have and give to the poor, and you will have treasure in heaven. Then come, follow me.' (**verse 21**)

When a friend moved from a three-bedroomed house to a one-bedroomed apartment, a process of shedding began. Transforming the church house where I lived into a retreat house meant moving into one upstairs corner for my living space, and I too began shedding. It was a crossroads and the question I had to ask was 'What do I really need to live well?' After an inner struggle, the answer, I discovered, is 'surprisingly little'! From a fully furnished four-bedroomed house I ended up with ten pieces of furniture and twenty-five paintings, the latter giving an idea of my ultimate priorities: sustenance for the soul. Interestingly, at that point of making choices of what to carry forward, I could not have foreseen the impact those choices would later have. But today, living as a Benedictine Solitary, what I chose as essential to carry back then has now become a source of freedom, a blessing.

Crossroads are moments when faith questions us, as the seeker who asked Jesus what else he needed to do quickly discovered. Giving up what he didn't need became a choice too hard to make! Socially, we are conditioned to believe that things are important and that stuff is what makes life worthwhile. Jesus challenged the seeker to re-evaluate that social value. After all, what is essential as we live and walk as disciples? Yet, perhaps finally, it is not even about things and perhaps more a question of faith. Confronted with crossroads as we follow Christ, how will we choose? What will hold us back? And what will free us to follow more completely?

† I long to follow you more completely, O Christ! Grant me wisdom and courage to choose to walk with you more faithfully.

For further thought

• What do I hold on to that is no longer life giving at this point in my life? Are there things that hold me back from exploring my faith more deeply?

Readings in Mark (3)

2 Conversations on the way

This week's notes are by **Daniel Oprean**

Daniel G Oprean is a Romanian theologian, living in Oravia, Romania. He is the President and Executive Director of Kenosis Association in Oravia, Romania. Daniel is married to Ana and they have two boys, Cristian and David. Daniel is involved in preaching and teaching in Evangelical churches in Romania.

Sunday 19 July

The possibility of entering the kingdom of God

Mark 10:23-31

Jesus looked at them and said, 'With man this is impossible, but not with God; all things are possible with God.' (verse 27)

The dialogue between Jesus and his disciples is a conclusion to the conversation with the rich man. Jesus shows how it is possible for one person to enter the reality of God's kingdom, and he makes crystal clear the fact that this will be impossible without God's own initiative. Christ contrasts the worldly spirit of being 'possessed by what you possess' with the renunciation of all you have for him and the gospel. Christ's saying is an important reminder of the fact that, as his disciples then and there, we must understand here and now that we have to receive the call to the kingdom, accepting that the only way to enter the kingdom is by the childlike self-renouncing trust in God.

† Our Father, God of all possibilities, we ask you today to give us the wisdom, through your Spirit, to accept our Saviour's way into the kingdom.

Monday 20 July
The model of living in the kingdom of God

Mark 10:32-45

Whoever wants to become great among you must be your servant, and whoever wants to be first must be slave of all. For even the Son of Man did not come to be served, but to serve, and to give his life as a ransom for many. (verses 43-45)

The request of the two disciples (verses 35-36) underlines a trap that could be detected many times in our living on the journey of discipleship. This trap is that of conforming to the 'lordship over' model shown often in the world and so often practised in our contemporary Christianity. It is rooted in the desire for personal elevation and characterised by being obsessed with one's own greatness and status.

In contrast, in his answer to the disciples, Jesus describes a different way of living – a 'self-emptying' model rooted in the desire to elevate the other and concerned with her salvation. This model is in fact the only one that is acceptable for the life in the kingdom of God. Fortunately, the two disciples, James and John, eventually understood the fact that suffering and death for Christ and with Christ are the two expressions of the real service of Christ's disciples in the world in every generation. For Christ, as the embodiment of the kingdom, sacrificial service is the only way to live out the kingdom's reality. For the disciples then and there, as well as for us here and now, the Christ model is the viable model of living in the kingdom of God.

† Dear Lord Jesus Christ, help us understand the uniqueness of your model of service and help us to accept that this is the way for us to live in the reality of the kingdom of God.

For further thought

• What is the model you follow in your journey of discipleship and in ministry to others? How can Jesus' self-emptying model inform the life of your community?

July

Tuesday 21 July
The light of the kingdom of God

Mark 10:46-52

'What do you want me to do for you?' Jesus asked him. The blind man said, 'Rabbi, I want to see.' 'Go,' said Jesus, 'your faith has healed you.'
(verse 51)

The cry of Bartimaeus to Jesus is an expression of his understanding of the fact that Jesus is the king promised for centuries, a king who comes to reign eternally on the throne of David. Bartimaeus becomes a signpost for the kingdom of God by acknowledging then and there the presence of the king of God. The way Mark organises the story is important, starting with Bartimaeus begging by the roadside, continuing with Bartimaeus hearing that Jesus is near (verse 47), and ending with him receiving his sight and following Jesus along the road. This way of constructing the story illustrates the way the people of God and all humanity can be transformed from spiritual blindness to spiritual sight, by acknowledging Jesus Christ as the light of the world. Moreover, the story emphasises the fact that nobody is too small or too unimportant to be heard by Christ, when he or she cries for help to him. Also, the story is a reminder of the fact that, just as Bartimaeus used his chance to meet Christ, so human beings should use the many occasions that God offers everybody in the world to be saved.

† Our Father, please help us acknowledge the truth that your son is the king of your kingdom, the only one who can restore our spiritual sight. We thank you that you always hear our cries.

For further thought

- How aware are you of the fact that God hears our cries and knows our needs?

The King of the kingdom of God

Mark 11:1-11

Many people spread their cloaks on the road, while others spread branches they had cut in the fields. Those who went ahead and those who followed shouted, 'Hosanna! Blessed is he who comes in the name of the Lord! Blessed is the coming kingdom of our father David! Hosanna in the highest heaven!' (verses 8-9)

What the blind beggar Bartimaeus acknowledged, the crowds also declared at the entering into Jerusalem of Jesus. He is the centre of the kingdom, as the eternal king of the Father; Christ redeems, concludes and redefines the kingly office for the people of God. And this is so because first, the King Christ redeemed the ways of the kings of Israel, becoming through his obedience the true way and, through his statutes, the kingdom itself. Christ concluded the kingly office for the people of God through his position. Finally, Christ redefined the kingly office through his life, being the king whose reign must be accepted.

† Our Father, please help us through your holy Spirit not only to declare but also to accept your son's office as the king and lord over our lives.

July

For further thought

• Reflect on the ways in which the lordship of Christ should be expressed in different domains of your life. What will be different?

The high priest of the kingdom of God

Mark 11:12-19

On reaching Jerusalem, Jesus entered the Temple courts and began driving out those who were buying and selling there. He overturned the tables of the money-changers and the benches of those selling doves, and would not allow anyone to carry merchandise through the temple courts. (verses 15 and 16)

The symbolic entry into Jerusalem as king is followed by Christ's actions in the Temple – an important reminder of another symbolic description of his high-priestly office. Christ is a unique high priest, being the sacrifice of the Father for the redemption of the whole of humanity (John 1:29). He is a unique high priest also because his sacrifice operates where the sacrifices of the Old Covenant could not, in the Temple in heaven, according to Hebrews 9:11-12, and in the human conscience, according to Hebrews 9:3-15. As such, his sacrifice covers the past – resolving the penalty of sin, the present – conquering the power of sin, and the future – opening the possibility of the eradication of the presence of sin. The story is an important reminder of the fact that the wrath of God is not the action of a capricious person against other persons; rather it is a profound opposition to godlessness and wickedness. God's wrath is directed towards the wrongdoings, not against people. Towards people God directs his 'riches of ... kindness, forbearance and patience' with the purpose that people will be led by 'God's kindness toward repentance', according to Romans 2:4.

† Our Father, we thank you for the uniqueness of our Lord's high-priestly office, and we give you praise for the efficacy of Christ's sacrifice over the past, present and future of our lives.

For further thought
• Reflect on how much the sacrifice of Christ conquers the power of sin in your life, and give thanks.

Friday 24 July
The prophet of the kingdom of God

Mark 11:20-25

Whatever you ask for in prayer, believe that you have received it, and it will be yours. And when you stand praying, if you hold anything against anyone, forgive them, so that your Father in heaven may forgive you your sins. (part of verses 24-25)

After the symbolic entry into Jerusalem as king, and the symbolic acts in the Temple as high priest, Christ speaks in the Temple as the prophet, in Mark 11:11 and 15.The way he speaks in the Temple is a reminder of the ministry of one of the greatest prophets in the history of Israel, Jeremiah. In the symbolic actions in the Temple, Christ is the prophet who recapitulates, concludes and redefines the prophetic office for the people of God. And this is so because he is the prophet and the prophecy at once. As such his word is obeyed by the entire creation; the cursing of the fig tree is another symbolic act expressing the failure of Israel, as God's people, to bear the desired fruits of their mission in the world. And this is an important reminder of the necessity for our obedience to Christ, expressed in following him, in his terms and way of thinking. Can we listen to Jesus' word, and let him dwell in us?

† Our Father, we thank you for your unique prophet, Christ, through whose message we are transformed and sanctified by your Spirit.

For further thought
• Ask yourself how much you accept to be modelled by the word of God.

July

207

Saturday 25 July
The authority of the kingdom of God

Mark 11:27-33

They arrived again in Jerusalem, and while Jesus was walking in the temple courts, the chief priests, the teachers of the law and the elders came to him. 'By what authority are you doing these things?' they asked. 'And who gave you authority to do this?' (verses 27-28)

The question of the chief priests and the teachers betrays their failure to acknowledge the uniqueness of the person acting in front of them in the Temple. The contrast is first with the blind beggar Bartimaeus, who received his sight and, second, with the people who acknowledged John the Baptist as a prophet in Mark 11. The answer of Jesus is in the form of a question about the origin of John the Baptist's baptism. It is a challenge to the chief priests and teachers to imagine the activity of John as a forerunner to the activity of Jesus. The challenge of Jesus aimed to prompt them to reach the redeeming conclusion that the one who sent John and gave him authority is the same one who sent Jesus and gave him authority. This dialogue is also a reminder that, for God, every person is important, even the ones who will not believe in him.

† Our Sovereign God, please help us to believe that your son has all authority and help us to live trusting this central truth of your kingdom.

For further thought

• Ask yourself how the truth of Christ's overall authority should be reflected in the way you think and live in the world.

Attentiveness
1 An attentive God

This week's notes are by **Michael Jagessar**

 Michael Jagessar is a minister of the United Reformed Church. He is currently serving as the Secretary for Intercultural Ministry and a moderator for the General Assembly of the United Reformed Church (2012–2014). More on Michael's biography and writings can be found at www.caribleaper.co.uk

Sunday 26 July
Creating, sustaining, renewing

Psalm 104:19-30

How many are your works, Lord! In wisdom you have made them all; the earth is full of your creatures. (verse 24)

I love holidaying in France every spring and summer. Whether walking, climbing mountains or simply lying in our garden in the nights with no electricity and studying the stars in the distance, the poetry of the psalmist come alive. The majesty of the Divine in the whole of creation is awesome. It simply piles up when we pay close attention to all around, even if we are bound to the domain of our 'concrete jungles' that we have erected. One cannot read Psalm 104 and not see resonance with the sentiments in the creation story in Genesis 1. In this vibrant song of creation, God created (and creates) with mastery and insight, with everything given detailed attention and purpose. It is as if the psalmist is saying to us: 'Look, pay attention. God is doing this.' Here is a song of praise to the Attentive One who creates, sustains and renews. The goodness and wonder of creation is poetry to the goodness of God. It is 'creation spirituality'. Behold! Seasons turn and change. Trees and children grow. The light comes from various directions, playing with the colours and shapes of leaves. Look and behold!

† Breath-of-Life, we give praise and thanks for, and delight in, your creating, sustaining and renewing of the whole of creation. Amen

July

Up close and personal

Psalm 139:1-18

You have searched me, LORD, and you know me. You know when I sit and when I rise; you perceive my thoughts from afar. (verses 1-2)

My Hindu grandmother, a devout woman who has been a tremendous influence on my faith journey, never read Psalm 139. Yet, the words of this psalm were reflected in her attitude to her life, relationships and spirituality. It was through her that I first journeyed through the psalms over and over again, tasting and drinking of the poetics of spirituality. Psalm 139 combines praise of, appeal to, and wisdom meditation on God who knows all and who encompasses all – who pays attention to every detail, down to knowing each of us! The psalm proclaims a relationship with God that is profoundly personal (not private). God knows me, cares about me, seeks me out, formed me in my mother's womb, knows my heart and soul, knows me inside and out, knows my worth. Perhaps, my grandmother's 'take' on this psalm is related to what my colleague Anthony Reddie refers to in the context of the 'Black experience' as 'some-bodi-ness'. In the presence of God in Christ, each of us is wonderfully and differently made and there is no need to pretend to be the imprint of someone else in order to be somebody. Such an assurance and recognition releases us to be ourselves – complex human beings whose identity is located in God who created and loves each of us.

† Searching-and-attentive God, you who know us better than we know ourselves, stir us to bring out the best of our gifts for your sake. In Jesus' name we pray. Amen

For further thought

• How does the knowledge of this all-attentive God who loves each of us intensely, shape your relationships and response to what you may be currently wrestling with?

Tuesday 28 July
A resting God

Genesis 1:31 – 2:3

Then God blessed the seventh day and made it holy, because on it he rested from all the work of creating that he had done. (verse 3)

In our world of 'created busyness', I warm to the idea that 'rested' may be more appropriately translated 'abstained' – that is, to catch one's breath. More important, there is a message here about abstaining from interfering with creation one day a week. God's 'resting' teaches us that we too need to make time for rest, intentionally abstain from 'work' one day of the week. Our 'groaning creation' urges this, given our inclination to manipulate and control our world. The habit of resting also says something about work. It is not an end in itself and we need to counter getting hooked on 'performance' and 'over-achieving'. Have we bought into what American spiritual leader Richard Rohr calls a sort of 'spiritual capitalism'? Resting on the seventh day, God connects the reality of working and resting with a deeper vision that accompanies it. Rest does not exist for the sake of work – it is about us, about our humanness – the ability to see life and the world as a whole. It is about seeing ourselves, others, creation not in terms of function but for who we are. It is about paying attention to the rhythms of our life that honour the image of God – an attentive God who rests and in whose image we are made.

† God-who-graces-us-with-rest, help us respond with gratitude, receiving the gift of a balanced life, which is our calling as your people. In the name of Christ! Amen

For further thought

• 'Come to me, all you that are weary and burdened, and I will give you rest' (Matthew 11:28). Consider scheduling a resting time in your diary. As communities of rest, what are spaces for rest that churches create/offer?

Wednesday 29 July
God chooses

Genesis 12:1-9

The LORD had said to Abram, 'Go from your country, and your people and your father's household to the land that I will show you. I will make you into a great nation, and I will bless you; I will make your name great, and you will be a blessing.' (verses 1-2)

My interfaith family (Muslim and Hindu) often reminds me that, while I could have followed another vocation, God had already 'had an eye on me' to become a servant of God's word. Hence, at my baptism I was given a list of names (Michael Nathaniel Emmanuel Samuel) to recognise this. I now use only two of these names!

My family would warm to this sort of specificity around the call of Abram. For them it suggests the attentiveness of God, even if it is being called out into nothing with nothing. What is important is that God has given the promise that God will make a great nation of this family. Hence, moving into the unknown is made easier knowing that God is with them.

From my experience, God's call (whatever form or shape it may take) is an invitation to move beyond our own fears: fear of the unknown beyond our control, fear of others who are different from us, and fear of powerlessness in the face of impossibilities. My family taught me that daring to step out is about throwing oneself at the mercy of grace. Though from different religious traditions, this is reflected in their understanding of both faith and faithfulness in God. I think their question to me will be: do you really believe that God, who knows each of us most intimately, can do the impossible in, for and through us?

† God-who-accompanies-and-sustains, where our hearts are fearful and worried, grant us trust, courage and hope. In the name of the one who frees and releases. Amen

For further thought

• 'Stand at the crossroads and look; ask for the ancient paths, ask where the good way is, and walk in it' (Jeremiah 6:16). Where and how is the call of God working in your life?

Thursday 30 July
Upsetting and saving

1 Samuel 2:1-8

There is no one holy like the Lord*; there is no one besides you; there is no Rock like our God.* (verse 2)

The routines of our day, including the lure of our wired world, are there to make us forget this deepest longing. Daily we are bombarded with the message that we find security in our achievements, family, friends and our own provision for the future. God, it seems, has become victim of a 'chronic displacement' movement.

Hannah's praise stands in direct contradiction to this tendency. She is praising God because God is giving her the strength and assurance she needs in the shifting circumstances of her life. One can read her song as saying that, while friends come and go, as do achievements, only God's presence satisfies the longing and hunger with what is good and enduring. God's specific presence in her life, personal and intimate, not only changes the immediate circumstances of her life; it also causes Hannah to look beyond herself to how God is working – at God's saving purposes in the world at large. Nothing is too small or too large for God who is always present and who saves. Hannah's prayer reminds us of our calling to inhabit a countercultural way of thanksgiving and praise, as we affirm our belief in God who gives, accompanies, frees, saves and sustains. She also reminds us of being attentive to the source of the gift!

† God-who-is-always-present, in the midst of competing voices, gift us with the will to stay fully awake and attentive to your assuring presence. Amen

For further thought

• Consider the subtle and overt ways in which God is being marginalised in our lives. Name some of the events/happenings/ people for which you wish to give God thanks. What would your version of Hannah's prayer be like?

July

She makes a feast

Proverbs 9:1-6

Come, eat my food and drink the wine I have mixed. Leave your simple ways and you will live; walk in the way of insight. (verses 5-6)

Among my interfaith inheritance is the imagery of tables and feasts and the high value placed on wisdom. My parents would agree that wisdom is more than intelligence: it is a matter of heart, head, hands and more. They would also add that 'wisdom is a craft that demands honesty'!

In Proverbs, wisdom's table is a metaphor for a space to enable mutuality in the giving and receiving of wisdom. In the Jewish tradition, wisdom is the Torah and so should be feasted upon like a banquet at wisdom's table. The invitation is to: 'come, taste and discover: eat and drink your fill; chew on, savour and swallow the sweetness of God's word; and be satisfied.'

Wisdom feeds us when we hear the word read and proclaimed, though we may not always find the flavour to our taste! When we gather for worship, in our prayers and meetings, Wisdom is there assuring, feeding, comforting, forgiving and challenging us – making us wiser. When we hear and speak the good news of abundant life, we are feasting upon Wisdom. Wisdom kisses and embraces us as we rise from her table and says to us: 'Now make me real in your life: go and feed others as I have fed you, and be sure to come back for more feasting. There is always enough for everyone.' Taste and see – God is generous!

† Wisdom-God, continue to feed us with your generous bread of life so that we may feed all with your offer of abundant life. Amen

For further thought

- Consider the places, spaces and moments you wish to name as wisdom-encounters. Imagine a 'come dine with me' TV show with Proverbs 9:5-6 as a strapline!

Saturday 1 August
Invitation to rest

John 1:35-42

Turning round, Jesus saw them following and asked, 'What do you want?' They said, 'Rabbi … where are you staying?' 'Come,' he replied, 'and you will see.' So they went and saw where he was staying, and they spent that day with him. It was about four in the afternoon. (verses 38-39)

I grew up at the home of my paternal grandmother. She was a Hindu and had converted one of her extra bedrooms into a worship space with an array of colourful Hindu icons. I recall often peering into this room, which I sensed as being quite 'other'. One day I was startled by the voice of my grandmother: 'What are you looking for? Come see!' I am glad I dared to enter this place of mystery to my young mind! I discovered a new and exciting world that has shaped my spirituality.

The question, 'What are you looking for?' is one of the greatest spiritual questions. It invites and provokes a response – stepping out, exploring and seeking. For John, questions about staying, abiding and seeing are questions of deep and enduring relationships. In Jesus, we encounter God in the invitation to belong. Entering the God-space (not a geographical location) in Jesus is entering a relationship with a purpose – to share in life in all its fullness. For me these questions of Jesus and the invitation are at the heart of our calling. Stepping out of our 'fear' and 'comfort' zones to come, see and experience the way of Jesus is a life-changing encounter. Come and see!

† God-who-invites-and-accompanies, journeying with us through our fears, grant us the courage to step out and let go into your way of abundant grace. Amen

For further thought

• Pay attention to what is happening around you. Take responsibility for changing it. Make a conscious effort to be present to the God who is present to you.

Attentiveness
2 Paying attention

This week's notes are by **Helen Van Koevering**

Living in Southern Africa for 18 years has challenged Helen, raised in England, to live differently in very real ways, and to see God at work in a context not of her roots. Apart from being the mother of three teenagers and the wife of the diocesan bishop, Helen presently works as the priest of a large lay- and youth-led parish in the largely Muslim town of Lichinga, and as Director of Ministry with the Anglican Diocese of Niassa in northern Mozambique, a diocese that has more than doubled in members and congregations since 2004.

Sunday 2 August
Paying attention to nature

Psalm 104:5-18

He set the earth on its foundations; it can never be moved … the trees of the LORD are well watered, the cedars of Lebanon that he planted. There the birds make their nests; the stork has its home in the junipers. The high mountains belong to the wild goats; the crags are a refuge for the hyrax. (verses 5, 16-18)

Plastic bags are the greatest source of litter in our Mozambican town. They're everywhere, caught in wire fences, blowing around in streets, thrown down on the pathways. The mantra 'reduce, reuse, recycle' is irrelevant here: only truly worthless rubbish is left on the streets, every bottle and paper is reused again and again.

The litter is so normal that it's hardly seen any more. It's only after our friend tells us her cows have died from eating plastic that we shake our heads. Another perspective is needed to see what's around us.

Being attentive to God's world means opening our eyes to the beauty and ugliness, stability and chaos, sustainability and healing. God has attended to the smallest details of life – that which gladdens and strengthens us, where animals find safe refuge and the seasons bring their changes. May we be attentive to these details of nature too and recognise our small responsibility in the beauty, stability and sustainability of God's world. And pick up our litter!

† Life-giving Lord, our creator and provider: transform us to see the details of your created beauty, stability and sustainability, and live to change ugliness and chaos. Amen

Monday 3 August
Paying attention to the mystery

Isaiah 40:12-17

Who has measured the waters in the hollow of his hand, or with the breadth of his hand marked off the heavens? Who has held the dust of the earth in a basket, or weighed the mountains on the scales and the hills in a balance? (verse 12)

For some in the world, our attention is given to many things in any one day or hour. Multi-tasking and communications with multiple persons is our pattern. Sound bites hit the mark. Time is of the essence. Knowledge is at our fingertips. For others, time is measured in events and seasons, and attention is given to one thing, one situation, one person at a time.

But, every now and then, something breaks through the hurried and event-filled existence. Something stops us in our tracks. Something hits home.

It could be an illness or death of a loved one, or it could be the birth of a baby. It could be the news of a tsunami, earthquake or flood, or it could be the sight of a rainbow, thunderstorm or sunset. It could be a TV documentary on the size of the universe, travel to distant lands, adventures in space and the oceans, or it could be a news report of war, trauma and devastation in known places. It could be in the taking of the communion cup and bread.

Then, somehow, we stand still, momentarily. With no answer of our own. Held in awe. Mystery opens us wordlessly, and we recognise who we are before God. Known and at home. In another's hand, with a new awareness.

The choice to allow Mystery's transforming touch or return to controlled answers of our own making is there, held in the balance.

† Holy Lord, open me to the presence of your mystery in my world, in all the big and small things of my life. You hold my world in your hand, and I hold you in awe. Amen

For further thought

• Gratitude forms hearts of awe. Take time today to consider your gratefulness for God's presence in your life, and to rest a little in that mystery.

Tuesday 4 August
Paying attention to suffering

Psalm 38:1-16, 21-22

Paying attention to suffering All my longings lie open before you, Lord*: my sighing is not hidden from you.* **(verse 9)**

The women round here say that life is tougher than it used to be. Who knows?

Hortênçia couldn't say how old she was as she's an orphan whose birth was unregistered. She was raised by her grandparents, who died recently. She sighed when asked about her new caregiver, her aunt - her eyes gave her away.

Maria, a young mother of three, has been abandoned by her soldier husband and now, for lack of rent, has only two weeks to leave their tiny shack home. She breathes deeply and shrugs her shoulders.

Felicia is in hospital, painfully emaciated by AIDS. Her eyes followed the priest's mouth as she spoke the words of prayer and blessing. Tears filled her eyes when she took the wine-dipped wafer of communion.

Joana, a widow at twenty-five, has just finished the usual 40-day ceremony since her husband died, and her in-laws have told her she must go back to her family, leaving her marital home. She smiles bravely.

Words may hide from us in times of suffering, unable to be spoken but seen in other small details that might easily be missed by another. But nothing is hidden from our attentive God, and no one shares our suffering as intimately as God. God doesn't wait for the right words, the correct response, the right attitude. When pain and suffering is deepest, our breath, our sigh, our slightest tear or smile, speaks for our hearts to our loving God. It is then that simply breathing, or crying, or smiling becomes prayer. And God knows.

† Lord, you are beside and within us in our pain and suffering. You know us and our deep need of you. Hear us when we pray, Lord. Amen

For further thought

- Remember that the people you meet today may be struggling in some way that you might not know, but God does. Pray for them.

Wednesday 5 August
Over the long night

Psalm 130

Lord, hear my voice. Let your ears be attentive to my cry for mercy.
(verse 2)

Psalm 130 is one of fourteen short psalms entitled the Songs of Ascents and reflecting concerns of and images from regular family and village life. The songs cover everything from protection to deliverance from gossip, harvest joy and happy homes, trust, thanksgiving and unity, as well as the desire for God's presence and voice in the depths of a dark night of a soul waiting for the morning of new hope.

Psalm 130 is also one of seven so-called penitential psalms. The early church sensed an extra note of urgency to be heard, and the certainty of the morning bringing God's keenly expected help. God's loving, hopeful, powerful response brings redemption from the soul's waiting night, and encouragement to the whole community that God lives in, with and for God's people.

But in among the poetry is a pilgrim's song. The journey from the family home to Jerusalem, the life of the village to the presence of the holy place, through the deep night to the light of morning, is the journey of a soul, too. God pays attention to our cries for transformation, and waits and watches alongside us for the hope-filled morning – with us and our communities as we confidently witness to God's presence in our lives.

† Lord, hear our voices and be there in our waiting and watching for the light of the new morning. Your kingdom come, Lord! Amen

For further thought

• Is there someone you know who might gain hope from hearing your testimony to God's love and power today?

August

Thursday 6 August
Paying attention to God's commands

Deuteronomy 6:13-25

The LORD commanded us to obey all these decrees and to fear the LORD our God, so that we might always prosper and be kept alive, as is the case today. (verse 24)

Between AD 1900 and 2010, the number of Christians in Africa grew from nine per cent to forty-nine per cent, from roughly seven million to over five hundred million. This enormous growth can be attributed as much, if not mainly, to the lives of ordinary men and women who have lived and taught their faith in their homes and villages as to any number of professional missionaries.

Today's passage of caution against disobedience to God follows directly on from the greatest commandment of all: 'love the Lord your God with all your heart, with all your soul and with all your strength' (verse 5). This is to be the key message we pass on to our children, that we ponder on our journeys, and the thought with which we begin and end each day. It is the message reflected in how we live, and essential to our testimony of God's presence with us.

The Israelites weren't the only ones in history surrounded by the impulse to be drawn into following other gods of our cultures – gods of materialism, violence, selfishness, greed. We confuse what we have with who we are, live to please anyone but God, and hurt what we were intended to be as God's imagers.

Turning to God and living God's commandments are one side of the coin of knowing who God is. The other side is remembering what God has done in our lives. Together, we are encouraged and strengthened to live rightly and truly, now and into the unknown future.

† God, you have worked through history to draw us to yourself. Let us be known as those who love you with all our hearts, souls and strength. Amen

For further thought

• How do we love God with all our heart, soul and strength?

Friday 7 August
What's better?

Luke 10:38-42

'Martha, Martha,' the Lord answered, 'you are worried and upset about many things, but few things are needed – or indeed only one. Mary has chosen what is better, and it will not be taken away from her.' (verses 41-42)

In this story, Luke shows both the liveliness of the stereotypical characters of Martha and Mary, and illustrates the command to love God above all things. Mary's quiet composure contrasts with Mary's busy fussiness. Martha is the activist who likes to fill every moment, who blurts out her frustrations, who sees hospitality in terms of providing for needs. Mary is the opposite – she sees attention to the guest, the importance of the personality of the guest, as more important than any entertainment or other activity at that moment.

Not that Jesus says being busy is wrong, just not the best thing at this time. Because attention to this guest is of prime importance right now.

In Christian spirituality, the two sisters have become the symbols of the contemplative and active life, where lives are centred on prayer and on translating prayer into action. In truth, it is more accurate to say the story contrasts two ways of attentiveness. The word Luke uses for Martha's service is the same as that used for the work of the first seven deacons who served the poor in the early church community. But Jesus is addressed as 'the Lord' here, strongly suggesting the Lord God to later readers. And in that small detail, we see that Luke is pointing us to the truth of Mary's listening – and her love of Jesus becomes an illustration of love of God with the whole heart. He's pointing us to the importance of being attentive to Jesus.

† Lord, give me the openness and tranquillity to listen to your word, and hear your word in my heart so that I may translate that word into action. Amen

For further thought

- Consider your own attentiveness to Jesus: are you more like Martha or Mary?

Saturday 8 August
Keep God honest

Luke 18:1-8

Then Jesus told the disciples a parable to show them that they should always pray and not give up. (verse 1)

Here, in a typical Lukan parable, we learn of perseverance in prayer. The chief character is the bad guy who ends up doing the right thing for the wrong reason, the powerful person that's expected to reflect God, but doesn't. And, once again, Luke encourages us towards a particular kind of action in the face of unjust power: prayer.

Throughout the Bible, orphans and widows are seen as the helpless vulnerable of our world. And they are. For them, God seeks the right thing. It is not the hopeless but the helpless who cry out to God 'day and night', and their faith in God is their hope-filled strength. The early church and Christians knew that persevering in prayer was vital in the face of persecutions, and has gained strength through the community of prayer around the world in the face of many troubles and hardships ever since. Look at the underground churches of various Communist countries and the growth of the church afterwards. Look at the faith of key leaders in South Africa that held the country and region during the apartheid years, and have seen peace and justice win through. Look at the faith-filled international debt campaigners in UK and Europe who finally saw the cancellation of debts with the millennium. Look at the work of various Christian organisations around the world in places crying out for peace and justice.

We pray in the expectancy of keeping God honest about God's very self in response to us, and particularly to the most vulnerable. Pray: 'let God be God'.

† Faithful Lord, hear our prayers for justice around the world. May we see your power to bring peace, right and good in places of suffering and injustice. Be who you are in our world always. Amen

For further thought
• Do you pray for justice for the most vulnerable? How are you involved in seeing justice come?

Attentiveness

3 Attentiveness in community

This week's notes are by **Jane Gonzalez**

Jane Gonzalez is a Roman Catholic laywoman and works as a pastoral assistant in Hertfordshire. She was awarded an MA in Pastoral Theology in 2012. She has a keen interest in studying scripture and is a visiting preacher at a local Anglican church. Other interests include singing, gardening and sewing and she looks forward to an active retirement one day. Ambitions for the future: visit all the English cathedrals and walk the Camino de Santiago.

Sunday 9 August
Singing from the same hymn sheet

Psalm 136:1-9

Give thanks to the LORD, for he is good. His love endures for ever. Give thanks to the God of gods. His love endures for ever. Give thanks to the Lord of lords: His love endures for ever. (verses 1-3)

I am a member of my church choir. A small community of singers! Recently we held a concert entitled Songs of Faith as part of a year-long initiative to grow in our faith and to increase our sense of being part of a faith-filled community. We invited parishioners and friends to listen and participate in an evening of music: hymns and secular pieces that spoke to us of living out our faith in contemporary society. A good time was had by all and it was uplifting to see everyone joining in the communal choruses. Afterwards, there were refreshments and the singers, musicians and audience got together and socialised. Singing builds community. Who can have failed to be impressed and moved by the TV programme featuring Gareth Malone that told the story of a choir in a run-down and deprived area, and the way singing promoted a sense of community? Community singing became a source of enrichment and empowerment for many people.

Praise is fitting for loyal hearts, the psalmist tells us, and praising together is about 'singing from the same hymn sheet' – recognising the enduring and faithful love of God made present through our coming together to bear witness to it.

† Thank you, God, that your love endures. Open our eyes to pay attention to it this week, together.

August

Monday 10 August
A trouble shared...

Psalm 74:1-11

We are given no signs from God; no prophets are left... How long will the enemy mock you, God? Will the foe revile your name forever? Why do you hold back your hand, your right hand? (part of verses 9-11)

This is lament that is angry and bitter – not merely sorrowful. It reflects a grief that questions God and his purposes. This is entirely natural when we suffer great loss or trauma. I wonder, though, if we really feel comfortable with anger that is directed towards God. Is it part of a wider reluctance in our society to address grief and its varied manifestations? We know from the outpourings of emotion at the death of well-loved figures like Diana of Wales, or when there has been a particularly brutal murder or accident, that people need to express – through flowers, candles, teddy bears – the sense of shared loss and suffering.

But for many individuals for whom there is not this public display, grief seems to be something that is challenging. There is far less 'formal' mourning – the communal acts of earlier decades that symbolised the community's sharing in the loss and spoke the words of condolence without actual speech. I remember how we used to close our curtains and blinds as a mark of respect when there was a funeral in our street. People can feel isolated in their grief. Even bereavement now has stages ... as if loss can be packaged neatly.

But grief is raw, not neat. It needs to be voiced so that the pain can be allowed to find a way out. The psalmist teaches us to be honest in our prayer. Only through that honesty can God work his healing.

† Loving God, keep us attentive to those in grief today, and to our own moments of sadness.

For further thought

• Reflect on Ecclesiastes 3.4: 'A time to weep and a time to laugh; a time to mourn and a time to dance.' Do we fail to pay attention to the griefs that inhibit our flourishing?

Tuesday 11 August
The seduction of safety

Luke 12:32-40

Provide purses for yourselves that will not wear out, a treasure in heaven that will never fail, where no thief comes near and no moth destroys. For where your treasure is, there your heart will be also. (part of verses 33-34)

In this passage, Luke exhorts his readers to remain alert and ready for the return of the Lord. It's part of the teaching of Jesus about trusting in God's providence and setting our hearts on the right course. Towards the end of the chapter Jesus will encourage us to read the signs of the times; to be attentive to what is really going on around us and to react and respond accordingly.

I suppose we have lost the sense of urgency that filled Jesus and the community for which Luke was writing. The second coming seems a long time in manifesting itself and in the comfortable confines of our families and parishes we can become complacent. We give in to what John O'Donohue calls 'the seduction of safety' and the 'grey promises' of sameness ('For a New Beginning', *Benedictus*, Bantam Press, 2007:32). We become happy with the restrictions that security imposes on us, as individuals and as communities. We may become churches concerned more with maintenance than with mission.

That is not our calling as followers of the way. Jesus wants us to be awake and alert and attentive to the needy world around us. He asks for an active anticipation of his return through real engagement with those who are desperate for good news. Faith in his message, hope as fruit of patient waiting, and love for those whom we serve in society – these are the treasures we should strive for. All else is mere dross.

† God of Abraham and Sarah, make us impatient to be a blessing for others.

For further thought
• Reflect today on the true meaning of Christian hope and trust.

The apple of my eye

John 15:12-17

You did not choose me, but I chose you and appointed you so that you might go and bear fruit – fruit that will last – and so that whatever you ask in my name the Father will give you. This is my command: Love each other.
(verses 16-17)

It has been a bumper year for apples – a rich harvest. The apple trees of my neighbours and friends have been groaning under the weight. We don't have any trees ourselves but we have been gifted with the fruits of other people's labours – bags of green, russet, gold and red apples. All different, all having a savour and scent of their own.

At harvest time, particularly if we celebrate it in our churches, it is a good thing, I think, to reflect upon our own gifts and talents. How best can these be used within the various communities of which we find ourselves members? We need to remember the words of Jesus about the harvest needing labourers – each of whom has a particular talent or calling to bring home a rich crop. So often, though, we waste precious time paying more attention to the gifts of others than to those many unique qualities that we possess. We dissipate our talents or fail to foster them – instead of polishing them like a lovely shiny apple!

Paying ourselves attention need not be self-absorption or selfishness. There is an Irish saying that 'the person attentive to herself is to her neighbour attentive'. How can we recognise the goodness in the other if we can't discern it in ourselves? Loving one another means really looking and really listening to each other – with a loving eye and an open heart. But first we need to practise on ourselves.

† Loving God, help me believe that, just as I am, I am the apple of your eye.

For further thought

• Where can I make time for myself? Where do I need love and attention?

Thursday 13 August
Help me make it through the night

Mark 14:32-42

He took Peter, James and John along with him, and he began to be deeply distressed and troubled. 'My soul is overwhelmed with sorrow to the point of death,' he said to them. 'Stay here and keep watch.' (**verses 33-34**)

I remember with great fondness an elderly parishioner, now dead, who rescued me emotionally one Sunday. I was troubled and upset but putting the usual brave face on things and nobody noticed that I was hurt, except this lady. She spoke to me and it was the fact that she had noticed that helped me get things into perspective and back on an even keel.

Here in his account of what we often call the 'agony in the garden', Mark is very explicit about how Jesus is feeling. He is deeply distressed and troubled. He actually tells the disciples that he is feeling overwhelmed by the magnitude of the situation and the decision he needs to come to. Although it is his decision alone to make, he needs the companionship of three of his closest friends to help him through. As the song says, 'All I'm taking is your time – help me make it through the night' (Kris Kristofferson).

How can Peter, James and John resist the plea? How is it that they miss the extreme anguish that Jesus is feeling? They don't give him the attention they should at this point – they don't notice. Jesus has talked about betrayal, about treachery and loss of faith. Maybe they get so wrapped up in their own emotions that they fail to empathise with his. Whatever the reason, they cannot – or will not – face up to the challenge of sharing this moment with him. They remain cocooned in sleep, cocooned from pain.

† Lord, when leaving seems easier, give us the strength to stay with you, and with each other.

For further thought
- Are we aware of the burdens that weigh others down? Where do we fail to notice and to act?

August

Friday 14 August
The tyranny of time

Exodus 23:10-12

Six days do your work, but on the seventh day do not work, so that your ox and your donkey may rest, and so that the slave born in your household and the foreigner living among you may be refreshed. (verse 12)

Sundays are not what they used to be here in the UK! I remember the long Sunday afternoons of my childhood and I appreciate why people campaigned to allow leisure and retail opportunities to be available Sundays. But have we thrown the baby out with the bath water? From there being precious little to occupy us on a Sunday, there is now precious little time for authentic rest and recreation. The 24/7 world of the twenty-first century precludes this. We fill our lives with activity and call it freedom and Christians are no different from others – often going from church to supermarket. The stresses and strains of a 24/7 life impact – often imperceptibly – on the way we look at each other and our relationships. We have less time to be generous towards the other – less time to spend honouring the dignity of the other.

The Sabbath, properly observed, is meant to be a day of liberation. Rest for all creatures – human and animal. Sundays, as many experience them nowadays, are an example of the tyranny of time. Anne Thurston, in her Advent book *A Time of Waiting* (Columba Press, 2004:18) says: 'If Sabbath time, defined as time to delight in God's creation, is given priority, then other things fall in behind. Time is no longer tyranny but gift. The Sabbath time defines the weekdays just as the feast makes sense of the fast.'

The Sabbath, if we let it, can give us the space to pay attention to God, each other and to the created world that speaks to us of God.

† Lord, make us attentive to your creation, for your name's sake.

For further thought

• Reflect on time as gift from God. Do I need to change my attitude to its use?

The heart of vision

John 2:1-11

On the third day a wedding took place at Cana in Galilee. Jesus' mother was there, and Jesus and his disciples had also been invited to the wedding. When the wine was gone, Jesus' mother said to him, 'They have no more wine.' (verses 1-3)

John relates the story of a wedding reception where Jesus performs the first sign – or miracle – of his ministry. It's a beautiful and very human story of a potentially embarrassing situation being avoided by one woman noticing that something untoward is happening. I have often been grateful in my life for similar attentiveness on the part of friends or family who become aware of things I have missed and who help me avoid giving offence or being hurt myself, by steering the situation away from dangerous waters!

Mary's intervention must result from this kind of attentiveness – the sort that sees to the heart of things, not just what is on the surface. And, through her intervention, she effects a transformation. There is, of course, the miraculous change of water into wine (and quality wine, at that!). But other things are transformed too. Jesus changes not just the water, but his mind. A wedding feast becomes a holy place. The disciples believe in him.

So, how we see is as important as what we see. Seeing, John O'Donohue says, is 'not merely a physical act; the heart of vision is shaped by the soul' (*Divine Beauty*, Bantam Press. 2003:28). If we see things from the perspective of a gracious and generous spirit, then our response will be transformative and full of joy. If not, through a lack of courage or insight, then we will fail in our mission, as disciples, to change the world.

† Beautiful God, give us a generous spirit in which to behold your beautiful world.

For further thought
- What are my blind spots? Where do I fail to see, as my Creator sees, with a loving and kindly vision?

August

Jonah

This week's notes are by **Kate Hughes**

Kate worked for the church in Southern Africa for 14 years. Since her return to the UK she has worked as a freelance book editor, initially specialising in theology but more recently widening her work (and her mind) to include books on gardening, dog training, climate change, sociology and gender studies. She lives in a small council estate in Coventry and is involved in her local community and preaches regularly at her local Anglican church.

Sunday 16 August
The runaway

Jonah 1:1-3

But Jonah ran away from the LORD and headed for Tarshish. He went down to Joppa, where he found a ship bound for that port. After paying the fare, he went aboard and sailed for Tarshish to flee from the LORD. (verse 3)

Jonah is one of my favourite books in the Bible – it's such a good story. Whether there actually was a whale or whether the whole thing is fiction doesn't really matter. Its insight into human nature challenges all of us when we try to run away from the demands of God, or when we forget that the church is for sinners, not the smug righteous.

Perhaps Jonah had vivid memories of other occasions when the Lord had spoken to him and he had made a mess of it. Anyway, this time Jonah didn't even stop to find out what the Lord had in mind for Nineveh; he just ran. He ran as fast and as far as possible.

We may not get such direct instructions from the Lord, but there are times when the Holy Spirit drops a crazy idea into our mind, or a friend makes a comment or suggestion, or a Bible verse leaps out at us, and we know that God is asking us to do something big for him. Like the tennis player John McEnroe and the prophet Jonah, our immediate response is all too often 'You cannot be serious!' As we shall see with Jonah this week, God has ways to persuade us to co-operate.

† Lord, help us not to run away from what you ask us to do, but to trust your grace to support us through it.

Monday 17 August
Disaster

Jonah 1:4-17

'Pick me up and throw me into the sea,' he replied, 'and it will become calm. I know that it is my fault that this great storm has come upon you.' (verse 12)

Jonah knows what he's doing. His refusal to do what God asks is not a moment of panic but a deliberate choice. He heads for Tarshish, knows where to get a boat, has the money for his fare – and is pretty sure that God won't let him get away with it. So it's no surprise to him when a storm hits and the ship gets into difficulties.

Like most of us, Jonah is a mixture of doubt and faith. On dry land he doesn't trust God to support him in going to Nineveh. But he has no doubt of God's care when on the sea. He sleeps through the beginnings of the storm and, when confronted by the sailors, immediately says that he's to blame and they'd better throw him overboard. Perhaps even drowning seems easier to Jonah than the inevitable confrontation with God. It's the sailors who try their best to avoid sending Jonah to his death in the sea. But the storm just grows wilder and into the sea Jonah goes – and apparently accepts quite calmly being swallowed by a huge fish and staying inside it for three days. No panic, fear or discomfort, no running away – in contrast to his behaviour back home on dry land, when God only had to mention a difficult assignment and Jonah was off.

† Lord, help us to have faith in your loving care wherever we are and whatever you ask us to do.

For further thought

• How difficult do you find it to trust God to care for you in hard places?

Back in touch

Jonah 2

But I, with shouts of grateful praise, will sacrifice to you. What I have vowed I will make good. I will say, 'Salvation comes from the LORD.' (verse 9)

To me, Jonah comes across as a bit of an actor. He dramatises what happens to him and, when it doesn't get the attention or the result he hopes, he sulks. Jonah is sitting safely – though probably not very comfortably – inside a huge fish. A fish swimming in a turbulent ocean may make him seasick but he was not actually in the water, where, according to him, 'The engulfing waters threatened me ... seaweed was wrapped around my head' (verse 5). But by providing the fish, God had ensured that Jonah didn't simply drown when he got thrown overboard, and Jonah isn't going to stay inside the fish for ever. So after running away from God, his narrow escape from death is enough to start Jonah talking to him again and recognising his care in saving him from death and providing the fish. This resumption of talks is enough for God to get Jonah out of the fish, which spits him out onto dry land, though still a good walk away from Nineveh, the capital of Assyria. After all Jonah's rushing about and his experience of the fish, the Lord just quietly starts again with him. At the beginning of chapter 3, he again tells Jonah what he wants him to do.

† Thank you, Lord, for your patience with us when we are disobedient or careless or just stupid. Please be willing always to start again with us.

For further thought

• Can you recall an occasion when you were disobedient, careless or stupid and God started again with you? What happened?

Jonah gets to Nineveh

Jonah 3:1-5

Jonah obeyed the word of the L<small>ORD</small> and went to Nineveh ... The Ninevites believed God. A fast was proclaimed, and all of them, from the greatest to the least, put on sackcloth. (part of verse 3, and verse 5)

Finally, Jonah does what God asked him to do in the first place: he goes to Nineveh. He walks through the city, warning its people that God's wrath is about to destroy them. What he hadn't expected was that the people of Nineveh would believe him and take action to avoid destruction. Jonah was, after all, a prophet. He was proclaiming God's word and expected that word to come true. He would watch Nineveh being destroyed. But Nineveh proved him wrong. They didn't continue their evil ways; they took steps to turn God's anger away, with fasting and sackcloth.

There is something odd about the story of Jonah. Elsewhere in the Old Testament, God is very much the God of the people of Israel. Other people have their own gods, although the Israelite God is the only really effective one and controls history and political events. But here, God is interfering in the affairs of a completely different (and much more powerful) nation, Assyria. Presumably the 'God' that the Ninevites refer to is their god, not the God of the Israelites, whom they had no way of knowing about. But for the writer of the book of Jonah, God is concerned with every nation and prepared to act against anyone who is evil.

† Lord, may the powerful nations of the world know that they are under your rule and try to act with justice and compassion.

For further thought

• If God spares evil people who repent, what does this say about God's justice?

Thursday 20 August
Nineveh repents

> **Jonah 3:6-10**
>
> *When God saw what they did and how they turned from their evil ways, he relented and did not bring on them the destruction he had threatened.* (verse 10)

Without warning Jonah, God sees the good intentions of the people of Nineveh and decides to give them another chance. Jonah feels a fool. The people of Nineveh were terrible, so why had God changed his mind about destroying them? Why had he told Jonah to walk through the city shouting out that they were going to perish, and then not done it?

The contrast between Jonah and the people of Nineveh is clear. Jonah doesn't trust God to help him fulfil his commands, he argues with God, he gives God a lot of trouble and tries his patience, then finally does what God wants. The king of Nineveh, on the other hand, reacts immediately to God's warning. He orders all his citizens to 'call urgently on God' and 'give up their evil ways and their violence' (verse 8), and he believes in the compassion of God (verse 9). And the hope of the king of Nineveh in the compassion of God is justified.

This passage in Jonah reminds me of one of the parables that Jesus told (see Matthew 21.28-32), about the father who asked his sons to work in the vineyard. The king of Nineveh is the son who begins by saying no – ruling over an evil and violent city – but in the end obeys his father. Jonah is like the son who assures his father he will do what he asks, but then wanders off and doesn't do it.

† Father, so often I deserve your condemnation for my failures, evil and stupidity. Thank you that you are a God of compassion and forgiveness.

For further thought
• Which of the sons in the parable do you most resemble?

Friday 21 August
God does it again

Jonah 4:1-5

But to Jonah this seemed very wrong, and he became angry. He prayed to the LORD, *'Isn't this what I said,* LORD, *when I was still at home? That is what I tried to forestall by fleeing to Tarshish.'* (verse 1 and part of verse 2)

Jonah had looked a fool. He didn't see why the evil people of Nineveh should be spared. He had (finally) done what God had told him to do and then God had ignored Jonah's role and done what he wanted, given Nineveh another chance. Jonah knew God well enough to recognise that he would always come down on the side of compassion, forgiveness and avoiding calamity (verse 2). Jonah clearly feels he has been caught out by God before – that was why he ran away. But why, then, involve Jonah at all? Jonah is angry with God but perhaps also depressed, questioning his identity as a prophet. What's the good of a prophet whose words don't come true because God changes his mind and interferes? The evil deserve to be punished, so why does God let them off? Jonah had been so sure that God would destroy Nineveh that he had sat down outside the city to watch what happened.

Clearly, being a prophet, with a prophet's relationship with God, hadn't done Jonah much good. True, when in the fish's stomach, he had praised God – but that had all been about him, Jonah, me (see chapter 2). He had not learnt to share God's capacity for showing compassion and forgiveness. Letting bad people get away with it seemed to Jonah to be 'very wrong' (verse 1).

† Lord, teach me to share your compassion and forgiveness with everyone I meet, not just those I approve of.

For further thought
- How good are you at sharing God's compassion and forgiveness with everyone you meet, not just those you approve of? How can you do better?

August

235

Saturday 22 August
Learning compassion

Jonah 4:6-11

*But the L*ORD *said, 'You have been concerned about this plant, though you did not tend it or make it grow. It sprang up overnight and died overnight. And should I not have concern for the great city of Nineveh, in which there are more than a hundred and twenty thousand people?* (part of verses 10-11)

Jonah was sitting outside the city of Nineveh waiting for God to destroy it. Gradually he realised that it wasn't going to happen. God had decided to give them another chance. It was a hot day and Jonah had been sitting in the sun for hours, sweltering. So he was very grateful when a 'leafy plant' grew up to give him some shade. He happily slept under it that night – probably worn out by all his anger with God, as well as the day's heat. But the next day was even worse. The plant had withered and died, a scorching east wind blew up, the sun was hot again, and Jonah was even more angry. He was so angry with God and so hot that he wanted to die (verse 9).

But he gets no sympathy from God, who needs to teach his prophet a lesson. Jonah is angry because his useful plant has died, even though he had done nothing to plant or tend it. But he has no compassion at all for the human beings in Nineveh. So God tells him to get his priorities right. If Jonah is concerned about one plant, cannot he not also understand – and share – God's concern for the thousands of people in Nineveh? Jonah would have liked God to give the plant a second chance of survival, for his own comfort; God gives people a second chance, for their salvation.

† God, you give me so many second chances to grow more like you; help me to give second chances to others.

For further thought

• A notorious evildoer comes into your church and says 'I want to change. Can you help me to get to know God?' How would you react?

Fresh from the Word 2016

It may seem early, but *Fresh From the Word 2016* is now available to order.
Order now:
- with your local IBRA Rep*
- in all good bookshops
- direct from IBRA

To order direct from IBRA

- website: shop.christianeducation.org.uk
- email: sales@christianeducation.org.uk
- call: 0121 472 4242
- post: using the order form at the back of this book

Price £9.00 plus postage and packaging.

Ebook versions priced at £7.20 inc.VAT are available from our website.

Become an IBRA rep

*If you purchase 3 or more print copies, and you live in the UK, you can sign up as an IBRA Rep and claim the 10% IBRA Rep discount on all IBRA products. You will also receive a free poster and samples to help you share IBRA more easily with family, friends and others in your church. Contact staff at IBRA (email: sales@christianeducation.org.uk) to sign up now!

Would you consider leaving a legacy to IBRA?

What's valuable about a gift in your will to the International Bible Reading Association's International Fund is that every penny goes directly towards enabling hundreds of thousands of people around the world to access the living Word of God.

IBRA has a rich history going back over 130 years. It was the vision of Charles Waters to enable people in Britain and overseas to benefit from

the Word of God through the experiences and insights of biblical scholars and teachers across the world. The vision was to build up people's lives in their homes and situations wherever they were. His legacy lives on today in you, as a reader, and the IBRA team.

Our work at IBRA is financed by the sales of the books, but from its very start 100 per cent of donations to the IBRA International Fund go out to benefit our international readers. We guarantee not to spend any of it on general administration costs or our day-to-day overheads.

But to continue this important work would you consider leaving a legacy in your will?

Young IBRA readers in India

Find out more

Leaving a gift in your will to a Christian charity is a way of ensuring that this work continues for years to come: to help future generations and reach out to them with hope and the life-changing Word of God – people we may never meet but who are all our brothers and sisters in Christ.

Through such a gift you will help continue the strong and lasting legacy of IBRA for generations to come!

To find out more please contact our Legacy Adviser on 0121 472 4242, by email admin@christianeducation.org.uk or by writing to International Bible Reading Association, 1020 Bristol Road, Selly Oak, Birmingham B29 6LB.

- To read more about the history of IBRA go to page 26.
- To find out more about the work of the IBRA International Fund go to page 370.

Song of Songs

This week's notes are by **Robert Parkinson**

Robert Parkinson is a Baptist minister. Ordained in 1982, he has served congregations in the United States of America and the UK. He and his wife Dawn have three grown-up children. A student of the Hebrew Bible, Robert is passionate about biblical studies. In his spare time, he is an avid reader, a keen walker and a lover of the outdoors. He is minister of Didsbury Baptist Church in Manchester and an associate tutor with the Northern Baptist Learning Community.

Sunday 23 August
A song of love

Song of Songs 1

While the king was at his table, my perfume spread its fragrance. My beloved is to me a sachet of myrrh resting between my breasts. My beloved is to me a cluster of henna blossoms from the vineyards of En Gedi. (verses 12-14)

Traditionally, the Song of Songs has been read as an allegory about the love between God and Israel or Jesus and the church. In fact, it is about the love of a man and a woman. Still, it is not only readers but also translators who seem to have trouble with this.

Take the words above as an example. A woman imagines her lover as a king overcome by the fragrance of her perfume. So why does the translation have the man sitting at his table? The Hebrew word can mean either table or couch. The woman and her lover are locked in an embrace, so does it not make more sense to picture the king (and his lover) on his couch?

The NIV offers a fine translation of the Song of Songs but like most others it is cautious about the sensual content of the song. If you have access to other translations you might like to read them alongside each other this week. As we read, I hope we might see this most remarkable book of the Bible for what it is, a love song (or a collection of love songs).

† Gracious God, may your blessing be on all who are in love, all who long for love and all who have lost love.

August

Monday 24 August
A woman's voice

Song of Songs 2

My beloved is mine and I am his. (verse 16a)

At least three voices can be discerned in the Song: a woman's, a man's and that of a chorus. The NIV labels them, 'he', 'she', and 'friends'. The words quoted above, however, like the majority of the words of the Song of Songs, are those of the woman. In fact, so dominant is the female voice that numerous scholars have proposed that the entire composition was written by a woman. This is far from certain.

The opening ascription or title of the work might seem to assert that King Solomon wrote it. But the ascription is not without ambiguity. 'Solomon's Song of Songs' (NIV) may mean that the Song belongs to Solomon or was dedicated to him as readily as that he wrote it. In fact, much of the language of the Song suggests it was written many years after the time of Solomon.

We do not know who wrote it but the prominent female character, with the rest of the Song, celebrates a passionate love by which two people feel they belong to each other. Here the Bible is at its most egalitarian. For, if in other parts of the Bible, women are seen as the property of men, in the Song the woman and the man belong to each other in love. This interdependence of the sexes is a feature of the entire work.

† Gracious God, we thank you for the multiplicity of human voices in scripture; help us to pay attention to them all and especially to those less represented and too often ignored.

For further thought

• Are you listening carefully to women's voices and paying proper attention to the opinions and thoughts of women?

Tuesday 25 August
The power of love

Song of Songs 3

Daughters of Jerusalem, I charge you by the gazelles and by the does of the field: do not arouse or awaken love until it so desires. (verse 5)

This charge functions as a refrain occurring three times in the Song of Songs (here and in 2:7 and 8:4). I am intrigued by its content as well as by the objects by which the charge is made. Usually, in the Bible, an oath or charge is sworn in the name of God but here it is by the gazelles of the field. This is entirely in keeping with the rest of the Song. For, throughout, the Song of Songs rejoices in the natural world. It is a song of spring where the flowers are budding and the birds are singing. It is perhaps the greenest of the books of the Bible. It knows, even without recourse to God, that the world is good.

Yet the content of the charge, 'do not awaken love', seems counterintuitive. The Song of Songs praises love so enthusiastically that I would expect its refrain to proclaim, 'Awaken love as soon as you can!' In reality, however, the Song is not nearly as sentimental as we might suppose. It views love as an overwhelming force that may have deleterious consequences for those in its power. The immediate context imagines the woman in a frantic search for her beloved. The suspense created reminds us that if love brings joy it also brings pain in separation and fear at the thought that love may be lost. As in all the wisdom literature, everything has its proper place and time. Passion is as dangerous as it is wonderful and it should not be aroused prematurely.

† Patient God, help us to know that good things are worth waiting for and that valuable things often take time to develop or perfect. Grant us patience so that we might savour what is good.

For further thought
• If you are in a long-term relationship, are you giving it the time and attention it deserves?

August

Wednesday 26 August
Your lovemaking is better than wine!

Song of Songs 4

How delightful is your love, my sister, my bride! How much more pleasing is your love than wine. (verse 10)

A friend came to me recently, astounded. She had not long been a Bible reader and had just discovered the Song of Solomon. 'Is it really true', she asked 'that this love song is in the Bible?' She was astonished and delighted. A holy book that celebrated love and sex was a book worth reading!

Although the translations are restrained, it is very definitely sexual love that is praised in verse 10. The Hebrew can be rendered, 'How beautiful is your loving ... your lovemaking is better than wine!' Similar sentiments are expressed to each other by both the male and female characters throughout the Song. See, for example, 1:2-4 where the man's loving is comparably praised. Each gives and receives sensual pleasure in equal measure.

The Song of Songs was probably written as a secular love song. Perhaps it found its way into the Bible because of its association with Solomon and because it can be read as an allegory about God's love. It remains in the Bible as poetic testimony to the fact that sex is good and that men and women need each other. I wish the rest of the Bible were read more often in its light.

† Loving God, we thank you that you have made us sexual creatures. Let us, in our sexuality, express ourselves lovingly and caringly.

For further thought

• Do you think the Christian tradition too often associates sex with shame?

Thursday 27 August
Eyes like doves

Song of Songs 5:2 – 6:3

His eyes are like doves by the water streams, washed in milk, mounted like jewels. (verse 12)

The Song of Solomon borrowed a literary device from the Egyptians known as the *wasf*. A kind of praise-verse, it extols the parts of a lover's body in a set of similes drawn from the natural world. There are four of them in the Song (4:1-7, 5:10-16, 6:4-10, and 7:1-9).

Ever since Shakespeare wrote, 'my mistress' eyes are nothing like the sun', this kind of poetry has been out of fashion in the English-speaking world. The comparisons seem to stretch credulity and often appear contrived. Still, there are at least three aspects of its use in the Song that I greatly appreciate.

The praise-verse sections of the Song of Solomon extol the human body in all its physicality. They remind me that the only life we can live here on earth is an embodied one.

The *wasfs* of Song of Solomon celebrate human sexuality. Thus they praise not only head and feet, eyes and teeth, but breasts and thighs, navel and neck. Even the head, arms and feet are given a distinctly sensual treatment.

Finally, the *wasfs* are egalitarian in that they praise both the male and the female forms. What is more, they do so in similar terms. The woman's eyes are compared to doves but here the man has dove-like eyes too and this seems to me a little unexpected.

The praise verse of the Song of Solomon celebrates embodied human loving. It challenges some of our gender stereotypes and it treats men and women as equally worthy of praise.

† Thank you, God, for the beauty and attractiveness of the human body; forgive us when we are prudish about it and help us always to value what you have made.

For further thought
• Does not even the spiritual life require embodiment for its expression?

Love and longing

Song of Songs 7:1 – 8:4

His left arm is under my head and his right arm embraces me. (chapter 8 verse 3)

It is probably best to read these words as a cry of longing rather than a statement of fact: 'O that his left hand were under my head and that his right hand embraced me.' Here, as in many instances, the Song of Solomon is not only about love, it is also about longing.

In this passage the woman promises, 'I will give you my love' but the reader is left in suspense as to whether or not the promise can be fulfilled. This type of situation is repeated often in the Song. Impatient pleas such as 'take me away with you, let us hurry' (1:4) alternate with frantic requests such as 'if you find my lover ... tell him ... I am faint with love' (5:8). Here the plea, 'let us go to the countryside' seems potentially confounded by the cry, 'if only' (8:1). Heartache and yearning are part of the lovers' condition.

I think it is the quality of longing that so readily lends the Song of Songs to a mystical interpretation. The Song is a love poem but as such it may be allowed to express human longing for the divine. With Augustine, the Song might be heard to say, 'God, you have made us for yourself and our hearts are restless until they find their rest in you'.

† As one longs for a lover's embrace, so my soul longs for you, O God.

For further thought

• Do you think all human longing is an expression of our need for God?

Saturday 29 August
Love's worth

Songs of Songs 8:5-14

If one were to give all the wealth of one's house for love, it would be utterly scorned. (verse 7b)

Love in the Song of Songs is neither weak nor sweet. It is fierce as death, many waters cannot quench it nor can floods drown it. There is something irresistible, forceful and strong about love. It will bring the lovers together whatever may stand in the way. It cannot be manufactured, feigned or contrived. It can be elusive. It may bring pain as well as pleasure; it will cause suffering as well as delight but it is of all things most valuable. Love cannot be bought.

I do not know what the apostle Paul would have made of the Song of Solomon. He might not have approved of its passion. Still, I cannot help wondering whether he might have known and been influenced by this passage. The Greek translation of 8:7 uses the word *agape*, Paul's favourite term for love. Of course, Paul's famous words in 1 Corinthians 13 were not addressed to couples, but to the church in Corinth. He did not have passionate, sensual love in mind. Paul thought of love as something one could choose, the Song seems to think of love as an irresistible force that chooses you. Even so, his message was not a million miles from that of the Song. For Paul, love is patient and kind; it also endures all things and never fails, gives up or ends (1 Cor. 13:7). It is the greatest of all virtues (13:13) and must be sought above all else (14:1).

Paul and the Song agree. What matters most for any of us is love, for there is nothing in the world more valuable.

† Loving God, help us to know the value of love and nurture its many forms in all our relationships. Help us to live in your love.

For further thought

• Compare Songs of Songs 8:5-14 and 1 Corinthians 13. In what ways do the passages agree and in what ways do they differ?

Work

1 Earning one's living

This week's notes are by **Stephen Willey**

Stephen Willey is a Methodist minister involved in mission to the working world. His chaplaincies have included British Bakeries, CIBA Chemicals and the NEC Group. A desire to challenge exploitation and the illegal economy led him to establish and chair the West Midlands regional anti-trafficking network and the Adavu project in the period 2009–2013. Stephen is currently forming a property redevelopment company called Transform West Midlands, which will employ and work with young people in areas of urban deprivation.

Sunday 30 August
An early harvest festival

Deuteronomy 26:1-15

When you have finished setting aside a tenth of all your produce in the third year, the year of the tithe, you shall give it to the Levite, the foreigner, the fatherless and the widow, so that they may eat in your towns and be satisfied. (verse 12)

A new apple tree I planted in the Spring with my family had three red apples on it that I picked with delight one crisp autumn morning. There are three of us living at home, so that's one each, I thought. Then I reflected that these were first fruits. What would it mean to offer them to God? After all, I didn't do very much work to get these fruit to grow. I just bought a sapling, planted it, occasionally watered it, and God did the rest.

Celebration of the harvest is an acknowledgement of our dependency on soil, rain and sun to bring forth food for us in God's time. But a harvest festival means something more. Because each harvest is uneven – three apples on my tree while a neighbour has hundreds and another has none this year – harvest comes with a challenge: We did not decide how many good things God would bring forth from our labour and here, in Deuteronomy, we are reminded that we should share those good things so that the most vulnerable among us may benefit from the gifts God has given to us.

† Generous God, give me a heart so full of love that I might enjoy sharing the good things you have placed in my hands.

Monday 31 August
Jacob grows rich

Genesis 30:25-43

*Jacob said to [Laban], 'You know how I have worked for you and how your livestock has fared under my care. The little you had before I came has increased greatly, and the L*ORD* has blessed you wherever I have been. But now, when may I do something for my own household?'* (verses 29-30)

'I'll text you!' said the busy executive as she left my office. But I knew she wouldn't, she just found it hard to admit it. She couldn't imagine what value a chaplain might bring to her work, and outside work we meant nothing to each other.

Laban takes a similar line with Jacob. 'I'll pay you!' he says, but he's not willing to let Jacob have even one spotted sheep to start a flock. Outside his own business, Laban can't imagine Jacob having any value. When Jacob takes the matter into his own hands, using his wit and imagination, he becomes very rich.

Jacob is not alone. Joseph, Ruth, David, Nathan and many others in the Bible manage to turn things around in their workplaces using their imaginations. Working hard is not necessarily about being up late, typing frenetically or labouring with a huge physical task. At another point in Genesis, Jacob struggles with God for a blessing. He had imagined a future where he is blessed by God, and that vision moved him to struggle hard for God's blessing.

Those who seek change in the world in any way have to work in a similar manner. The Greenpeace activist, the anti-nuclear campaigner, the person challenging youth unemployment or domestic servitude all have to find ways of communicating to those who are unaware or actively opposed to them. Positive, eye-catching, imaginative, funny and sometimes disruptive actions make significant demands on creativity and wit.

God blesses our imaginative struggles and our wit as well as the work of our hands.

† God of Jacob, release in me an active imagination so that my struggles may lead to blessings.

For further thought
• With so many distractions in life, where could I go to imagine God's kingdom on earth as in heaven?

Tuesday 1 September
A hard-working woman

Proverbs 31:10-31

Charm is deceptive, and beauty is fleeting; but a woman who fears the LORD *is to be praised. Honour her for all that her hands have done, and let her works bring her praise at the city gate.* **(verses 30-31)**

In a children's address I asked what the children wanted to be or do in the future. I got the response 'Be famous' or 'Be on *The X Factor*' (the reality TV show). The girls talked about being dancers or celebrities. 'Does anyone want to be a surgeon, business leader or a politician?' I asked. Not one girl put up her hand.

The media's interest in women seems to be predominantly about how charming or beautiful they are. I wonder if this leads to women being taken less seriously in the workplace, and although teen movies like *Legally Blond* supposedly challenge perceptions in a humorous way, the young women and men in them still behave stereotypically most of the time.

As a child I remember seeing an old woman frowning (or at least she seemed to be frowning to me) on the front cover of a book entitled *Something beautiful for God* by Malcolm Muggeridge. She was not a typical 'cover girl', but Mother Teresa's work was life changing for some of the poorest people on the streets of Calcutta.

And Mo Mowlam's success while struggling with cancer... Throwing off her wig as a distraction, she corralled powerful intransigent men into a working relationship that brought the Good Friday Agreement in Northern Ireland into being. Now on the page of the BBC website entitled 'The Good Friday Agreement' eight men are mentioned and no women. Those women who started the peace movement and that remarkable politician, Mo Mowlam, who laboured to bring it to birth should, in the words of the Proverbs, 'be honoured' and praised 'at the city gate'!

† God, we praise and honour your name. Help us to praise and honour women among us who work hard to bring good things into being.

For further thought
• How are we distracted by good looks and charm (our own or others'!)?

248

Wednesday 2 September
Paul's day job

Acts 18:1-4

Paul went to see them, and because he was a tentmaker as they were, he stayed and worked with them. Every Sabbath he reasoned in the synagogue, trying to persuade Jews and Greeks. (part of verses 2-4)

Digging holes for trees on the newly completed Buxton bypass in late autumn was a challenging experience. It was hard physical work. The ground was a thin layer of topsoil and then rocky subsoil. Most days it rained and one day it rained very hard indeed.

That day, although we were expected to work in all weathers, our team leader suddenly ran to the van – 'Come on!' he cried, 'Time for lunch.' It was only 11am. We sat, cramped together, in the misted-up van, eating our lunches. We drank from our thermoses, and silently enjoyed the sound of rain, now on the van roof! Then I realised that, despite our differences, we had somehow become united by our work together.

For some time we didn't say anything. Then, slowly, we reflected on our reasons for doing this work. Each person had a story to tell – mine so I could afford the flight to Canada to marry my fiancée. This moment of meeting stayed with me.

Saint Paul brought a challenging message to Corinth – who would listen to him? He must have felt the enormity of that challenge and been aware of the isolation that it might bring. He also wanted to support himself by working, but that was a challenge too. Then he found Aquila and Priscilla, who had fled from persecution. These tentmakers could work together. They understood each other. Paul was not alone – he found friendship and support in the workplace – what a gift!

† Lord, lead me to those companions on the way who understand my day-to-day life and work. Help me to give thanks for times of common purpose and shared experience.

For further thought

• What motivations do I share with the people who work near me? What do the people in church each Sunday do during the working week?

September

249

Thursday 3 September
Who supports Paul?

1 Corinthians 9:1-14

Don't you know that those who serve in the temple get their food from the temple, and that those who serve at the altar share in what is offered on the altar? (verse 13)

I was talking to a young woman on a zero-hours contract. 'The trouble is,' she said, 'I'm the only one in my family working now and because I'm on the minimum wage, we're struggling.'

'How many of you are in the family?' I asked.

'Four,' she said, 'My brother's at college and my parents worked at that big store that closed on the main road.'

Temporary work and flexibility in the workforce create a climate, for many, where certain opportunities never occur. The thought of having further education, buying a home or other opportunities to grow and develop were not in this young woman's mind: she was wrapped up in supporting the family. Her story is repeated throughout the world.

Paul was thinking about earning his keep in Corinth. He clearly felt that he deserved to receive a material reward for his spiritual work. His words 'Who plants a vineyard and does not eat its grapes?' (verse 7) resonate with Isaiah's promise that 'they will build houses and dwell in them; they will plant vineyards and eat their fruit' (Isaiah 65:21).

Just reward for labour is something to long for. Many people work hard but see little reward, while some others earn far more than they need. Paul stands with the prophets when he challenges the way things are. He knew that he deserved the Corinthians' support and he was willing to ask for it.

† Pray by name for someone you know on a low wage or unemployed. Bring to God all who suffer as a result of poverty or injustice.

For further thought

- Do I accept a level of unfairness in my workplace? Are there ways I could challenge unfairness without causing more harm than good?

Friday 4 September
Work with your hands!

1 Thessalonians 4:9-12
You should mind your own business and work with your hands, just as we told you, so that your daily life may win the respect of outsiders and so that you will not be dependent on anybody. (verses 11b-12)

I remember the praise I got when I showed my parents a wooden bowl I'd made by hand at school. The delight was enhanced when my mother put some sweets in it!

Forty years later, when I entered a huge new open-plan office, I have to admit, my heart sank. The restructuring and office moves were complete and more than ten departments had relocated into just two offices. Faced with banks of computer monitors, with scores of people in front of them, I wondered how I could offer chaplaincy in this environment. Who would talk with me when so many eyes were on me and so many ears were listening in?

These days many people sit at a desk in large commercial organisations doing 'invisible' jobs integral to the functioning of the company. Sometimes they have nothing physical to show for their work, which may be part of a bigger picture over which they have no control. In such a context, when the day is over, they can miss out on the satisfaction of being able to see what they have made by the work of their hands and respect from others cannot come from showing what they have created that day.

In such a setting, so distant from that of Saint Paul, a colleague, a manager or a chaplain can still show respect towards those who do the 'invisible' work. The recognition of a smile or a short conversation can indicate to each person that their work is respected and that they are appreciated.

† Lord, when I feel I'm not respected or I feel unvalued, help me to be confident that I am a source of delight to you every minute of the day.

For further reflection
• Who do you know that works in front of a computer a lot? How might you show them that you respect their work?

Saturday 5 September
Paul justifies himself

2 Thessalonians 3:6-13

We were not idle when we were with you, nor did we eat anyone's food without paying for it. On the contrary, we worked night and day, labouring and toiling so that we would not be a burden to any of you. (verses 7b-8)

I received a little brown envelope from the boss. For a moment I wondered what it was. Then I realised. For the first time in my life I had my own pay packet. A week's work on Scarborough's sea front had earned me £22, and I was more than content!

In the days of Ruth, although times were hard, there was the possibility of doing some work. In Ruth's case, gleaning in the field after the harvesters were done for the day, she managed to scrape together enough to live on (and a bit more, when supported by Boaz). In a different time, Paul obviously had plenty of work to do, which was rewarded so he was able to pay for their food and not be a burden on anyone. Hundreds of years later John Wesley said, 'Make all you can, save all you can, give all you can.'

But what happens when we feel we are a burden? The writers of the report 'I am one in a million', on youth unemployment (produced by the Church Urban Fund), discovered that among young people there was a desire to work, and a spirit of real determination, with some making hundreds of job applications. But there was another side to young people's experience: a sense of abandonment. At such times depression can set in. An increase in suicides has been directly linked to unemployment, especially among young people. Paul was willing and able to work hard to pay for his food. What can the church say to those who do not have that opportunity?

† Pray for young people overwhelmed by the difficulty of finding work. Thank God for St Paul and all those who worked hard, creating with God so many examples in the Bible that point us to the kingdom.

For further thought

- How important is it not to feel like a burden to others? What is the best work a person can do?

Work

2 Blessing or curse? Work and rest

This week's notes are by **Sister Paula Fairlie OSB**

Paula is a Benedictine nun living in Chester, England. From the time of her childhood in Germany she has been catching glimpses of God in nature, in other people, and in memories, as well as in prayer and wordless awareness. Poetry has heightened this perception, and so has music. Having completed her studies, she was received into the Catholic Church in 1965. She received the gift of faith in Italy. This was accompanied by the call to seek God in the monastic life. The quest continues.

Sunday 6 September
God's handiwork: our responsibility

Psalm 8

LORD, *our lord, how majestic is your name in all the earth! You have established a stronghold against your enemies... What is mankind that you are mindful of them... You made them rulers over the works of your hands; you put everything under their feet.* (verse 1 and part of verses 2, 3, and 6)

In our Benedictine tradition there are two sorts of work. First and foremost is 'the work of God', that is, our daily liturgical prayer. This is interspersed with and balanced by spiritual reading, manual work, personal prayer and meals in common and recreation. Our speech is to be used for 'edifying words'. The Psalter, from which we pray, describes our human struggles, our sinfulness, our pride and our humiliations. It also describes God in different ways, sometimes based on our projection of anger, vindictiveness or our pride. From this we can learn about our basic nature, our need for God and mutual forgiveness. Prayer can indeed be work!

Our manual work, either working alone or with others, helps us concentrate on practical matters on which our earthly well-being depends: cooking, cleaning, sewing and mending, hospitality. We are urged to treat everything, and everyone, with reverence. We are reminded, 'Idleness is the enemy of the soul'.

According to the psalmist, in pronouncing the name of God, we share in his glory. We know that we have impaired the image of God within us. Have we thus failed to appreciate the blessings of service?

† Let us ponder and pray our Lord's Prayer.

Monday 7 September
God's Spirit: active in creation

Genesis 1:1-2, 2:1-3

By the seventh day God had finished the work ... and he rested from all his work. Then God blessed the seventh day and made it holy. (chapter 2, part of verses 2 and 3)

It was during the Babylonian captivity that the priestly creation account was recorded. The Babylonians celebrated a holy day every seventh day, starting with the new moon. The Jews celebrated every seventh day as a holy day of rest from their work, as described in Genesis 1:1 to 2:3. This was unique to the Jews. Monotheism was central to Jewish belief at a time when many 'false gods' were worshipped by other nations. Yahweh was believed to be the sole creator of the universe. The Spirit of God hovered over the dark water, like a bird. God spoke the creative word: 'Let there be light'. God, like a tired man, rested on the seventh day. Does this account foreshadow our later belief in the Holy Trinity?

We should not ignore the importance of the second creation account. It tells us why work became a burden, and why relationships failed. Expulsion from the garden could be compared to being expelled from our mother's womb: we have to learn personal responsibility. Christian theologians interpret this as the consequence of disobedience, while centuries later it was seen as a 'happy fault' when God became man and 'dwelt among us'. Through the pain of separation, of loneliness, of our sin, may we return to God. He offers us freedom within boundaries, another Garden of the Soul, in which we may encounter him in peace and love.

† We are told that God rested on the Sabbath. We are encouraged to do the same, but also to pray together, and to relax together in loving harmony.

For further thought
• Imagine God's Spirit hovering over a chaotic part of your life or the life of the world.

Tuesday 8 September
Come to me, all you who are weary

Matthew 12:1-13

At that time Jesus went through the cornfields on the Sabbath. (part of verse 1)

Jesus was challenged by the Pharisees because his followers did not observe the minutiae of Sabbath observance. His hungry disciples had picked ears of corn on that day. Jesus reminded the Pharisees both of David's companions who ate consecrated bread, and of the priests who worked harder on the Sabbath than on any other day of the week: 'If you had known what these words mean, "I desire mercy, not sacrifice", you would not have condemned the innocent. For the Son of Man is Lord of the Sabbath' (verses 7-8). Jesus justified the subsequent healing of a man's withered hand on the Sabbath by comparing his act to the rescue of a sheep in danger of death.

It may help us to understand this section by looking at the parable of the self-righteous Pharisee and the humble Publican. In the monastic life we learn a discipline called 'the custody of the eyes', which leads to the custody of the heart. We are further told 'With a quiet heart hold on to patience'. This is to encourage us not to criticise our neighbour, as criticism is corrosive.

On the day of the Lord we are told that 'idleness is the enemy of the soul'. Suitable work in silence is provided for those who cannot read or pray. This monastic wisdom has been gleaned from the scriptures. Chapter IV of our Rule is headed 'The Tools of Good Works', all of which are drawn from the teaching of Jesus and amplified by our predecessors the Desert Fathers. They can be a guide for us all.

† Reflect upon the above text and pray that we be granted humility as we serve others in peace.

For further thought

• Which of the Benedictine maxims above appeal to you, or speak to a habit that would help you in your working day?

September

Wednesday 9 September
The intermingling of blessing and despair

Ephesians 6:5-9

Slaves, obey your earthly masters with respect and fear, and with sincerity of heart, just as you would obey Christ ... Serve wholeheartedly, as if you were serving the Lord, not people, because ... the Lord will reward each one for whatever good they do, whether they are slave or free. (part of verses 5-8)

We see graphic pictures of the tragedies throughout the whole world, of 'man's inhumanity to man' and despair. Has the Incarnation been in vain? In faith we say 'No' but the atheist says 'There is no God.' It has been so throughout recorded time, as historic documents reveal. The Christian response to foreign occupation, to slavery and servitude, is found above. That response is heroic. Abuses of every kind are taking place in secret, as they always have been. Can we really repay good for evil, as Jesus did on the cross? All the legislation in the world will not prevent abuse. What can we do? Does knowing that we all have the same Master in heaven, who has no favourites, really help? Isn't it this that led to the taunt that 'Christians believe in pie in the sky'?

We all have to find the answer granted to us. In the Benedictine Rule we are urged 'to patiently persevere' in times of distress, to show respect and courtesy to all. But what about people in the world who are falsely accused, tortured in captivity, killed? Perhaps Jesus says to us, as he answered Peter's question about John, 'Lord, what about him?' by replying '...what is that to you? You must follow me' (John 21:21 -22).

† Amid the confusion and pain of the world may we persevere in faith, hope and love.

For further thought

• Find a copy of the recent critically acclaimed movie *12 Years a Slave* and watch it to gain insight into the way Christian faith was used to support nineteenth-century slavery.

Thursday 10 September
The grace of the present moment

Matthew 6:25-34

Therefore I tell you, do not worry about your life, what you will eat or drink; or about your body, what you will wear. Is not life more than food, and the body more than clothes? (verse 25)

In the 1970s, after Vatican II and before the rapid changes in society and instant communication, our religious life was based on 'the grace of the present moment'. Those of us who came from academic backgrounds had time to read the scriptures slowly and meditatively, finding spiritual nourishment. We trusted in providence because all our basic needs were already provided.

Jesus was not speaking to privileged people: he was speaking to poor people who worked for their living, whose families were dependent upon them. How did they respond to the following: 'I tell you, do not worry about your life'? For many centuries, until the present day, many individuals have entrusted themselves to providence in their pilgrimage through life. There has been an increasing number of wanderers, migrants and refugees in our disturbed world, due to natural disasters, ethnic conflict, and the misuse of natural resources – as well as the persecution of ethnic minorities. Would Jesus have spoken to them in the same way? Possibly, because his people were under Roman rule, and some indigenous officials were corrupt.

Many poor and needy people do seem to have an awareness of God's providence, perhaps more than we do, and interpret any act of kindness as his gift. Often the one who gives receives something more lasting: a smile that warms the heart and lingers in the memory.

† Ponder how we react to those who arrive at our doorstep at inconvenient moments.

For further thought
• Where in your life do you need to trust in God's providence?

September

Friday 11 September
God's ways are not our ways

Matthew 20:1-16

For the kingdom of heaven is like a landowner who went out early in the morning to hire workers for his vineyard. (verse 1)

This parable shows us clearly that God's ways are not our ways. By keeping his word to the first labourers, and then showing great compassion to those who had perseveringly waited to be hired, God showed that he had understood their anguish and their need. When we work, knowing that we will be able to look after our dependants, we are blessed. When we lack work and have no means of supporting others, we become desperate. The men in the parable had waited almost the whole day but did not lose hope. Perhaps that is a message for our times, when so many young people are unemployed. People seeking work in the UK come from poorer areas of Europe, from the former Commonwealth, and work hard and uncomplainingly, even knowing that they are not receiving the legal rate.

The landowner was also persevering in his quest for labourers: the grapes were ripe for harvesting and any delay could have meant that they would rot on the vine. Could we interpret this as God caring for the fruit of the earth, for all his creation, with the vocation of human beings to be those who tend it? (Genesis 2:8 'Now the Lord God had planted a garden in the east, in Eden ... And the Lord God made all kinds of trees grow out of the ground – trees that were pleasing to the eye and good for food.')

† The justice of God is not limited by human concepts: his love and compassion surpass all human thinking.

For further thought

• What is the church doing about unemployment in your town, city, or country? What could you do?

Saturday 12 September
The bread from heaven is the Word of God

John 6:25-34

*Then they asked him, 'What must we do to do the works God requires?'
Jesus answered, 'The work of God is this: to believe in the one he has
sent.'* (verses 28-29)

The texts and commentary given for this week have now come full
circle for a Benedictine nun. Our life, our liturgy, our prayer – from
the time our Rule was written by Saint Benedict in the early sixth
century – has been regulated by the *opus dei*, the work of God. We
have been gathered together through a vocation based on faith
in Christ as the Son of God. Christ is at the heart of our monastic
life. The abbot or abbess is depicted as his representative in the
community – now as Christ reigning in glory, now as the Good
Shepherd – leading and guiding the community (the flock). I prefer
the role of the Shepherd, who seeks out the one who has strayed.
We all of us stray, including the shepherd, and sometimes it is the
loving sheep who seek him/her in the wilderness.

We receive abundant spiritual food in our life, not only through
the sacraments but through mediated grace. Some comes from
spiritual reading, some from listening attentively to the Word of
God, and some comes from relationships. It is often through those
who come for spiritual accompaniment that we learn how our life,
our ordinary daily life, is a source of peace and a sign of hope. I still
marvel at this: God still makes good use of imperfect disciples, as
Jesus did with his first followers.

We pray 'Let us not lose sight of Jesus, the pioneer and perfecter
of our faith'.

† Through patience may we share in the sufferings of Christ that we may deserve
to share in his kingdom. Amen

For further thought

• Circumstances beyond our control, and our attitude, will decide
what was a blessing and what was a curse.

September

Work

3 Joseph: rags to riches

This week's notes are by **Jules Gomes**

Canon Dr Jules Gomes is Canon Theologian at St German Cathedral, Peel, and Vicar of Castletown and Arbory on the Isle of Man. He earned his doctorate in Old Testament from the University of Cambridge and taught biblical studies at the United Theological College, Bangalore, the London School of Theology and Liverpool Hope University. Formerly a journalist in Bombay, he now contributes to Manx Radio and has written five books. Jules enjoys literature, art, classical and jazz music, target shooting, walking and golf.

Sunday 13 September
Hey Joe, don't make it bad!

Genesis 37:2-14a

Now Israel loved Joseph more than any of his other sons, because he had been born to him in his old age ... When his brothers saw that their father loved him more than any of them, they hated him. (part of verses 2b-4)

Joseph can be seen as the 'good guy' and his brothers as the 'bad guys'. But the story introduces Joseph as a snitch. He tells tales about his brothers. Was Joseph justified in bringing back a 'bad report' to his father? The Bible is silent on what the brothers were doing. The Hebrew for 'bad report' can be translated 'defamation'. The word occurs in Proverbs 10:18: 'whoever spreads slander is a fool'. A 'fool' is someone who makes bad choices.

Joseph has made a bad choice. It will take a long time before his character is transformed – from one who sets himself above his brothers to one who is willing to eat at the same table with them.

It took a long time before his father's character was transformed – from Jacob to Israel. True character is revealed in the choices a person makes under pressure. As you read through this week, watch for how the story puts greater and greater pressure on Joseph to make more and more difficult choices. It is this that changes him into an agent of salvation for both Israel and Egypt – the Jews and Gentiles.

† Almighty God, you call us, like Joseph with all our flaws, to be transformed into the image and likeness of your Son Jesus. Grant that we may not esteem ourselves better than others, but in humility value others above ourselves. Amen

September

Monday 14 September
Is there a bomb under your bed?

Genesis 37:14b-28

But they saw him in the distance, and before he reached them, they plotted to kill him. (verse 18)

Zinaida Bragantsova lived with a Second World War bomb under her bed for 43 years. The unexploded bomb was detonated only when Ukrainian authorities were laying a telephone cable in the area.

Hatred is a ticking time bomb waiting to explode. Three times we are told of Joseph's brothers: 'they hated him'. The first time we are told 'they hated him and could not speak a kind word to him'. The third time there is an intensification of hatred: 'they hated him all the more', not just for his dreams but 'for his words' as well. There was a bomb ticking under the family bed. How does one move from sibling rivalry to sibling shalom? Was this story meant to be a lesson to the Israelite tribes when they were tempted to quarrel and fragment the unity of God's people?

Did Joseph need to share his dream with his brothers? How did he narrate his dreams? Humbly? Pompously? Did Jacob need to display favouritism for his youngest son by parading him in an ornate robe and then sending him to oversee them shepherding? Didn't that make it worse by stoking the hatred and jealousy?

In the Sermon on the Mount, Jesus equates anger against a brother to murder. Cain was angry with his brother and murdered him. The sons of Jacob were angry with their brother and murdered him. Almost. If not for Reuben, Joseph would have been dead. No doubt, God had something to do with it, too!

† Almighty God, you have made us ambassadors of your reconciling work in Christ Jesus. Forgive us when we exalt ourselves, when we let the sun set on our anger, when we provoke anger in others. Amen

For further thought

• Are there longstanding disagreements in your family that need forgiveness and healing? Act now to defuse the bomb. Be reconciled.

September

God's promise, God's plot and God's people

Genesis 39:1-6

From the time he put him in charge of his household and of all that he owned, the LORD blessed the household of the Egyptian because of Joseph. The blessing of the LORD was on everything Potiphar had, both in the house and in the field. (verse 5)

I've made the mistake of settling for a mere moralising of Joseph. I've asked myself what virtues can I imitate, what vices can I reject. But that's missing the bigger picture. I need to ask myself a bigger question to help me understand the bigger picture. How does Joseph fit into God's plan for Israel's salvation and the salvation of the world?

Today's text is beginning to answer this question. Today's text takes us back to God's promise that God would bless the whole world through Abraham and his seed (Genesis 12:1-3). God is now blessing Potiphar, an Egyptian, 'because of Joseph', Abraham's seed. There is no doubt that Joseph prospers because the Lord is with him, but Joseph is not to selfishly hoard that blessing of wellbeing. The blessing through Abraham's seed is for 'every family on earth'.

The word 'blessing' occurs three times in this chapter. God's promise of blessing the nations will be fulfilled – sometimes through the faith of the patriarchs and matriarchs; but most often in spite of the flaws, the fears, the faithlessness, the failures and the family rivalries of the patriarchs and their children. God writes straight with crooked lines. Israel as God's agent impacts the affairs of the nations, even though the bearer of the promise is sometimes the enemy of the promise. It's all about God. It's all about the world. It's all about how God uses God's people as God's agent to bless God's world. That blessing will be fulfilled when another Joseph is forced to flee to Egypt and find favour with God because God is with him.

† God of Abraham, you called Israel to be a blessing to the nations. Grant that we who are grafted into your vine may bear fruit and share the blessings of Abraham with the nations, through Jesus our Lord. Amen

For further thought

- Read through Genesis and trace the plot of God's promise to Abraham. How many Gentiles respond positively to Abraham and his descendants and receive God's blessing?

Derailing the plot, betraying the promise

Genesis 39:7-20

How then could I do such a wicked thing and sin against God? (verse 9)

Joseph is faced with two choices: adultery or integrity. He makes the right choice for two reasons. First, he wishes to honour the trust his master has placed in him. Second, and more important, he does not wish to 'sin against God'. The fear of the Lord is the beginning of wisdom. Faced with the pressure of a huge sexual temptation, Joseph's character is being transformed through his choice to resist. This is not a one-off simple choice. The seductress is 'day after day' knocking at his door in her attempts to lure him into bed. The echoes of wisdom literature are heard in the seductive voice of the adulterous woman who says to the 'youth who has no sense', 'My husband is not at home; he has gone on a long journey' (Proverbs 7:7, 19).

Of course, the story goes beyond highlighting Joseph's morality. The patriarchal stories are full of attempts to derail the promise. If Joseph yields to temptation, the promise is at risk! Honesty is not always the best policy. Joseph's choice lands him in prison.

There is a naïve assumption among some Christians that if we are God's people and if we live lives of holiness according to God's will then our lives will be trouble free. Nothing could be further from the truth! On the contrary, we can expect more trouble. But what we can be certain of is that God's ultimate purposes will never be derailed. All things will indeed work together for the good of those who love the Lord and are called according to his purposes (Romans 8:28).

† God of pit and prison, God of Israel and Egypt, God of patriarch, prophet and sage, give us wisdom to discern between right and wrong and courage always to do what is right in your sight. Amen

For further thought

• Beware of the prosperity gospel! When was the last time you heard a sermon suggesting that those who trust in Jesus will live trouble-free lives?

September

Thursday 17 September
Joseph vs Joseph

Genesis 39:21-23

The warder paid no attention to anything under Joseph's care, because the LORD *was with Joseph and gave him success in whatever he did.* (verse 23)

Does the Bible guarantee success if we are faithful? Joseph faces his fair share of setbacks. But he is ultimately successful and victorious. What if such were not the case? For when we turn to a New Testament Joseph we discover that there are no guarantees. He, too, is a 'dreamer'. He, too, is an instrument in God's plan. He, too, is just, merciful, loyal and obedient. He does not disown Mary after discovering she is pregnant. He does not have sexual relations with her until after Jesus is born.

But this Joseph is not successful. Things only get worse for him. He is forced to flee as a fugitive from a genocidal tyrant. In Egypt he has another dream. The angel asks him to return to Israel; Herod is dead. He returns but now has to face another tyrant, Archelaus. When Jesus' family is mentioned, Joseph is not even named. He is simply called 'the carpenter' (Matthew 13:55).

There is simply no happy ending for Joseph in the Christmas story. All the other characters around the crib receive their Christmas gifts: Mary gets the baby, Zechariah and Elizabeth are blessed with John, the shepherds receive glad tidings of great joy, and the magi are given a star; Joseph gets nothing. Joseph is not given a single line to speak in the Gospels. There is no proper ending to the story of Joseph. We are not told what happens to him. Fairy tales end happily ever after. True stories often do not. We may not always be successful, but the good news is that God is always with us.

† Almighty God, give us the wisdom to define success according to the standards of your kingdom. Keep us from being disheartened when success eludes us and remind us that your accompaniment is guaranteed even if success is not. Amen

For further thought

- Look up the hymn 'O Love that wilt not let me go' written by George Matheson. Read through the words and try to find the story behind the hymn.

September

Joseph remembers to forget

Genesis 41:46-57

Joseph named his firstborn Manasseh and said, 'It is because God has made me forget all my trouble and all my father's household.' (verse 51)

From pit and prison Joseph has been catapulted into the palace – the pinnacle of prestige and power. His barns are bursting with abundance. Joseph is a prince. He could marry a princess and live happily ever after. Almost. Joseph marries the daughter of the priest of Heliopolis. Heliopolis was Egypt's centre of sun worship. Joseph names his firstborn son Manasseh, 'causing to forget'. Has God made him forget? Or does Joseph want to forget? Ironically, naming his son 'causing to forget' will cause him to remember! Joseph ceases to use God's specific name 'Yahweh' after he enters Pharaoh's service. Is Joseph forgetting the God of his ancestors?

At the very moment Joseph is seeking to forget, God is fulfilling his promise to Abraham and through his seed is blessing Egypt and all the famine-stricken nations of the earth. A hint of this is found in the description of grain like the 'sand of the sea' (verse 49), a description previously applied to the descendants of Abraham. Is the promise to the patriarchs about to be jeopardised? If God does indeed cause Joseph to forget his father's household, they will starve to death and the promise will come to an end.

It is a cliffhanger and a nail-biting read until we see how Joseph does actually respond to his family in the coming chapters. God is faithful and will work through Joseph, with Joseph, and in spite of Joseph. God will work with Joseph's reluctance to remember but also with Joseph's willingness to reconcile when the time comes.

† Almighty God, we too often try to blot out the memory of a tragedy and then you remind us of it. But it is then that the power of your redemption bursts through. Help us remember what you will have us remember and forget what you will have us forget. Amen

For further thought

• As you read through the book of Genesis have you ever noticed that different chapters use different names for God? What do you think is the reason for this?

September

Saturday 19 September
Countdown to slavery

Genesis 47:13-25

'You have saved our lives,' they said. 'May we find favour in the eyes of our Lord; we will be in bondage to Pharaoh.' (verse 25)

A biblical hero who was sold into slavery by his brothers is now responsible for nationalising the institution of slavery! Tragically, famine serves as an opportunity to turn food into an instrument of state policy and foreign policy. Joseph exploits hungry people, turning them into slaves.

The countdown is ruthless and relentless. First, Joseph collects monetary payment for the grain. Then he takes over the livestock in exchange for food. Next he takes over the land belonging to his starving citizens and turns them into debt-slaves. Even that is not enough. He obliges them to pledge one-fifth of their future produce to Pharaoh. 'Joseph reduced the people to servitude from one end of Egypt to the other.' This is precisely what Pharaoh will do to the Israelites in the book of Exodus. The only concession Joseph makes is to the priests. He does not force them to sell their land. In any case, they have an allotment from Pharaoh to buy food. But Joseph has a vested interest here. His wife is the daughter of the most important priest in the most important religious city of Egypt. Earlier we are told that Joseph has provided food for his own family who have emigrated from Canaan.

Some may see Joseph's fiscal strategy as that of a wise and shrewd manager and administrator. But wisdom literature is punctuated with calls to treat the poor with fairness and justice. Has Joseph forgotten God? It is perhaps no coincidence that God is not mentioned anywhere in this chapter.

† God of the Magnificat, we thank you that you fill the hungry with good things and send the rich away empty. Forgive us for so often condoning oppression and tolerating the exploitation of the weak and vulnerable. Amen

For further thought

- In what way does the Sunday school version of the Joseph story differ from its biblical version? How can we present an unsanitised version of Joseph's character to children?

September

266

James, Jude and Philemon
1 Life in the early church

This week's notes are by **Elisa Gusmão**

Born in Brazil, Elisa belonged to the Presbyterian and the Methodist Churches before moving to the UK with her Scottish husband in 1987. From then on, while constantly taking theology courses for lay preachers and serving the United Reformed Church as an elder, she has worked as a freelance translator. Her web site is www.gusmao-translations.co.uk. Eric and Elisa have family living in Switzerland, the UK, and Brazil.

Sunday 20 September
On the basis of love

Philemon 1-14

I always thank my God as I remember you in my prayers, because I hear about your love for all his holy people and your faith in the Lord Jesus … Your love has given me great joy and encouragement, because you, brother, have refreshed the hearts of the Lord's people. (verses 4-5, 7)

In the past, commentators wondered why a personal letter like Philemon became part of the Bible. Truly, this most beautiful epistle, inundated with brotherly love, contains lessons for us all. Paul wrote it in prison, to a rich young man in Colossae, Philemon, converted by his preaching. Being between 50 and 60 years old, and an apostle, Paul could have ordered Philemon to receive Onesimus – a runaway slave who had somehow done him wrong – back into his household. Under Roman law, Onesimus was subject to severe penalties, such as being sent to a gladiators' school, being forced to turn a corn mill with his bare hands, being lashed with a whip, or even being crucified.

But Onesimus had met Paul and become such a good Christian that Paul wanted to keep him as a helper in his mission. Although Paul loves him, he understands that Onesimus is Philemon's slave, in an age when slaves were their masters' property. Paul exercises his authority neither commanding nor breaking the social codes of his time: he appeals to Philemon's Christian love. The man he is sending back is not the same 'useless' one, but brother Onesimus. And, curiously enough, this name means 'useful'.

† 'And when you stand praying, if you hold anything against anyone, forgive them, so that your Father in heaven may forgive you your sins' (Mark 11:25).

September

Monday 21 September
Even more than asked

Philemon 15-25

I will pay it back – not to mention that you owe me your very self. I do wish, brother, that I may have some benefit from you in the Lord; refresh my heart in Christ. Confident of your obedience, I write to you, knowing that you will do even more than I ask. (verses 19b-21)

We know about the slave trade in the seventeenth and eighteenth centuries from Africa to the rest of the world. A few years ago, a Brazilian social worker from Rio travelled to a meeting in a country town where her great-grandparents used to own a large Brazil nut plantation. She was very proud because, on her way there, she had noticed one of the local streets had her family name. So, at introduction time, she said her name loud and clear to the group.

During the coffee break, a colleague took her aside and said, 'If I were you, I would use a different name. Your family were the most cruel slave owners in the region, people the like of whom can only cause revulsion in any social worker.'

Reading the letter to Philemon, we wonder why Paul didn't shout against slavery, and the awful social structure around him. But he did. He filled this epistle with the names of loving brethren – who would be expecting Philemon to act big-heartedly. Paul even promised to visit him soon, to see how things were going. Colossae, after all, was not far from Ephesus, where it seems his prison was.

By addressing Philemon the way he did in the verses above, and returning a slave to his master on completely different terms than usual, he started a revolution. Paul's words 'you will do even more than I ask' may imply that he was telling Philemon to emancipate Onesimus.

† Father, help us to change the shameful fact that to this day children are exploited in sweatshops, as are immigrants and young women in hidden places of our big cities. In Jesus' name. Amen

For further thought

• Does the church tolerate the forms of slavery existing in your country? Has it been vocal against it, or has it also acted as slave master?

Tuesday 22 September
Mature and complete

James 1:1-11

Let perseverance finish its work so that you may be mature and complete, not lacking anything. If any of you lacks wisdom, you should ask God, who gives generously to all without finding fault, and it will be given to you.
(verses 4-5)

This may have been the first New Testament letter to be written, by James, who was Jesus' brother and leader of the Christians in the Jerusalem Temple. It is a letter for you, and for me, as he wrote it for Christians in general, by then already 'scattered among the nations' (1:1b).

James' letter is a pastoral message telling Christians how to relate to each other. In the first eleven verses, he gives an idea of the points he will develop further on, such as the strength essential in testing times, the need for a firm faith, and the perpetual presence of rich and poor people in society. Addressing his readers warmly as 'dear brothers', he delivers powerful teaching, meant to encourage Christians to act like Christians, and live a life that proves the gospel is at work.

However, it is the idea of perfection that binds together all the concepts in this letter. James, who probably grew up beside Jesus and is described by historians as a righteous and respected man, was totally devoted to Christ. He called himself, and truly was, a servant of the Lord.

James embodies Christ's teachings to such a point that his words at times echo Jesus' very words, for example, in the Beatitudes (Matthew 5:10-12). As Jesus said, 'Be perfect, therefore, as your heavenly Father is perfect' (Matthew 5: 48), so James directs us to strive for perfection in our discipleship, by rejoicing in our trials, and persevering in our growth towards spiritual maturity.

† My God and Father, may I strive for perfection, both in happy days, and in testing times. Help me remain always faithful to you, receiving from you the wisdom and strength I need. Amen

For further thought

• Think of the areas of your life where your actions could be improved, better to reflect your Christian faith.

September

The greatest prize

James 1:12-18

Every good and perfect gift is from above, coming down from the Father of the heavenly lights, who does not change like shifting shadows. He chose to give us birth through the word of truth, that we might be a kind of first fruits of all he created. (verses 17-18)

Throughout the Olympic Games hosted by the United Kingdom in 2012 (and to take place in Brazil next year) we all watched the finest athletes in the world perform at their best. Idolised by the crowds, they won the medals they had coveted so much – the prize for achieving perfection in their particular sport.

To get there, though, each one of these people had to go through rigid discipline and training, and sometimes a great amount of psychological and bodily stress. In ancient Greece, where the games had their origin, winners were given a laurel wreath to wear on their heads, which symbolised glory and honour – like the 'crown of life' mentioned by James in verse 12.

We, too, are tested in our Christian life. James is not talking of our own inner temptations and weaknesses but of the trials we have to go through in our life, defeating each obstacle, persevering in our willingness to obey God. And it is our Father who awards us the greatest, most perfect, gift: a new birth through Jesus Christ.

† I know that, however severely my faith is tried, however sad the events I go through, you, Lord, will be with me. May this knowledge give me strength, confidence and peace. Amen

For further thought

• Like an athlete getting ready for a competition, we too need spiritual preparation for the trials of life. What do you do in this respect? Are you getting good results?

September

Thursday 24 September
Listening is not enough

James 1:19-27

Do not merely listen to the word, and so deceive yourselves. Do what it says. Anyone who listens to the word but does not do what it says is like someone who looks at his face in a mirror and, after looking at himself, goes away and immediately forgets what he looks like. (verses 22-24)

There are listeners whose attention to the word is very limited – like a quick glance at a mirror. There is no chance they will prepare good ground in their hearts for the seed to produce fruit (Mark 4:8). Some of them can even have a talent for preaching the word but cannot apply it even in their personal relationships, let alone in society or at work.

James insists in teaching his 'dear brothers' that simply listening is not enough. He even uses harsh language, which was common in those days: 'Therefore, get rid of all moral filth and the evil that is so prevalent and humbly accept the word planted in you, which can save you' (verse 21b).

Lillian, my first Sunday school teacher in Rio de Janeiro, was a very sweet-natured spinster who finally married a widowed church minister with four children. Besides working as a school teacher, she became their dedicated mother and, after her husband's death, the matriarch whom the children and grandchildren loved deeply and could always count on. Her great, constant contribution to church life was remembered with gratitude when her long life came to an end.

The word Lillian heard in her early years was deeply planted in her heart, and produced abundant fruit. Vital to her, the word was part of her very being.

† 'Blessed is the one who does not walk in step with the wicked … but whose delight is in the law of the Lord, and who meditates on his law day and night' (Psalm 1:1-2).

For further thought

- Which things in my life are proof that I have accepted the word planted in my heart? Is this word truly part of me?

September

All are one

James 2:1-13

If you really keep the royal law ... 'Love your neighbour as yourself', you are doing right. But if you show favouritism, you sin and are convicted by the law as law-breakers. For whoever keeps the whole law and yet stumbles at just one point is guilty of breaking all of it. (verses 8-10)

The Lord's Supper was always a regular part of Christian meetings, which, in the early church, took place mainly in people's houses. The groups of Jewish Christians were very selective in allowing people to take part in this ritual but, as Christianity spread, the restrictions of the fellowship changed. The whole community was admitted. Jew and Gentile, slave and free, men and women, rich and poor, shared a single loaf at the Eucharist.

At the time, the known world consisted of the Roman Empire, where discriminatory rules applied: upper and lower classes were heard by separate courts, higher classes received lenient penalties if convicted of crime, had the front seats at shows, received from the state more money, food or wine than the poor. The 'honourable' ones mocked the 'humble', who lived in squalor and servility. At meals or public banquets, a person's place and what he ate depended on his status. No one would invite to 'come up higher' someone of unsuitable status.

Two thousand years have passed since those days, yet many of these things have not changed. Our societies still allow forms of prejudice similar to the ones above, which give us more reason to hear again James' message. He makes clear that, in a Christian setting, discrimination is totally unacceptable. James places at the same level as adulterers or murderers the host at a Christian meeting.

If only we could see others as God sees them! As his children, it is time for us to eradicate injustice and prejudice – we have waited too long!

† Lord, who lived on earth without having a place to rest your head at night, forgive our indifference and prejudice against the weak and poor. Help us to bring equality to our society, we pray. Amen

For further thought

- How is social life organised in your neighbourhood, town, place of work, church? Is there room for changes? Who will take action?

Faith in action

James 2:14-26

In the same way, faith by itself, if it is not accompanied by action, is dead. But someone will say, 'You have faith; I have deeds.' Show me your faith without deeds, and I will show you my faith by my deeds. (verses 17-18)

Today's reading has been the object of many discussions among Christians, as apparently James is contradicting Paul. While this apostle talks of justification by faith in Galatians 3:24 and Romans 3:28, James insists that 'faith without deeds is dead' (verse 26).

In my young days, I once had the privilege of travelling in the same plane as Dom Hélder Câmara, and having the chance of seeing 'live' the way that man – a Catholic Bishop, author of dozens of Christian books, recipient of many honorary doctorates – related to the people around him.

Hélder Câmara wasn't simply a man of faith but a fierce fighter for the cause of social justice, who became an icon of the so-called 'church of the poor', and worked tirelessly to change the conditions of people living in 'favelas' – Brazilian slums.

In 1970, while the country was still under a dictatorship, he was accused of treason and stopped from talking to the media, and his house was shot at twice.

This gentle little man's life clearly showed that faith and deeds go hand in hand in Christian life. Paul and James, after all, thought the same way, even though they had different ways of expressing themselves: Paul insisted that faith takes us to God, coming before deeds. James insisted on the absolute need of deeds, as a result of faith.

† Father, remembering Jesus' life on earth, I recognise that neither I nor my church serve each other as Jesus expected. Help us to grow in love, to also serve the world beyond church walls.

For further thought

• Is the Christian group I belong to looking inside our church walls, occupied in keeping our practices and traditions, or facing the outside world and its needs?

September

James, Jude and Philemon
2 Living the Christian life

This week's notes are by **Selina Samuel**

Selina is from New Delhi, India. She is a housewife and a freelance editor. She attends a local Methodist church in New Delhi and with her husband mentors young adults aged 25 to 35. They also work with postgraduate and doctoral students at Jawaharlal Nehru University. Selina is a frequent contributor to a local Christian magazine.

Sunday 27 September
The kingdom's speech

James 3:1-12

Anyone who is never at fault in what they say is perfect, able to keep their whole body in check. (verse 3:2b)

We begin this week's study on 'kingdom character' with 'speech'. Jesus never wasted words. He portrayed kingdom character. The tongue is a revealer of character. Though it is small, slippery and boneless, its potential for evil is huge. It can cause healing and reconciliation or major destruction with just a few words.

It has become fashionable to use bad language, curse words and swearing. This does not portray a pure heart, but silence is not the answer. Jesus spoke. Jesus taught. As children of God's kingdom it is our responsibility to guard the tongue. Words of wisdom appropriately spoken bring life.

'What Would Jesus Do' badges and wrist bands have been popular for some time now. What Would Jesus Do is a good question to ask, but 'why' does Jesus do what he does? This week our focus is on the Christian life. What do we mean by this? Is it a life of good works or is it asking 'WWJD' and doing likewise? Jesus has the kingdom character. He was filled with the Holy Spirit for this purpose. We as his children are kingdom people, portraying the kingdom character with the help of the Holy Spirit.

† Dear God, touch my heart and let my tongue show kingdom character. Help me not to blame situations or my background for quick or hurting words but to be a new creation in the Lord.

September

274

Monday 28 September
Sowing peace

James 3:13-18

Peacemakers who sow in peace reap a harvest of righteousness. (**verse 18**)

Two kinds of wisdom are mentioned here, revealing the kind of heart we have. The earthly wisdom springs from selfish ambition and an envious heart. What is envy? It is simply being unhappy or unable to enjoy life because someone else has what you do not have, and you want it. Selfish ambition changes life's goals into self-gratification at any cost. This kind of wisdom is the cause of disorder and every evil practice, because only 'me and my' desires are considered in everything I do. Envy blinds and cripples us from being truly wise.

The wisdom from heaven portrays the kingdom character of humility and pure motives. It is not selfish. Neither is it someone who just maintains silence. True wisdom is proactive in caring for the other, in reconciliation and in good works. Jesus said 'blessed are the peacemakers for they will be called children of God' (Matthew 5:9). Relationships are important, first with God and then with each other. Make every effort to live in peace and create peace.

So we have a choice to make. We can be envious and crippled, or we can enjoy being transformed into God's image. We can create communities of righteousness by being peacemakers wherever we are.

† Father God, help me today not to miss out on any opportunity to be a peacemaker. Help me to miss out on all opportunities for envy and selfish desires. Amen

For further thought
• How can you sow peace today?

Decisions, decisions

James 4:1-17

When you ask, you do not receive, because you ask with wrong motives, that you may spend what you get on your pleasures. You adulterous people, don't you know that friendship with the world means enmity against God? (part of verses 3-4)

Why adulterous? Because we claim to be in a relationship with Christ but in daily decisions we allow Satan or the world's values to have control over us. What is the world? It is portrayed in the Bible as the values, ethics and lifestyle that are under the direction of Satan and hostile towards God. 'Enmity against God'? These are strong words but to love the lifestyle of the world that is in enmity with God is to hate God. Why enmity? These are two different kingdoms altogether. We can belong to only one.

Our prayer life is yet another indicator of what we love. First, we do not have because we do not ask God. Do we pray at all or do we just wish and worry? Second, the content of our prayer many times exposes our selfish motives and love for pleasure. Is this not adultery? This is yet another test to check out our faith by our life.

James gives us five ways of living correctly: submit to God's authority, don't be deceived by Satan, desire God's purity, be genuinely sorry about your sins and be humble before God. In drawing near to God our desires will become pure and our prayers will be powerful.

Is your tongue busy again boasting about your future? Remember God is in control. You are not the manager of your future. Some of the words in this passage are strong and even violent but they only emphasise God's desire for us to walk in his ways and not be deceived by Satan.

† Dear God, help me to be focused in my pursuit of your kingdom. Amen

For further thought

- In what part of your life do your allegiances and priorities need reconsidering?

The ears of the Almighty

James 5:1-12

Look! The wages you failed to pay the workers who mowed your fields are crying out against you. The cries of the harvesters have reached the ears of the Lord Almighty. (verse 4)

The Bible says 'the money in the pocket is crying'. Can money cry? Yes, and it is crying against the rich man who hoards at the expense of his labourers. Is having money wrong? Is it wrong to have investments? Is it wrong to have savings? This passage talks about savings that do not belong to you, but to someone else.

Read carefully and you will notice that there are two cries that reach the ears of God. The first is the cry of the wages that have been withheld. Yes, the money that actually belongs to the worker is crying. The money wants to belong to a worthy owner. The labourer may be happy for what you pay as otherwise he or she may not have anything at all. But God notices and holds us accountable for what we withhold. Remember James also admonishes us to help the brother or sister who is in need.

Second, it is the cry of workers who have been denied their wages. Cheap labour is what worldly-wise, selfish people look for. Whether it is big corporations or small daily chore payments, 'just wages' is the hallmark of a kingdom person. The cry of the labourer gets the attention of God's ears.

Truth is an important characteristic of a kingdom person. Be known as a trustworthy person and try not to have a reputation for lying and exaggerating. A kingdom person's presence will increase the truth component in any conversation or walk of life.

† Father, I want to be truthful and just in all my relationships and situations. Amen

For further thought
• Investigate and consider supporting a local or national campaign for a living wage.

September

Elijah's prayer

James 5:13-20

Elijah was a human being, even as we are. He prayed earnestly... (**verse 17**)

Prayer is a privilege, a unique gift of God, available to all. We can call on God if we are in trouble. We can praise him in song if all is fine. We can depend on the community of God's people to pray for us and on our behalf. No one in the church should be alone. Prayer helps us to confess and seek forgiveness where needed, both with God and with each other.

Prayer is the most powerful resource for a kingdom person. It is also important to learn the discipline of striking a balance between demanding God to answer all our prayer requests and often not expecting any answers at all. Verse 16b says 'The prayer of a righteous person is powerful and effective'.

F B Meyer writes, 'The greatest tragedy is not unanswered prayer, but unoffered prayer'. How true. Elijah was a man like us, ordinary, and yet his prayer changed the course of the nation. Notice that he did not pray for prosperity. Despite the good economy of the nation, Elijah prayed for tough times so that they might acknowledge God.

We need blessings, healing and provision but the desire of all prayer should be our transformation into God's likeness. Prayer is to learn that dependence on God is our way of life. Another purpose of prayer is for people around us to acknowledge God and know that God is all powerful. Prayer is an act of faith in asking God to help us achieve the extraordinary with the help of the Holy Spirit.

† Teach me, God, to use this great resource of prayer without wavering and without selfish motives. Give me the boldness to achieve great things for you by the power of the Holy Spirit. Amen

For further thought

• For what aspect of God's coming kingdom will you pray today?

October

Friday 2 October
Faith entrusted

Jude 1-13

I felt compelled to write and urge you to contend for the faith that was once for all entrusted to God's holy people. (verse 3b)

Living the Christian life is action. In the Christian life there is a deep sense of respect and awe for God, a sincere study of the Word to know our faith and an active vigilance to contend for our faith against false teachers. Jude calls the ordinary members of the church, and not just pastors and theologians, to contend for our faith. This is the responsibility and privilege of all who are the called ones, loved by God and kept by Jesus Christ. Contending for our faith means looking out for those who use God's grace as an excuse for immoral living and deny Jesus Christ. It means opposing heresies and recognising the dangers of false teachers who have a way of using any sphere of influence to twist God's word and distort our thinking. Their only desire is self-gratification.

Jude reminds us of God's character: though he rescued the Israelites from Egypt, he also punished them for disobedience. Do not take God's holiness lightly, overlooking the awfulness of sin. Jude reminds us of the disobedient angels and of Sodom and Gomorrah. If they are punished, how much more the false teachers and those who promote and tolerate sin? He then gives another three examples, of Cain for vengeful disobedience, of Balaam for greed and Korah for disrespect for God's appointed leaders. These signify sinful attitudes.

The church cannot be used for selfish ambition or to bring disunity among the members. We need to protect each other from false doctrine – through a life of action for the kingdom's sake.

† Help us, dear God, to be faithful students of your word and defenders of the faith.

For further thought

• Which of your own motivations can you identify as being for your own gain?

October

279

Build yourselves up

Jude 14-25

But you, dear friends, by building yourselves up in your most holy faith and praying in the Holy Spirit, keep yourselves in God's love as you wait for the mercy of our Lord Jesus Christ to bring you to eternal life. Be merciful to those who doubt; save others by snatching them from the fire... (part of verses 20-23).

As kingdom people we are called to build ourselves in faith by studying the Word and keep ourselves in God's love. Jesus said 'If you keep my commands, you will remain in my love, just as I have kept my Father's commands and remain in his love' (John 15:10). Obedience is the key to remaining in God's love. To enable obedience, God has given us the Spirit. Praying in the Spirit requires a willing heart. It is a prayer in accordance with God's character.

Jude also entreats us to be kind to those who doubt. They are portrayed here as those who speak harsh words, grumblers, fault finders, those who follow evil desires, those who are boastful and flatter only for personal benefits, are divisive and follow their natural instincts. The Bible is definite about punishment of the ungodly.

But 'he who began a good work in you will carry it on to completion until the day of Christ Jesus' (Philippians 1:6). So live the kingdom life and God will keep us and present us without fault on the last day. What an awesome God we have! It is natural, then, for us to bless God with all glory, power, majesty and authority. God's love made the provision of God's word and the Holy Spirit for direction and power. We owe it to God to live a worthy Christian life.

† God, I want to thank you for your love, for the Bible, the Holy Spirit; for clear guidance for those whose hearts are inclined to obedience. Amen

For further thought

- Imagine a gathering of God's kingdom people, and then picture the camp of the grumblers and fault-finders. Which would you rather be in?

Birds in the Bible
1 Birds in the Old Testament

This week's notes are by **Rachel Montagu**

Rachel Montagu teaches Judaism and Biblical Hebrew. She believes teaching people to understand the Bible in Hebrew, without translators' interpretations, empowers them as readers. She has been involved in interfaith dialogue for many years. She trained to be a rabbi at the Leo Baeck College, London. She lives in London with her husband Francis Treuherz, a homeopath, their two sons and the family's combined library of more than 15,000 books.

Sunday 4 October
On a wing and a prayer

Genesis 8:1-12

He waited seven more days and again sent out the dove from the ark. When the dove returned to him in the evening, there in its beak was a freshly plucked olive leaf! (verses 10-11)

The land of Israel has a wide variety of resident bird species and is also on many migration routes; over 500 million migrant birds cross twice a year. This wealth of birdlife means it is natural that the Bible often mentions birds, either in analogies or in stories.

The story of the flood has parallels in other ancient literature, which suggests that memories of devastating floodwaters were passed down. In our biblical version, the flood is a tragedy for God; the creation God saw as 'very good' was soon so marred by people's senseless violence against each other that God reversed the process of creation. God washed away the carefully created birds, animals and people, all except for the ark, Noah, his family and breeding pairs of each species.

The raven, a carrion-eater, could survive away from the ark if corpses were still floating in the remaining floodwater. When the dove came back with some olive leaves Noah knew that the waters had receded enough for life to be resumed.

We can match God's promise of 'never again' to flood the earth with our determination to create a more peaceful world. Today the dove's olive branch symbolises peace.

† May God who makes peace in the highest, make peace for us, for Israel and for the whole world.

October

Monday 5 October
Manna from heaven

Exodus 16:9-21

The Israelites did as they were told; some gathered much, some little. And when they measured it by the omer, the one who gathered much did not have too much, and the one who gathered little did not have too little. Everyone had gathered just as much as they needed. (verses 17-18)

In Jeremiah, God says, translating from the Hebrew, 'I remember the loving-kindness of your youth, the love of your bridal promises as you followed me in the wilderness' (Jeremiah 2:2). We wonder at this because we remember the people's grumbles, their disobedience and their difficulty learning God's commandments during their desert wanderings. But I love this verse from Jeremiah because it shows how, for God, the romantic mutual love of the years in the wilderness outweighs the people's frequent uncooperativeness.

In Exodus 16 the people yearned for the Egyptian fleshpots, and insulted their Redeemer; they preferred their assured rations while enslaved to being free. In response they received quail to eat: flocks of quail do sometimes appear in the desert. God always provided for the people, yet they found it hard to trust God.

Manna, their miracle food, was not just about nutrition. God used manna to train them in social justice and sabbath observance – only on Friday could they collect more than they needed for one day so they could rest on the sabbath. Everyone got the same, even if they tried to collect more or couldn't collect the standard ration. Medieval Jewish interpreters said one of many miraculous characteristics of manna was that it tasted of whatever the eater wished and added that, in the wilderness when all had equal rations, giving charity meant the rich who had eaten more interesting food in Egypt described flavours to those who had a more restricted diet while enslaved to help them imagine more variety in their manna. Literally true? Maybe not, but this story teaches kindness, helping and sharing.

† We should always thank God for everything we eat and drink. If you can't think how, try this: Blessed are you Eternal our God by whose word everything exists and who provides food for all.

For further thought

• In much of the developed world much food is thrown away, wasting environmental resources used to produce it. Try to buy only what you will use this week.

Miraculous food and hope for a needy prophet

1 Kings 17:1-6

Then the word of the Lord came to Elijah: 'Leave here, turn eastward and hide in the Kerith Ravine, east of the Jordan. You will drink from the brook, and I have directed the ravens to supply you with food there.' (**verse 2**)

We can see in Samuel and Kings the early development of prophecy as an institution. Some prophets simply proclaimed God's word to the people; some, like Elijah, demonstrated their closeness to God by doing miracles. Elijah not only performed miracles, he was sustained by miracles: first the ravens fed him and then his landlady's oil and meal jars stayed full during the famine.

Ravens are birds of prey. We might not associate raptors with benevolence and nurture, but ornithologists have found ravens devoted parents. Here God used them to feed Elijah until his water source dried up when God stopped all rain to punish King Ahab; Elijah then moved to Zarephat. But even if the Bible's instructions for kosher eating divide birds into carnivores (don't eat them) and domesticated birds that eat grain (fine for eating), the Bible describes admiringly the way all birds (well, almost all – see tomorrow) care for and nurture their young, as well as any stray prophets in need of a steady food supply. In one memorable passage from Deuteronomy 32, the eagle that hovers protectively over its young became a metaphor for God's care for the children of Israel.

Rabbi Hugo Gryn, one of my teachers, described how in a concentration camp he was upset to see his father using some precious margarine as a makeshift Chanukah lamp. His father said, 'You can live three weeks without food, three hours without water but you cannot live properly for three minutes without hope.' The food the ravens brought kept Elijah fed and also gave him hope, constant reassurance of God's support while he prepared to confront Ahab.

† Blessed are you Eternal our God who provides for me everything I need.

For further thought

- Find a way to give encouragement or support to someone who needs it, either by giving food or time or a listening ear or money.

October

Wednesday 7 October
Complex wonder

Job 39:13-18, 26-30

Does the hawk take flight by your wisdom and spread its wings toward the south? Does the eagle soar at your command and build its nest on high? (verses 26-27)

Reading Job reminds us that the world is complex and bad things do happen to good people. More important, it warns us that the distressed need the best comfort we can provide and we visit them to help them feel better, not to make us feel good. Job's 'comforters' didn't deserve the name. Petrified by the disasters Job has suffered, they assumed a simplistic world view – the good are rewarded and the bad punished. They were sure Job had done something dreadful and showed too prurient an interest in having him confess all. But Job knew he had done nothing wrong. He knew the world is complicated and that understanding God is beyond humanity. God says to Job and his friends that Job is right. In a long speech from which today's reading is extracted, God describes the complex wonders of our world.

Look at any bird book or film or in any aviary. Birds, their variety, their colours, their sounds, their shapes are truly amazing. No wonder God included them among the wonders too great for those 'comforters' to understand. However much modern science has increased our knowledge of the world and its creatures, we still marvel.

Unlike the many Bible references to birds' devoted care of their young, the author of Job compared the ostrich's parenting and wing-power unfavourably with the stork (whose Hebrew name means 'kindly one') and deplored its stupidity, but still admired its astonishing land speed.

† 'I call on you, my God, for you will answer me; turn your ear to me and hear my prayer. Keep me as the apple of your eye; hide me in the shadow of your wings' (Psalm 17:6, 8).

For further thought

• Look up the website of the Society for the Protection of Nature in Israel; see pictures of the many beautiful birds that visit or live in the country.

October

Thursday 8 October
Flying free

Psalm 84:1-12

Even the sparrow has found a home, and the swallow a nest for herself, where she may have her young – a place near your altar... (part of verses 3-4)

This psalm is sung at Jewish weddings, and for me it brings back happy memories of weddings I've attended or at which I officiated. The Jewish wedding service says the couple are undertaking to build for themselves a faithful house among the Jewish people and make a covenant of love and affection with each other. The main theme of this psalm, however, is God's house and the joy of being in God's presence.

In *Bird Walk Through the Bible*, Virginia C Holmgren (New York, Dover Publications, 1972) suggests that the psalmist is contrasting sparrows – small, home-loving, staying close to the ground, hopping from bush to bush – and swallows, which can fly for hours, needing to nest only to rear young.

The Hebrew word translated 'sparrow' is *tsippur*, a generic word for bird. The Hebrew for 'swallow' means 'freedom'. When God freed the Israelites from Egyptian slavery, they were to use their new freedom to serve God. So the swallow, the freedom bird, which migrates across the earth but returns each year to nest, is a good symbol for the pilgrims who annually visited the Temple to serve God, and enjoyed their freedom to worship God there. They complement the sparrow, representing the local population who kept the worship going year-round. In Hebrew Bibles, the word for 'nest' is written with a large initial letter, stressing the importance of a resting-place in God's presence, even for free-spirited travellers.

† 'Happy are those who dwell in your house, who are ever praising you. Happy are the people whose life is thus; happy are the people whose God is the Eternal' (from Psalms 84 and 144).

For further thought

• Is there something you can do to make your home or your church a more pleasant place to serve God, either through prayer or by hospitality to others?

October

Friday 9 October
Eagle-like strength

Isaiah 40:25-31

...those who hope in the L<small>ORD</small> *will renew their strength. They will soar on wings like eagles; they will run and not grow weary, they will walk and not be faint.* (verse 31)

These verses round off a long prophecy. Isaiah said God wants prophets to comfort the people and give them good news: the exile in Babylon is over and they will be restored to their land.

But the people may feel this promised return a mixed blessing. The journey will be long and difficult; any uprooting, however yearned for, is painful. At the start of this chapter, Isaiah promised easy travel. Isaiah described God with many metaphors here, including as a shepherd who leads his flock gently on the road, in verse 11. Isaiah promised that, because God never tires, and God's awareness is unlimited, God will constantly be alert to help the exhausted. Those who hope for the Eternal will have their strength renewed; Isaiah used the same words for their weariness and faintness as he did to describe God's endurance in verse 28. Imitation of God, whether in holiness or inexhaustibility, is a constant biblical theme. The power and stamina of eagles' flying here represents what the people can hope for themselves.

Soon after the 1948 United Nations' vote authorising the creation of the State of Israel, planes were sent to airlift Yemen's Jews to Israel because many Yemenite Jews had been murdered in conflicts during the previous few years. Never having seen planes before, they were nervous, but all knew their Bible and were reassured when the aircrews mentioned both Exodus' covenant promise, 'I carried you on eagles' wings' (from chapter 19, verse 4) and this chapter. Jews read this on Consolation Sabbath, which follows Tisha b'Av, the day the Temple's destruction is mourned.

† 'Behold God is my salvation, I trust and will not fear, because the Eternal, my strength and divine song, was my salvation and you will draw water with joy from the wells of salvation' (Isaiah 12:2-3).

For further thought
• List twenty things that tire you and thirty things that encourage your stamina and wellbeing. Can you improve their balance in your life?

Saturday 10 October
The partridge and the tree

Jeremiah 17:5-11

Like a partridge that hatches eggs it did not lay are those who gain riches by unjust means. When their lives are half gone, their riches will desert them, and in the end they will prove to be fools. (verse 11)

Jeremiah preached God's messages of social justice and monotheism and the exile the people will bring on themselves by their sins. Jeremiah had to compete with false prophets who assured the people all would be well; unsurprisingly, the people preferred their message of peace. Realising that this would ensure the people's punishment lent passion and urgency to Jeremiah's prophecies. After contrasting the fate of those who trust only in people and those who trust in the Eternal, Jeremiah said God searches the heart and the kidneys (at that time it was believed that rational intelligence was found in the heart, and love and emotion in the kidneys).

The partridge (her Hebrew name means 'calling bird') was believed to brood over and hatch eggs laid in her nest by other birds. Jeremiah made her an example of wickedly stealing other people's property, but he might have had this wrong. Virginia Holmgren (see Thursday's notes) thinks the partridge's strategy may be to lay some eggs in a neighbouring nest for another partridge to hatch, thus increasing their chance of successfully raising chicks. Perhaps one nest will escape predators if the other is lost. On a bird-watching walk with my grandfather, I remember a partridge's distraction display, leading us from her chicks, showing not greed but potentially self-sacrificial mothering.

† 'The Eternal is the hope of Israel, the fountain of living waters. Heal me and I will be healed, save me and I will be saved because you are the one I praise' (from Jeremiah 17:13-14).

For further thought

• Learn more about birds and bird-watching by reading books, watching films or YouTube, visiting bird reserves or aviaries. Consider putting out grains and nuts as birdfood.

October

287

Birds in the Bible
2 Birds in the New Testament

This week's notes are by **Jan Sutch Pickard**

Jan Sutch Pickard is a poet and storyteller living on the Isle of Mull. A lay member of the Methodist Church, she is now privileged to preach in local Church of Scotland congregations. A Member of the ecumenical and dispersed Iona Community, she served for six years on that island, latterly as Warden of the Abbey, and enjoyed working collaboratively on liturgies that 'find new ways to touch the hearts of all'. Since leaving Iona Jan has served twice with the Ecumenical Accompaniment Programme in Palestine and Israel.

Sunday 11 October
Set free!

John 2:13-17

To those who sold doves he said, 'Get these out of here! Stop turning my Father's house into a market!' (verse 16)

Imagine it: the chaos of crashing tables, scattering coins, fluttering wings. There, in a place of worship, the ugly sounds of a whip cracking and voices raised in anger. But wait, what had been heard in the Temple day after day? Bellowing of cattle, competing money-changers bawling out exchange rates, the chink of money being piled up and the calling of pigeons and doves destined for sacrifice.

This was a moment of liberation. Not just literally – for birds suddenly uncaged, flying up into the rafters of the Temple – but also symbolically, for that ancient building that had been so misused and degraded by politics and greed. And for the ordinary people, of different nations, who, when they came to worship there, had been pushed to the margins and financially exploited. After all the noise, the silence of the Temple rang in their ears. What was it telling them?

The Gospels often draw attention to plants and birds, which both receive and show God's care. This week's readings remind us of birds in Jesus' story – and in his teaching. So these freed birds can be a sign of Jesus coming to bring freedom of spirit and hope to all humankind.

† Holy and disruptive God, break into our structures of injustice; drive out those practices that exclude others and set our imprisoned spirits free. Amen

Monday 12 October
Like a dove

> ### John 1:19-34
>
> *Then John gave this testimony: 'I saw the Spirit come down from heaven as a dove and remain on him.'* (verse 32)

John the Baptist's words bear witness to an experience that gave everything else in his life meaning. Over the centuries, religious artists have invited us to become witnesses, too, as they depict this scene: John, and Jesus, the moment of baptism and the presence of God.

In a corner of the rebuilt cloisters of the Abbey on the isle of Iona, off the west coast of Scotland, a modern sculptor has carved the scene in detail. At eye level, we see the River Jordan – though running waves and a leaping fish make it look more like the Sound of Iona! Two men have waded into the water. One, John, stands and pours water on the head of Jesus, who receives the blessing, while into his cupped hand a dove is settling. The bird is lifelike, resembling those that live in the Abbey tower and fly round above the cloister, sometimes landing on the grass. In this dynamic image, the dove at the centre, with wings spread, connects heaven and earth, the flowing water and the two men immersed in it.

Looking at it, we too become immersed: glimpsing – at a turning point in human history – the gentle, empowering presence of God.

† Ever-present God, in the spread wings of a dove, in arms outstretched on a cross, you show us the connection between heaven and earth. Learning about your love, may we witness to it. Amen

For further thought

• Think of a work of art that has brought a biblical story or theme alive for you. If possible, find a copy and reflect on it.

October

Birds have roosts

Matthew 8:18-22

Jesus replied, 'Foxes have dens and birds have nests, but the Son of Man has nowhere to lay his head.' (verse 20)

Jesus and his followers are on the move again, compelled by the restless Spirit. An educated man, a scribe, comes to Jesus, saying, 'Teacher, I will follow you wherever you go.' Jesus points out that there is no security and little common sense in following him. Animals and birds have their lives better organised.

I stroll in late afternoon autumn sunshine, reflecting on this passage. Rooks are flocking together to roost for the night, though the nests of the rookery have long been empty. The swallows' nest is empty too: they and their brood have made the long journey to Africa, their other home. Small birds that overwinter here chirp and chatter in a red-berried hawthorn – having found bed and breakfast there! A wren takes shelter from the wind in a crevice of the old stone wall. I imagine Jesus observing the little lives of God's creatures in the Galilean countryside – seeing how these reflect the diversity of people. Some come together in noisy communities, others keep themselves to themselves; some cherish the old familiar places and others are restless, migrants, always moving on; for some home is a safe place and for others not.

And for Jesus himself – however welcoming the homes he visited, however much his disciples wanted to be with their families – there was no chance to stay in their 'comfort zone'. Into the streets, on to the next village, to a town where they were strangers, to the hostility of Jerusalem: God's urgent Spirit drove them on, to challenge people's comfortable assumptions and to bring good news.

† In our restless lives, God, help us to follow the prompting of your Spirit, but also help us to find rest when we need it, in your love. Amen

For further thought

• Nesting, or migrating? How do you see your own life reflected in the lives of the birds described above?

Wednesday 14 October
When a sparrow falls

Matthew 10:26-31

Are not two sparrows sold for a penny? Yet not one of them will fall to the ground outside your Father's care. And even the very hairs of your head are all numbered. So don't be afraid; you are worth more than many sparrows. (verses 29-31)

Imagine a place where two sparrows are sold for a penny. This is not the landscape in which we reflected on yesterday's reading – an environment where birds are watched for pleasure, where wildlife is valued, where the survival of species is a matter of concern, where sparrows are no longer two-a-penny.

In Jesus' time, as in many developing countries today, the tiny body of a sparrow means nourishment. Boys with slings bring down as many as they can. Birds are shot and snared and sold in the street: human greed is one reason, but so is human need.

There are too many places in our world today where human life is held cheap, too. Some babies are abandoned when they are born, by mothers who cannot care for them.

Desperately poor families sell older children to human traffickers, and they become domestic slaves, or exploited in sweatshops, or sex workers. In developed countries social services sometimes overlook the breakdown of family care, the abuse and suffering of a child. Sparrows are very small – they can be overlooked by busy people dealing with big issues.

But God sees the fall of a sparrow and the suffering of each child – God sees and grieves. For every single one of us is loved and valued.

† I feel small, weak, helpless. Worse still, I feel worthless. Weighed down by the world's suffering: Why does God let terrible things happen? Look – an injured bird cradled in gentle hands. 'Don't be afraid.'

For further thought

• Do you need to hear those words 'Don't be afraid'? Think about why – and thank God.

Think of the birds

Luke 12:22-31

Consider the ravens: They do not sow or reap, they have no storeroom or barn; yet God feeds them. (verse 24)

How easy is it to think of ravens? Where I live, as I write this, I see them daily, crossing the skies with the beat of their powerful wings, calling to each other with a deep 'cronk'. For people living long ago, in Europe or the Middle East, it was natural for these birds to come to mind and come into stories: they were a known part of the natural world. Ravens seemed signs of God's compassion – working both ways – the Creator hears the young ravens crying out and feeds them (Psalm 147) but also sends ravens to bring bread to Elijah in the wilderness (1 Kings 17).

But in our twenty-first-century urban society, where are the ravens? Instead some versions of the Bible urge us to think of 'the birds of the air' – imagining those with which we are familiar. Here is a true story about a robin and a blackbird.

It was told by the sculptor who carved an image of John's baptism of Jesus in Iona's cloisters – a task that took weeks to complete. As he worked away each day, two of the birds that take shelter in the cloisters kept him company. They perched nearby and watched him with bright inquisitive eyes. When he took a break to eat his packed lunch, they hopped nearer and picked up his crumbs. He fed them and enjoyed their companionship. When the biblical scene was complete, there was a corner left blank – but not for long. The dove is not the only bird in the picture. There are two lovingly-carved witnesses: a blackbird and a robin.

† Creator God, small as we are in the scheme of things, you watch us with care; you meet our daily needs. We are beautiful in your eyes, blessed like the birds of the air. Amen

For further thought

• Today, wherever you go, keep your eyes open for creatures or growing things. How are they blessed by God? How does their existence bless us?

Friday 16 October
O Jerusalem, Jerusalem...

Luke 13:31-35

How often I have longed to gather your children together, as a hen gathers her chicks under her wings, and you were not willing. (part of verse 34)

This city has many names, and the names have many meanings. 'Jerusalem' contains the powerful concept of 'shalom' – meaning peace, wholeness. But today it is a fragmented city, and certainly not a place of peace.

In Jesus' time, too, it was a place of conflict and danger. We hear Jesus lamenting 'Jerusalem, Jerusalem, you who kill the prophets and stone those sent to you'. He himself could not be deflected on his way to Jerusalem, knowing that was where he must meet his death. Yet he spoke with compassion of its people.

And he used an image from village life that his hearers would recognise. These words speak to us, too, of a down-to-earth God with a mother's care and courage.

The poultry flock ranges freely around the farmhouse, and further afield, searching for seeds and grains and grubs. They take dust baths in the sunshine, then go back to their gleaning, clucking contentedly. From time to time a triumphant call announces that an egg's been laid. One hen has led her newly-hatched chicks out into the open meadow. Suddenly she's calling, but on a very different note – harsh, urgent. The chicks hesitate and then run to her. She spreads wide her speckled wings, and they take shelter. The shadow of a buzzard passes overhead. She has risked her own life to save her chicks.

† Careful God, with danger in the air, we run this way and that in panic, but you are still there for us. Wayward, we scatter. Call us back, and spread your sheltering wings. Amen

For further thought

• Free-range chickens are a less familiar sight for many of us. What word-picture (instead of the mother hen) would you choose today to show Jesus' love?

Faith faltering

Luke 22:31-34

Jesus answered, 'I tell you, Peter, before the cock crows today, you will deny three times that you know me.' (verse 34)

In the dense darkness of the small hours, a cock crowing is an unwelcome sound. It may signal the approach of dawn – but that may still be several hours away. It would be good for human beings to sleep longer. We do not want to be wakened to the anxieties and regrets of these dark hours. But farmyard birds have their own logic.

A night is coming when no one will sleep. Jesus will be betrayed by one of his companions and arrested. His other friends (the men among them – the women are more steadfast at the end) will run and hide. Peter, their natural leader and spokesman, the Rock on which the church could be built, will deny that he ever knew Jesus.

At their last supper together, Jesus looks ahead to what is about to happen. He warns Peter (as the cock crowing will also be a warning and a reminder). But this is not a message of blame, but of encouragement. Jesus says that he has been praying – and will still do so – that Peter, whose courage and faith is about to falter, will find himself again and be a source of strength to the others.

† Compassionate Christ – in our frailty we pray to you, and we give thanks that your constant prayer for us lifts us out of all our failings so that we may find ourselves again. Amen

For further thought

- Read on: Look at the way that Peter's triple denial of Jesus (Luke 22:54-62 – found in other Gospels too) becomes his triple affirmation when he meets the risen Jesus (John 21: 9-17).

October

Readings in Mark (4)

1 In Jerusalem: parables and teaching

This week's notes are by **Julian Bond**

Julian Bond is Director of the Christian Muslim Forum for England (www.christianmuslimforum.org). He has a degree in Theology from the University of Aberystwyth and previously worked for HM Revenue & Customs. He has a passion for 'translating' the themes of scripture into a range of contexts. He meets regularly with imams, rabbis and other Christians to study scripture together. He is currently writing a book on the humanity of Jesus.

Sunday 18 October
Taking aim

Mark 12:1-12

Then the chief priests, the teachers of the law and the elders looked for a way to arrest him because they knew he had spoken the parable against them. But they were afraid of the crowd; so they left him and went away. (verse 12)

Jesus tells a few 'loaded' parables that are directed at people in positions of power and authority, or to those impressed with their own piety (usually hypocritically). They are not usually as violent as this one but Jesus' life and ministry is reaching a violent culmination and the leaders are more visibly against him. Trouble is brewing. It looks as if he foreshadows this in the story of the vineyard and the vineyard owner's son.

Jerusalem is a difficult place. It is also, as the parable states, a city 'with a wall around it'. Jesus is not making it too difficult for people to grasp his message. The leaders know that he is talking about them and they are only too aware that the people do, too. Jerusalem is where the prophets come with their difficult messages – either God is going to save the city when everyone has given up hope and begun bargaining faithlessly with the invaders, or God is going to wipe it out when the inhabitants think that the city walls will save them.

This story would have been written down, most likely, after the fall of Jerusalem. The fateful power of death, destruction and collapse hangs over Jesus' parable.

† Pray for those seeking to gain through violence, and for a change of heart where religion is supporting hatred.

October

295

Monday 19 October
Trapped?

Mark 12:13-17

Later they sent some of the Pharisees and Herodians to Jesus to catch him ...They came to him and said, 'Teacher, we know that you are a man of integrity. You aren't swayed by others, because you pay no attention to who they are; but you teach the way of God in accordance with the truth.' (part of verses 13 and 14)

In today's reading the leaders try to turn the table on Jesus. They set out to catch him in their trap, banking on the difficult political tension between hatred of a pagan occupying empire and imperial crackdown on insurrection. Where does Jesus place himself – as a rabble-rouser or an appeaser? Note how shifty they are, complimenting him twice, on his integrity and impartiality. They ask the question twice also, in their impatience and excitement, thinking that they have got him. But trickery and dishonesty create and ultimately fall into traps that are never any risk to the genuine and authentic. In our day these may be offered in one hundred and forty characters on Twitter, where we may be flattered and provoked in turn by those who want to trick us away from peaceful interaction.

A single coin is all Jesus needs to subvert their spurious argument. 'Whose coin is this?' 'Caesar's.' 'Yes, it has his head on it'. And God? 'God doesn't use money, God is interested in people.'

Native Americans revere a character called the 'Trickster'. Here, Jesus is that trickster, puncturing the attitudes and arguments of the highly educated with (another Americanism) homespun wisdom – a coin, a bird, a handful of corn. He makes jokes at their expense while they feed him the lines with straight faces, kicking themselves and boiling with rage as he does it again! It's worth noting their one-word answer that is the only honest and genuine thing that they say: 'Caesar's'.

† Lord, enable us to follow our teacher Jesus in being authentic, genuine and honest. Give us the straightforward outlook that enables us to follow his way.

For further thought

• How do we best serve God with all our resources? And, more important, what does God want from us?

A different approach

Mark 12:18-23

Then the Sadducees, who say there is no resurrection, came to him with a question. 'Teacher,' they said, 'Moses wrote for us that if a man's brother dies and leaves a wife but no children, the man must marry the widow and raise up offspring for his brother.' (verses 18-19)

Absurdity is a well-known way of making what is hoped to be a 'killer argument'. Massive exaggeration and poking fun, while humorous, don't achieve a great deal in meaningful dialogue. But it is Jesus who is interested in dialogue and his opponents who are more interested in point-scoring. Jesus is surprised when the rich young man in chapter 10 embarks on a serious conversation, taking the trouble to listen to Jesus rather than trick him.

The Sadducees, accepting only the Torah (the 'books of Moses'), expect that Jesus will agree with their (implied) assessment of the ridiculous situation they describe. They want (while not believing in it) to know how earthly relationships will be reflected once the resurrection takes place. It is easy to think of the Sadducees as great sceptics but they put us in touch with the ancient beliefs of the Jewish people when there was no clear idea of an afterlife. A developed understanding of the afterlife – resurrection, heaven/hell, final judgement – emerged among the Jewish people, and writers of the Hebrew Scriptures, while they were in captivity in Babylon. Their own experience, and exposure to the beliefs of others, led them to think and believe differently.

There is perhaps a cautionary aspect to this encounter. If what we believe, or share, is so unrealistic or ridiculous that even people of faith cannot take it seriously, we may succeed only in putting them off. Jesus, on the other hand, brought things down to earth by taking a different approach.

† Lord, help us not to be committed to believing 'six impossible things before breakfast' but to both earthly and spiritual realities. Help us to share what we sincerely believe with sensitivity. Amen

For further thought

• How do we respond to those who believe differently? Do we avoid treating as ridiculous what they believe and insisting on the rightness of our beliefs?

October

Wednesday 21 October
A treasury of tweets

Mark 12:24-27

Have you not read in the Book of Moses, in the account of the burning bush, how God said to him, 'I am the God of Abraham, the God of Isaac, and the God of Jacob'? He is not the God of the dead, but of the living. You are badly mistaken! (part of verses 26-27)

Jesus is typically blunt in putting his challengers straight – of course they're wrong! He uses their own text (the Torah) against them. His response – you have a very human perspective, it's not like that in heaven – is surrounded by scriptural appeals. Do we aspire to killer putdowns? Especially backed up by a Bible verse? Typically, Jesus is inventive with scripture. We learn from him a habit of using scripture creatively, whatever its original meaning, to make a point. More scholarly approaches to scripture rule out some of Jesus' uses than adopt them; Jesus is riffing on scripture here! Scripture is not a code, or rulebook, but a treasury of tweets, as Anglican Archbishop Justin Welby has suggested. Old scripture in new context creates new impact. This is Jesus' message.

Sometimes we can't take Jesus' liberty with texts, but we should be alive to the tradition that nourished him – Midrash. Midrash is the tradition of interpretative story used by the Jewish rabbis, adding colour, making people think. Have we tamed scripture by putting it in a book and offering tame lectionary portions? If it is going to 'work', or 'be fulfilled in your hearing today', it should create a shock, wake us with a start, give us new thoughts. The risk with the Gospel stories is that we look down on the challengers and think, 'they've got it wrong, not us ', when the purpose of the account is to make us ponder whether we have fixed ideas. Are we looking for the sceptics, when we're the modern Sadducees?

† Lord, help us not to be so right that others must be wrong. Help us to read your word creatively, alive to its life. Amen

For further thought

• How inclusive or exclusive are we? Do we pick up ideas of openness and imagination from Jesus' words? How would he challenge us today with new things?

Thursday 22 October
In praise of appreciation

Mark 12:28-34

Noticing that Jesus had given them a good answer, [one of the teachers of the law] asked him, 'Of all the commandments, which is the most important?' ... When Jesus saw that he had answered wisely, he said to him, 'You are not far from the kingdom of God.' (verses 28 and 34)

Appreciation of others is very important, and it is sometimes lacking. Very few of the encounters Jesus has with leading members of his society are marked by appreciation, so this story really stands out. This scholar comes forward, and note how his approach is described – he approaches Jesus with scholarly respect, not as an opponent or an enemy. He comes with an honest enquiry. He offers Jesus an opportunity to set out his message; a master was defined by his own take on the core of religion (devotion to God). It is a formulaic question and Jesus responds with the expected answer – the shema ('Hear, O Israel') and the accompanying responsibility towards human beings.

Jesus is speaking to the scholar in his own language, a tailored response that he could appreciate. He responds in kind, mirroring and paraphrasing to show both understanding and agreement, raising the stakes with a prophetic acknowledgement of what matters most to God. He speaks Jesus' language back to him and Jesus notes it appreciatively. Jesus must have been impressed by someone speaking from the heart without trickery. It brings to an end the series of tests and questions that Jesus has passed with no difficulty.

Jesus always appreciated people's spiritual journeys, encouraging them at times of shaky doubt and gently urging them on to trust and commitment.

† Reflect on the 'Great Commandment'. How significant is it to us? Is it the driving force in our lives? How do we engage with the journeys of others, and our own?

For further thought

- Are we able to answer the questions about life and faith that others put to us, with a straightforward gentle response that engages with people?

Friday 23 October
'Son of David'

Mark 12:35-40

While Jesus was teaching in the Temple courts, he asked, 'Why do the teachers of the law say that the Messiah is the son of David? David himself, speaking by the Holy Spirit, declared: "The Lord said to my lord: 'Sit at my right hand until I put your enemies under your feet.'"' (verses 35-36)

Jesus goes on the offensive ('How can the teachers of the law say?'), making their ideas seem ridiculous. We may get some satisfaction from Jesus beating his opponents at their own game, but his approach is difficult. If we look at David's psalm without any expectation of 'prophetic fulfilment' we will not think that he is talking about another, especially a more exalted figure; David is talking about himself, or his son Solomon. In fact the idea of a Messiah, described in Davidic monarchical terms, is a longing for a return to the stature and piety of a leader like David, who ruled a united people.

Today, some read Jesus' words as indicating that the Messiah is 'the Lord', i.e. of actual divine status (which the writer of the psalm would not have had in mind) and that he is pointing out that the Messiah is not the 'son of David' but 'the Son of God'. Is Jesus here, as on other occasions, wrestling with the idea of the Davidic Messiah in order to distance himself from Messianic status? Jesus as Messiah is the opposite of what we see in Jesus' last days in Jerusalem. In fact, he is thrust into the Messianic expectation of the people. He crashes into the objections of the religious elite, who see him as more as an anti-Messiah, and is broken by Roman 'justice'. He will soon share in the eventual fate of the people of David at the time when the Gospel is written – death and destruction at the hands of the brutal Romans.

† Pray about our own misuse of scripture and how we speak of the 'Messiah' to those who do not follow Christ.

For further thought

• How ready are we to challenge common 'Messianic' thinking among Christians and how does this issue impact on relations with Jewish believers?

Saturday 24 October
Jesus' bias

Mark 12:41-44

Calling his disciples to him, Jesus said, 'Truly I tell you, this poor widow has put more into the treasury than all the others. They all gave out of their wealth; but she, out of her poverty, put in everything – all she had to live on.' (verses 43-44)

This final section of the chapter links to yesterday's mention of the teachers in their fashionable clothing (as I write this, the 'bling bishop' has been disciplined for his wealth and excess). Jesus implicates the wealthy, and the religiously wealthy, in this story of the widow's last penny (less than a penny in fact): Jesus talks about them 'eating up the property of widows'. We read often in the Gospels of the contrast between the rich and the poor but, with Jesus' customary twist (bias), those who are materially rich are spiritually poor and those who have nothing are spiritually rich. This is challenging for those who are well off, and even those who are poor in our society are much more prosperous than Judaean peasants living under occupation in grinding poverty.

The gospel is for the marginalised. We can take it in only when its expression includes those who are on the edge. It is tempting, in some parts of the church, to draw this line marking the edge according to particular moral judgements (perhaps forgetting that Jesus reserves his criticisms for the morality of the wealthy and the religious). Instead, the gospel tells us that the church should be for the poor. As we look around at middle-class congregations, we need to ask ourselves – where are the poor? Sometimes this question is answered by the churches' involvement in foodbanks. This is why we should hold Jesus' saying about the first being last close to our hearts.

† Pray for the poor – our own scripture tells us that they will always be with us, but we should not be content with that.

For further thought

- Where do people of other faiths fit in? Whether or not we're looking for their conversion, are they seeing the gospel in action in us?

Readings in Mark (4)

2 Signs of the end

This week's notes are by **Jember Teferra**

Dr Jember Teferra was the founder, co-ordinator and fundraiser of a project known as Integrated Holistic Approach Urban Development Project. The project's dedicated team focused on the poorest six slums in Addis Abeba, with a population of 52,000. She has now scaled down to focusing on an institute that is training disciples in the hope that they will replicate the original vision of poverty alleviation and promotion of social justice. She is a widow with three children and four grandchildren.

Sunday 25 October

Jesus' warning

Mark 13:1-8

'Look, Teacher! What massive stones! What magnificent buildings!' 'Do you see all these great buildings?' replied Jesus. 'Not one stone here will be left on another; every one will be thrown down.' (part of verse 1, and verse 2)

This week's readings focus on what we lay people describe as 'the second coming'. Our Lord's first response to his disciples was regarding the great Temple in Jerusalem that only King Solomon was privileged enough to build. Today many Christians are confused as to whether or not the fall of Jerusalem in AD 70 was what our Lord was referring to. The other warnings of false 'Messiahs' coming in his name throughout the centuries – 'nations against nations', 'kingdom against kingdom' – have gone on beyond the Roman Empire and into the last century. Two world wars, present-day racism and tribalism, religious divisions leading to war, terrorism, unrest in the Middle East, riots and crimes ... distressing events still go on, as do natural disasters such as famine, drought, floods and typhoons in all four corners of the earth. Even though our Lord says 'the end is still to come', as Christians are we ready to meet our Lord here and now if he came today?

† Heavenly Father, as we see great famous buildings thrown down, wars and various disasters destroying different parts of the world, please help us to listen to your warning and be ready to meet you as and when you come.

Monday 26 October
Faithful to the end

Mark 13:9-13

...but the one who stands firm to the end will be saved. (part of verse 13)

Unlike Paul of Tarsus, my own political imprisonment, between 1976 and 1981, by the military Marxist government, gave me a humbling experience as a Christian. In a 7 metres by 17 metres prison barrack we were 140 mixed prisoners: some from the two communist parties: Marxist and Maoist (extreme left), and our group – the ruling class – the so-called oppressors! I initiated, against opposition, evening devotions and morning prayers. One morning, unexpectedly, the Marxist military prison administrator came to our compound of 485 women prisoners. I did not know that I was the reason for his visit, since I was reported to have been continuing my 'oppressive' behaviour – not respecting the rights of the atheists, the Muslims and other non-Christians. The administrator gathered us all and asked us to listen to the spokesperson's accusation. He then, unexpectedly, expressed his surprise as to how a health worker who served 485 persons around the clock could be accused this way.

God triumphed! The administrator asked for those who opposed the devotions to raise their fingers. Only five did, versus 480 (including those not even in my barrack) in support. The administrator concluded by saying 'Sister Jember, the large majority has given you permission to continue your devotional time for breakfast, lunch and dinner!' Such an accusation could have resulted in serious action. Mark 13:13 just came to my mind, especially since 'the red terror' had killed thousands. We awaited execution every day. Praise the Lord for that attitude in that context and for helping us to be faithful throughout that experience.

† Only you, Lord, know how we, in different circumstances and contexts, find it hard to remain faithful to the end. Help us all the way and all the time to be faithful to the very end.

For further thought

• Do we believe that, with the help of the Holy Spirit, we will remain faithful to the end when faced with situations that challenge our faith?

Tuesday 27 October
Crisis and horror

Mark 13:14-23

At that time if anyone says to you, 'Look, here is the Messiah!' or, 'Look, there he is!' do not believe it. For false messiahs and false prophets will appear and perform signs and wonders to deceive, if possible, even the elect. So be on your guard; I have told you everything in advance.
(verses 21-23)

Whenever I read this portion of Mark, it reminds me of war films and books written about horrific occurrences. Recently, typhoons have caused horrific damage and killed thousands (e.g. in the Philippines). Aeroplane pilots have emergency instructions in case of any accident: passengers must leave everything behind and focus on saving their own life. Is our Lord warning us of the end for each one of us if we are victims of an awful crisis? Or is he warning those who will still be alive and still be on earth when he comes?

It is mind boggling, as I mentioned yesterday, that during the Marxist revolution we political prisoners used to say to each other, 'If I am a victim of the "red terror" before you, please pass this and that to my family' – a will, personal belongings, etc. We were expecting death – we had our minds set to face the crisis and horror with a calm spirit. We were ready to meet the Lord. It was a healthy attitude!

† King of Kings and Lord of Lords, help us never to be complacent but to be on our guard every day of our lives – not only when forced to be by health problems, war, or natural disaster and crisis.

For further thought

• As practising Christians, do we seriously take our Lord's warning to be on our guard every day of our lives?

October

304

The return in glory

Mark 13:24-27

At that time people will see the Son of Man coming in clouds with great power and glory. (verse 26)

When world events go terribly wrong I feel like saying, 'Yes, Lord, please, come now; Jesus, come soon.' In the middle of this perplexing, detailed chapter it is absolutely clear that the suffering Messiah, Jesus, will ultimately return in his full power and glory – even though it is not very clear as to whether or not those who are being addressed by him will see it (he does not specify). But our Lord's description of his coming makes it really exciting, especially in this terrible era in human history. Daily we read of crimes even against the innocent, like child victims of war, crime, and trafficking.

Throughout the New Testament, after the death of Jesus, and beyond the resurrection, all his followers clearly looked forward to his return to earth in his glory and full power and triumph. What a privilege to be among God's chosen people, whom he will send the angels to gather from one end of the world to the other – 'the ends of the heavens'. This portion of Mark 13 should make each practising Christian look forward to the triumphant coming of our Lord and pray to be his 'chosen person'.

† Heavenly Father, while we long for you to come and gather us into your everlasting kingdom, we pray that your Holy Spirit will help us to live Christlike lives in order that we might deserve to be one of your 'chosen people'.

For further thought
• Do we, daily, examine ourselves and ask if we deserve to be considered among 'the chosen people'? How do our standards compare with the biblical standard?

October

Thursday 29 October
Signs of the end of the age

Mark 13:28-31

Now learn this lesson from the fig-tree: As soon as its twigs get tender and its leaves come out, you know that summer is near. Even so, when you see these things happening, you know that it is near, right at the door. Truly I tell you, this generation will certainly not pass away until all these things have happened. Heaven and earth will pass away, but my words will never pass away. (verses 28-31)

One of the lessons a medical doctor learns is how to recognise the accompanying signs and symptoms of specific diseases or illnesses. It's the same with the meteorologist forecasting the weather. Our Lord's lesson of the fig tree is similar in that he is teaching his disciples to look out for the process of events and changes of situations leading to his coming. For some Christians the destruction of Jerusalem in AD 70 was seen as the end, but our Lord's saying, 'This generation will certainly not pass away until all these things have happened' (verse 30) still remains a mystery for those of us Christians who are here in the twenty-first century. But one thing is certain: what we see and hear here and now, today, is what our Lord has foretold.

† Lord, we believe that all things will pass away but your word will never pass away. Help us to recognise the signs of your coming and be ready, with great expectation, joyfully to receive you whenever you come.

For further thought
• How attentively do we, with spiritual insight, discern the unfolding of God's purpose in the changing panorama of events? What signs do you see you around you today of the coming of the kingdom?

October

Friday 30 October
Watch!

Mark 13:32-37

If he comes suddenly, do not let him find you sleeping. What I say to you, I say to everyone: 'Watch!' (verse 36 and part of verse 37)

My first career was nursing in the UK. As a junior nurse in my second year I was going to visit my recently widowed mother, having not seen her for more than five years. To get my visa and arrange my trips I was running around, and then I had to work for seven consecutive nights. On my last night I had difficulty in staying awake and, even worse, when I was left alone in charge of a geriatric ward I got what was known as 'night nurse's paralysis'. I sat on the chair with eyes wide open but I was unable to move. When two patients called me I could not go to them. Even when the senior night sister walked on to the ward I could not accompany her or talk to her. Just as she did her round alone and was about to leave I somehow miraculously forced myself to get up and run to apologise to her. She was so angry that, even though she recognised my problem, she reported me to the Matron.

Just before I was packed to leave for the airport, I was called and given a warning (for the first and last time!!). The Matron sympathised but pointed out the seriousness of my not watching and caring. Every time I read this portion of the Bible I go back to that experience and, if I speak anywhere on our Lord's second coming, I tell of my failure or irresponsibility on that occasion. For me, it speaks of our lifelong responsibility as Christians – to watch, as our Lord has warned.

† Our caring and understanding Father, help us never fail in watching around the clock, as you may come here and now – any minute or any second.

For further thought
• Have you ever been negligent and failed to watch every second of the day, as our Lord repeatedly ordered us to do?

October

Saturday 31 October
A beautiful thing

Mark 14:1-9

*Why are you bothering her? She has done a beautiful thing to me ...
She did what she could. She poured perfume on my body beforehand
to prepare for my burial. Truly I tell you, wherever the gospel is preached
throughout the world, what she has done will also be told, in memory of
her.* (part of verses 6 and 7, and verses 8-9)

In the Ethiopian Orthodox Church, it is customary to put perfume
on a dead body before burial. What is surprising in this story is
what inspired the woman to go to Simon's house, and how Jesus
chose to spend his time. Jesus in his last days goes to the house of
Simon – a healed untouchable leper – for dinner; he then accepts
the anointing by a socially unacceptable woman. Our Lord was
gracious enough to accept both hospitality and anointing with
great appreciation, and told off his disciples for the ungracious
comments some of them made.

Although it is nothing new for our compassionate Lord to reach
out to the poorest of the poor – the rejected, the unwanted and
the untouchable, it is very interesting still that, on his last day, as he
was being watched by the Jewish religious leaders plotting to kill
him, he would be in an environment that would offend them most.

However, the woman, in discerning how near the end was,
amplified the 'fellowship of his suffering' through her love, faith,
and humility.

† Thank you, Lord, for teaching us that it is not just the 'respectable' and socially
accepted who are offered your love, but that you know every detail of every one
of our lives, and offer all sinners your love and forgiveness.

For further thought

• What has Jesus taught us by spending time with the outcasts of
society on his last days on earth? How would we have spent our
time if we were in his place?

Tears

1 Tears in the Old Testament

This week's notes are by **Nicola Slee**

Nicola Slee is a theologian and poet based at the Queen's Foundation, Birmingham, where she teaches contextual and feminist theology, and supervises research students. Author of many books and articles, she was editor of *Words for Today* from 2002 until 2011. Her most recent publications include *The Faith Lives of Women and Girls* (Ashgate, 2013) and *Making Nothing Happen: Five Poets Explore Faith and Spirituality* (Ashgate, 2014). She is a lay Anglican, living in Stirchley with her partner and two cats.

Sunday 1 November
Weeping and rejoicing belong together

Psalm 30

You turned my wailing into dancing; you removed my sackcloth and clothed me with joy, that my heart may sing your praises and not be silent.
(part of verses 11-12)

Although some act as if the life of faith is one long party, Christians are no more immune to tragedy than anyone else. On the other hand, there are some who suggest that Christians are morbidly addicted to suffering! Liberation and feminist theologians have critiqued theologies of suffering that keep the poor and the oppressed in their suffering rather than seek to change it. As we consider the theme of 'tears' in this and the following week, we will need to steer a path between an unhealthy glorification of suffering on the one hand, and a facile optimism that denies the depth of human pain, on the other.

Both elements are present in today's psalm: there is weeping in the night, and rejoicing in the morning (verse 5); there is wailing and dancing, sackcloth and festal garments (verses 11-12). The psalm balances tears and laughter very closely, so that it is difficult to imagine one without the other. The exaltation of being raised depends on the prior experience of having gone down into the depths; the joy experienced in the new light of morning would not be so intense were it not for the suffering endured through the night.

† Teach me, dear God, to weep and to laugh with my whole being, denying nothing of my humanity – that I may find you in both.

November

309

Monday 2 November
Weeping as political act

Psalm 137

By the rivers of Babylon we sat and wept when we remembered Zion. There on the poplars we hung our harps... How can we sing the songs of the LORD *while in a foreign land?* (verses 1-2, 4)

One of the most memorable Bible studies I have experienced was a dramatic re-enactment of the Babylonian exile, involving a hundred students and staff. I was part of a group of Israeli deportees taken captive. Shoved in a basement, tied up with ropes and 'beaten' with makeshift prods, we were left to ferment in darkness. Our student captors evidently enjoyed the switch of power and a couple of visiting bishops got more than they bargained for! This is the nearest I have come to being displaced by an enemy – a far cry from the reality of those who have seen their homes and cities besieged and destroyed. Yet it did provoke some measure of identification with the powerlessness of people taken into exile and I can still remember the smarts from the 'beating'!

This psalm is a prayer by people who have been displaced from their homeland and sit weeping by a foreign river, reliving the scenes of destruction they have experienced, and crying vengeance on their enemies. Their tears are not simply for personal loss of home and livelihood but for the collapse of their whole universe, what Kathleen O'Connor describes as 'narrative wreckage' (see Thursday's notes). Land, Temple, religion, security and ownership of their communal lives – they have been rudely dispossessed of all.

The reality of which this psalm speaks is a common one in our world, when weeping becomes a response of anger, brokenness, loss and revenge. But tears may also be a form of resistance, steeling the will to refuse compromise with captors and keeping the pain of loss alive.

† Teach us, sorrowing God, to weep tears of resistance with those who have lost everything, and to refuse the easy comfort of compromise.

For further thought

• Who might be praying this psalm in the world today? Read the newspaper or listen to the news with this psalm in mind and heart.

November

God as wailing woman

Jeremiah 8:21 – 9:2, 17-21

Consider now! Call for the wailing women to come; send for the most skilful of them. Let them come quickly and wail over us till our eyes overflow with tears and water streams from our eyelids. (part of verses 17-18)

Mourning in ancient Israel, as in many cultures today, was primarily the work of women, who tended and embalmed the body and performed the rites of mourning, keening in the streets as the body was carried to its burial place. Funerals in such cultures can go on for many days, with the ritual weeping continuing 'day and night' (9:1).

L Juliana M Claassens, in her remarkable book *Mourner, Mother, Midwife* (Westminster John Knox, 2012), suggests that God is the speaker in this passage of Jeremiah, presenting to us an image of God as divine wailing woman who shares in the work of the mourning women in verses 17-21 keening for the dead. 'The dead' in this case is 'the slain of my people' (9:1), the hundreds killed by the invading armies of Babylon in the late sixth century BCE.

This work of tears performed by God and women is theologically significant, according to Claassens. It is a work of witness, testifying to and magnifying the pain of a broken people whose land and city have been devastated. It is, too, a therapeutic work that enables a people to come to terms with and express their grief. More than this, it is a prophetic work, giving expression to the fact that things are not as they should be, and therefore calling for change.

Such an image of God is startling to many of us, very different from the male warrior God portrayed in scripture. How does it change my relationship to God if I imagine her weeping with me in my sorrow, and that of my people?

† Show us, Wailing Woman God, how to mourn with you and share your work of tears.

For further thought
• Spend some time considering the image of God as wailing woman. What new insights does this offer?

November

Wednesday 4 November
A mothering God who weeps

Jeremiah 31:15-20

*This is what the L*ORD *says: 'A voice is heard in R*AMAH*, mourning and great weeping, Rachel weeping for her children and refusing to be comforted, because [her children] are no more.'* (verse 15)

The wailing woman God is also a mother, weeping for her slain children. This is the image we are presented with in this text, through the vivid portrayal of Rachel, weeping for children who are 'no more'. Rachel was the mother of Joseph and Benjamin, who represent through their offspring the two kingdoms of Judah and Israel and thus the whole nation. Rachel laments in Ramah, the place at which Nebuchadnezzar assembled the people for their long trek into captivity (Jeremiah 40:1), thus a place of bitter loss for the nation. Jeremiah recalls Rachel's grief some thousand years after her death; long dead, she is still in mourning for the terrible suffering of her 'children' in the prophet's time.

No mother expects her children to die before her own death, and the grief of a mother for a dead child is a grief that refuses to be comforted. Such is Rachel's grief and such is the grief of the mother God whose womb aches with compassion for her exiled children. She can never cease her weeping until such time as her bereaved offspring are gathered into her arms and their hurts are healed.

While the passage evokes the poignant image of a mother God who cannot cease weeping for her wayward offspring, it also anticipates a time to come when maternal tears will cease and the scattered children of Israel will be regathered. Until such time, the maternal longing of God will not cease. And we too, God's children, are called to share in that maternal longing for all who weep in misery and exile.

† Hold us, Weeping Mother God, and all who weep, in your compassionate arms.

For further thought
• Where, when and how have you experienced the maternal longing of God?

Thursday 5 November
A topography of pain

Lamentations 1:1-6, 11-12, 16-17

How deserted lies the city, once so full of people! How like a widow is she, who once was great among the nations!... Bitterly she weeps at night, tears are upon her cheeks. Among all her lovers there is none to comfort her. (part of verses 1-2)

It is not only people who weep: places can grieve too. Houses, villages, cities, landscapes and even countries may mourn because of the ravages that have taken place in them and the neglect or abuse they have suffered. We are increasingly aware of ways in which the earth itself weeps and groans in lament.

In Lamentations, the besieged and captive city Jerusalem is depicted as a suffering woman who has fallen from the condition of a princess to that of a slave, 'from fully inhabited city to a lonely widow on a hill' (Kathleen M O'Connor, *Lamentations and the Tears of the World*, Orbis, 2002:28). She has been betrayed by her false lovers, raped and abandoned. Her pain is acute, and there is no comforter to assuage her pain. Every part of her body participates in her suffering: her eyes weep endlessly, her mouth cries out in anguish, her very bowels constrict with pain. Like a survivor of abuse, she is marked and marred by all that she has suffered. In a shocking and graphic image, woman Jerusalem has become as stained and spoiled as a 'menstrual rag' (verse 17b, literally, rather than NIV's generic 'unclean thing') – an image speaking of ritual defilement and shame.

The book of Lamentations charts with searing honesty and detail the topography of a land and city's pain. As we read this passage, let us bring before God the devastated places of our world and lament with them.

† In place of words, let your whole body lament with the suffering cities and lands in the news.

For further thought
• Where are the places in your neighbourhood that are weeping?

The body's tears

Lamentations 2:11-22

My eyes fail from weeping, I am in torment within; my heart is poured out on the ground because my people are destroyed, because children and infants faint in the streets of the city. (verse 11)

In today's passage, the description of the city's grief is visceral: it involves the running tears of the eyes (verses 11, 18), pouring out of the heart (verse 11), holding pain in the arms (verse 12), stretching out of hands (verse 19), the piercing of the very flesh (verse 13) in agony. The body cries out where words fail. There is no question of saying or making prayers to God: the whole person becomes a tortured prayer, writhing and moaning in its suffering, demanding to be seen and heard. The dominant prayer of Lamentations is not for comfort or healing so much as simply to be seen, beheld in all the agony of one's plight. 'See, Lord, how distressed I am' (1:20). 'Look, Lord, and consider' (2:20).

Some people cry more readily than others; I will readily weep at music, films, art, and when deeply touched by another person. Yet there is a form of the body's weeping that I have experienced rarely that is different from all of these, when the whole body becomes lament, rather than merely expressing it. It is difficult to write about, since such weeping comes out of depths beyond words. It is a manifestation of soul pain as much as physical pain, a crying out from profound dislocation, a shuddering of heart and body. There is no answer to such prayer other than the absolute regard of the One who beholds and loves us in our pain.

† Take some time to be attentive to any grief or pain within your body-soul, and offer it to God.

For further thought

• As you go about your day, look out for bodies that seem to be weeping, and hold them before God.

November

The touching of tears

Isaiah 25:6-9

On this mountain ... the Sovereign LORD *will wipe away the tears from all faces; he will remove his people's disgrace from all the earth.* (part of verses 6, 8)

One of the most intimate acts we can perform for another person is to touch their tears; in such a moment we come as close as it is possible to come to another's pain. A three-part drama series is currently being televised, entitled 'Don't ever wipe tears without gloves'. These words are spoken in the opening scene by one nurse to another as they dress the wounds of a young man covered in suppurating sores and evidently near death. The drama narrates the AIDS epidemic of the early 1980s, exploring its effects upon the lives of gay men as well as on wider society. It evokes vividly the rampant fear at that time of the bodies of gay men. Even though it was known that AIDS could not be contracted except through close sexual contact or the sharing of needles, many did not want to touch the bodies – or the tears – of those affected by the disease.

In today's well known passage from Isaiah, God comes close enough to touch the tears of those who grieve and are in pain. Gloves come off, and the touch is flesh to flesh, body to body. God's tears mingle with our tears and, out of that mingling, there is hope of healing. This is the reality of which the incarnation speaks. God does not keep any kind of distance from human bodily pain but comes as close as it is possible to come. God puts on flesh in order to weep human tears, feel human sorrow and, ultimately, die a human death.

† Teach us, fleshy God, to touch each other's tears with tenderness, as you have touched ours.

For further thought

- Where is the need for gloves to come off in your life, or in the lives of those with whom you have to do?

November

2 Tears in the New Testament

This week's notes are by **Nicola Slee** (see page 309)

Sunday 8 November
The gift of tears

Matthew 5:1-6

Now when Jesus saw the crowds, he went up on a mountainside and sat down... and he began to teach them. He said: 'Blessed are the poor in spirit, for theirs is the kingdom of heaven. Blessed are those who mourn, for they will be comforted. Blessed are the meek, for they will inherit the earth.' (verses 1-5)

The Eastern Orthodox tradition speaks of 'the gift of tears', regarding tears as a prized virtue, earnestly to be desired and prayed for. This tradition looks to Jesus' teaching in the Beatitudes, particularly his saying in verse 4.

It may seem strange to think of desiring tears, when we might more naturally regard weeping as a painful condition to be avoided. Yet, in the Orthodox tradition, tears are regarded as integral to the state of contrition and self-knowledge that is essential for any true prayer. Orthodox writers look to the early desert fathers and mothers who also prized tears, seeing them as a silent way of learning and loving, a form of surrender to God. Tears are a sign of our human frailty and weakness, an embrace of our spiritual poverty.

The kind of tears we are speaking of here are those in which we acknowledge our fallibility and distance from God. Such tears can soften and prepare the heart for receiving God's grace. This is exactly in tune with Jesus' teaching in the Beatitudes, where it is those who know their poverty and need who are blessed, in contrast with those who think they are rich or well-resourced and therefore have no need of God.

† God of tears, teach me the grace of weeping so that my heart may be softened to receive you.

Tears more precious than gold

Luke 7:36-48

A woman in that town who lived a sinful life learned that Jesus was eating at the Pharisee's house, so she came there with an alabaster jar of perfume. As she stood behind him at his feet weeping, she began to wet his feet with her tears. (verses 37-38)

Perhaps because she has no reputation (other than a very bad one) to preserve, the woman in this story can act in such an outrageously abandoned way. Unlike Simon and the Pharisees, who are only too well aware of their religious status and are highly self-conscious about how they present themselves in public, her being and action are oriented towards Jesus, with little regard for herself.

The woman weeps freely, and her tears are precious gifts, mingling with the costly ointment to anoint Jesus' feet. Jesus receives her tears with gratitude, knowing that they are worth more even than the precious ointment, because they are an offering from the very depths of her soul. We know nothing about this woman, other than that she 'lived a sinful life' (verse 37) – generally taken to refer to a life of prostitution. While we know nothing about her other than what is presented here, we can imagine that she has plenty to weep about: compelled perhaps by poverty to sell her body, doubtless treated with disdain and shame by the men who have used her, and quite possibly subject to physical violence, she will have known the tears of shame, powerlessness, helplessness and hunger. But her tears in this story are different – they are the outpouring of deep love and adoration, and they witness to her profound spiritual discernment. Unlike the men present, she knows in whose sacred presence she is, and she acts accordingly: she gets to her knees, weeps and pours out her very soul.

† God of tears, teach me not to judge harshly the tears of others, but to receive them as costly gifts.

For further thought
• Whose tears have been most precious to you, and why?

Tuesday 10 November
The tears of Jesus

John 11:30-36

When Jesus saw [Mary] weeping, and the Jews who had come along with her also weeping, he was deeply moved in spirit and troubled. 'Where have you laid him?' he asked. 'Come and see, Lord,' they replied. Jesus wept. (verses 33-35)

Jesus does not only receive the tears of others as precious gift – he also weeps tears himself, and the Gospel offers us these tears as a reflection of his intense love for humankind: for Lazarus, in the first instance; for Mary and Martha whose grief he shares; but also for us, who seek, albeit stumblingly, to be his friends.

This is not the only place in the Gospels where Jesus laments; he mourns over the city of Jerusalem (Luke 13:31-35), and we are told in a number of places of his 'pity' or compassion on those who come to him for healing. In Gethsemane, he wrestles in an agony that may have included tears (Luke 22:44). But this is the only place in the Gospels where we are shown Jesus weeping at the death of a friend.

His tears are prompted in the first place by Mary's weeping and the tears of the other mourners (verse 33). It is as if, in seeing their grief, his own grief is released, and he weeps freely for the beloved friend he has lost. But his tears are also in solidarity with the sorrow of the two sisters. Jesus knows this household well, and has often been a visitor there; he loves each of them as friends and feels keenly their loss, as well as his own.

John gives us an image of Christ whose own heart can be broken in sorrow and who can therefore weep with us when we sorrow and grieve.

† God of tears, thank you for the tears of Jesus that speak to the depths of my pain.

For further thought

• What makes Jesus weep today, in your local context as well as in the wider world?

Wednesday 11 November
Baptism of tears

Luke 22:54-62

The Lord turned and looked straight at Peter. Then Peter remembered the word the Lord had spoken to him: 'Before the cock crows today, you will disown me three times.' And he went outside and wept bitterly.
(verses 61-62)

In Bach's *St Matthew* and *St John Passions*, this scene is one of the most poignant in the whole oratorio. Verse 62, sung by the Evangelist, is a musical rendering of weeping that is unparalleled in the musical canon. The word 'bitterly' is extended over a long series of descending notes, in the minor key, that evoke more powerfully than any words could do the intense sorrow and bitterness of Peter's tears. I am generally reduced to tears when I hear a performance! Peter's tears, taken up and interpreted by Luke, then interpreted again musically by Bach, have the power to provoke fresh tears in those who listen (I am sure I am not alone in weeping at this part of the *Passion*).

In Orthodox tradition, tears are highly prized because they are an expression of repentance and therefore a part of the pathway to forgiveness and renewal of life. They form part of the 'pasch' that is the pattern of Christian life: a continually renewed dying and being reborn, that is also the pattern of baptism. Indeed, tears are often compared to baptism by Orthodox writers. John Climacus says that tears 'resemble a bath', in which sins may be washed away (*Patrologia Graeca* 88:808). So, perhaps, in this heart-breaking scene where we see Peter crushed and broken by his own betrayal of Jesus, we may discern in his tears a profound baptism of sorrow that turns his heart back to the one he has just disowned.

† God of tears, wash me, baptise me, renew me, in the sorrow of my weeping.

For further thought

• Listen to Bach's *St Matthew* and *St John Passions* and pay particular attention to his setting of today's text.

The fertility of tears

Luke 23:26-31

A large number of people followed him, including women who mourned and wailed for him. Jesus turned and said to them, 'Daughters of Jerusalem, do not weep for me; weep for yourselves and for your children.' (verses 27-28)

We are back with the wailing women, and with Simon of Cyrene, unknown strangers and aliens who accompany Jesus on his way to the cross. His friends and disciples, who might have been expected to be with him on the Via Dolorosa, sharing his tears, are nowhere in sight. Others perform that ministry for him; there is a reality in this, as it is sometimes strangers who can share our tears in a way that those nearest and dearest cannot.

Jesus turns to the women and tells them not to weep for him, but for themselves and their children, foreseeing a coming cataclysm when they will wish they had never given birth, for the terrible suffering that is coming upon their offspring. It is terrible to imagine women in such pain for their families that they wish they had never been born; yet our television screens regularly show women in such a plight, having to witness their children ravaged by disease, poverty or war, or abused by those who should protect them.

Jesus turns away from his own suffering, acute as it is, in order to speak to those whom he perceives to be more vulnerable and at risk than himself. May we have the compassion and insight to do the same.

† God of tears, teach me to reach out in my own pain to those who are in greater distress.

For further thought

- Think of a time when a stranger ministered to you, and give thanks.

The anguish of tears

2 Corinthians 1:23 – 2:4

For I wrote to you out of great distress and anguish of heart and with many tears, not to grieve you but to let you know the depth of my love for you. (verse 4)

It is obvious from 1 and 2 Corinthians that Paul's relationship with the Corinthian church was a stormy one, beset by a number of tensions and difficulties. In particular, 2 Corinthians charts the twists and turns of a painful dynamic – half of the total New Testament references to 'pain' occur in this one letter! Paul's pain included physical hardship and torture, despair, 'deadly peril' (2 Corinthians 1:8-10), but also mental distress and anguish, the grief when a loving relationship has turned sour or causes great pain. It is out of such distress that Paul writes now, even with 'many tears'.

In turns, Paul chides and upbraids them, but he is also capable of remarkable tenderness and patience. He puts off visiting them in order that they can have time to absorb the hard things said in an earlier letter (presumably 1 Corinthians) so that, when he does come, they can relate to each other in love and mutual fellowship.

Relationships that endure over the long haul are very likely to undergo times of tension, misunderstanding and painful difficulty – whether we are speaking about the relationships within a community or more personal ones. Honesty in the expression of what is painful and difficult needs to be held in balance with gentleness and a respect for difference – not an easy balance to achieve.

† God of tears, teach me when to speak of my anguish and when to keep silent.

For further thought
• Where are the tensions and difficulties in relationships in your own life and that of your local church? How are you responding?

November

321

The end of tears

Revelation 21:1-4

[God] will wipe every tear from their eyes. There will be no more death or mourning or crying or pain, for the old order of things has passed away. (verse 4)

When we are in deep grief, it is impossible to imagine our suffering ever coming to an end. Indeed, there are many wounds from which we do not fully 'recover', if such a term can be used. The death of a partner, child or friend is a pain we do not want to cease feeling, for to do so would indicate the death of love.

Nor is it generally possible to hear or grasp the hope of our pain easing or transforming when we are in the place of deep grief, which is why it is usually unhelpful to try to cheer a sufferer up with upbeat messages of healing or comfort. Paradoxically, it increases their isolation and pain, because the sufferer feels their pain has not been taken seriously or entered into.

How, then, can we hear these words at the end of the Book of Revelation, which speak of the end of pain and death, mourning and weeping? They signal a transformed reality that stands in absolute contrast to our present world, submerged as it is in pain, death and tears. They speak of a God who will remake all things, bringing the old order to an end and initiating a new one. At present, we can catch only glimpses of such a world, in vision and art, perhaps, or in the free play of children.

Meanwhile, for as long as we weep, God continues to walk among us, touching our tears and wiping them away – not just once, but over and over again, for as long as tears continue to fall.

† God of tears, while we long for a transformed reality in which all pain will cease, do not leave us but stay close to our tears.

For further thought

• Think of a time when God has wiped your tears away, and give thanks.

Rejoicing

1 Rejoicing in the Old Testament

This week's notes are by **Rachel Montagu** (see page 281)

Sunday 15 November
Gratitude unto delight

Deuteronomy 12:5-12

There, in the presence of the Lord *your God, you and your families shall eat and shall rejoice in everything you have put your hand to, because the* Lord *your God has blessed you … you, your sons and daughters, your male and female servants, and the Levites from your towns...* (verse 7 and part of verse 12)

This week's readings start with gratitude for God's gifts to us, move on to delight in how we perceive God, and end with joyous anticipation of the perfect future age for which we wait. The Hebrew language is blessed with many words for rejoicing; several are included in these readings.

By now Moses knew he couldn't enter the Promised Land and had one last chance to impress the lessons he had been trying to teach on the children of Israel, throughout the 40 years in the wilderness. We hear how far he has grown since he told God at the Burning Bush that he was inarticulate, literally 'with lips closed over' (Exodus 3:10). Deuteronomy repeats many commandments given already and adds more, to give the children of Israel a framework within which to live their covenant with God in the land under Joshua's leadership.

Deuteronomy often mentions the future Temple. Thanking God by animal sacrifices may be a form of worship hard for us to understand. But we can understand the sense of achievement that comes from harvest, the comradeship of celebrating that with other farmers and sharing God's bounty with the Levites, who served in the Temple and did not own land to farm.

† 'My mouth will praise you with lips uttering cries of joy, when I remember you upon my bed and meditate about you during the night' (Psalm 63, part of verses 5-7; translation author's own).

November

323

Let the heavens rejoice!

1 Chronicles 16:7-12, 23-27, 31

For all the gods of the nations are idols, but the LORD made the heavens. Splendour and majesty are before him; strength and joy are in his dwelling-place … Let the heavens rejoice, let the earth be glad; let them say among the nations, 'The LORD reigns!' (verses 26-27, 31)

This psalm from Chronicles, paralleled in Psalms 105 and 96, delights in praising God.

Because David is traditionally the author of most of the psalms, many illuminated medieval Bibles show him playing a typical medieval harp; what David actually played is more likely to have been a lyre with a soundbox made of animal skin. We first hear of David's skill as a musician banishing Saul's depression. Later we see how he rejoiced when bringing the ark of the Eternal to Jerusalem, even if his wife Michal thought his leaping and dancing undignified and not regal. This psalm suggests that, even before the establishment of Solomon's Temple, his father David wanted to establish a regular regimen of praise for God.

For David, praising God involves both direct praise to God and also telling the surrounding nations about God, source of salvation. David also contrasts God, the creator of all, with the gods – mere idols – which the surrounding nations are foolish enough to believe in.

In verse 11, we can read 'Seek his face always' as 'seek God's presence always'; an injunction to try to feel ourselves constantly in God's presence.

For David, when we praise God we are attuned to the cosmic hymn of joy in which all the universe God created unites in praising the Eternal: let the heavens rejoice...

† 'Let the field rejoice and everything in it, then let all the trees of the forest shout joyfully; at the presence of the Eternal who comes to judge the earth, judging the earth in righteousness…' (Psalm 96:12-13).

For further thought

- List twenty-five things that make you want to praise God, either in your own life or historical events from the Exodus until now.

Tuesday 17 November
Sensational God

Psalm 34:1-10

*Of David. When he pretended to be insane before Abimelek, who drove him away, and he left. I will extol the L*ORD *at all times; his praise will always be on my lips. I will glory in the L*ORD*; let the afflicted hear and rejoice.* (verses 1-2)

We sometimes divide people into those oriented towards sight and those more inclined to get information from their hearing. The Bible frequently uses both senses close together so both visual and hearing oriented people are included. Here we also get the command in verse 8 to taste and see that the Eternal is good.

The psalm heading says David pretended to be insane before Abimelek. During the time when God had decided to make David king to replace Saul but Saul was still alive and frightened of being displaced, David fled from place to place for refuge while Saul pursued him. When he was recognised, even though his heroic fighting was mentioned, he pretended to be mad rather than acknowledge who he was, as described in 1 Samuel 21. Having escaped with his life, he sang in praise of God. However, the king of Gath before whom he feigned madness was called Achish not Abimelek. Commentators suggest that perhaps Abimelek (the Hebrew means 'my father is king') was a title rather than a proper name.

This psalm is an almost complete acrostic of the Hebrew alphabet. Alphabet acrostic chapters such as those in Lamentations or psalms often suggest either completeness or bringing order in a distressing and chaotic situation. There is an extra verse at the end of the acrostic here describing God as redeemer and rescuer. David rejoiced because his prayers for rescue and safety were answered.

† 'Let them call joyfully, and be happy ... and always say, "May the Eternal be great who delights in the wellbeing of God's servant. My tongue will meditate on your righteousness and your praise all day"' (Psalm 35:27-8).

For further thought
• Think whether there is an organisation near you for people who feel at risk that you could help with your time or money.

November

325

Thank the Eternal

Psalm 118:15-24

Shouts of joy and victory resound in the tents of the righteous: 'The Lord's right hand has done mighty things!'... the Lord has done this, and it is marvellous in our eyes. The Lord has done it this very day; let us rejoice today and be glad. (verses 15, 23-24)

Yesterday's psalm was about David rejoicing when God saved him from Saul's murderous rage and pursuit. Today's psalm reminds me of when I felt very much under God's protection when giving birth to my children; I was in less danger than David but still felt in need of help. I read about a Jewish woman chanting a verse 'open the gates', which I thought must have been Psalm 118:20, and I included it in my birth plan to remind me to keep saying it during labour!

Psalms 113–118 are chanted in synagogues on festivals, so I remember several times a year the way I used this verse and my gratitude to God for my children's safe delivery. They are also part of the Passover service said at home to teach children about the Exodus from Egypt; they were among the first psalms I heard as a child.

The message of the importance of thanking God as part of joyous festive celebrations, as well as trusting in God's constant loving-kindness, runs throughout Psalms 113–118, even if individual psalms have a different emphasis. This psalm celebrates the return from exile; the Jews who had been rejected and exiled were returned to the land and their worship in the Temple was now the cornerstone, the vital centre of praising, thanking and rejoicing in God manifest in their world.

† 'I love the Eternal who listens to my voice, my supplications ... Gracious is the Eternal and just; our God is merciful. My soul, return to your rest for the Eternal has treated me with kindness' (from Psalm 116:1-7).

For further thought

• If you have computer access, listen on YouTube to the choir of Lauderdale Road Synagogue singing Psalm 118:26-29 in Hebrew to a cheerful festival tune. www.youtube.com/watch?v=9PMzn7q1-tc

Thursday 19 November
Gladness and joy overtake

Isaiah 35

The desert and the parched land will be glad; the wilderness will rejoice and blossom. ...and those the LORD *has rescued will return. They will enter Zion with singing; everlasting joy will crown their heads. Gladness and joy will overtake them, and sorrow and sighing will flee away.* (verses 1 and 10)

Isaiah talks constantly of the divine punishment of destruction and exile the people will suffer if they do not cease doing wrong, but also frequently mentions the rescue and return that at least a remnant will enjoy, when God brings them from exile back to the land. If they are scared of the perils of the return journey – wild animals, roadside bandits and thirst – Isaiah promises them a magical highway, free of wrongdoers, that will make the journey a blessing. He also promises miraculous cures for the disabled; it's not enough that the lame walk and the mute speak – the lame leap and the dumb shout for joy. A further promise is that the desert through which they travel will be a place of water and green growing things. In a dry climate, water and the plants it enables to flourish are an evident blessing.

The Hebrew word for highway in this chapter is unique in the Bible. Isaiah uses a similar word in chapter 11 where he promises a return from the exile in Assyria as miraculous as the journey back from slavery in Egypt. Isaiah tells of God's promise that the returning exiles' journey will be straightforward and 'the glory of the Eternal will be revealed'.

† Happy are those who delight in the Eternal's teaching, meditating on it day and night. They shall be like a tree planted by streams of water, producing fruit in due season (from Psalm 1).

For further thought

• Think of something you have been postponing because you are afraid. Do it, discover whether it is more straightforward than expected. Rejoice in your achievement once it is done.

Joy for all the world

Isaiah 61:1-7

The Spirit of the Sovereign Lord is on me, because the Lord has anointed me to proclaim good news to the poor. He has sent me to bind up the broken-hearted, to proclaim freedom for the captives and release from darkness for the prisoners …and everlasting joy will be yours. (verse 1 and part of verse 7)

Isaiah has an urgent message from God for the people. The people had ended a time of exile and tribulation, and they hoped for a return to a very different life as well as an opportunity to rebuild what had been shattered. They hoped for everlasting joy from God.

Isaiah describes himself as 'anointed'; prophets, like kings, were anointed for their role.

In verse 3 we see the sort of wordplay that doesn't survive translation – the Hebrew words for ashes – *aphar* – and garland – *pha'ar* - are very similar. Mourners would sprinkle ashes on their heads, so turning ash to garlands on the head was a sign of the end of grief. Similarly, mourners would refrain from anointing themselves with oil. 'Oil of joy' promises a very different time from the terrible era of destruction when many were killed and all suffered during the siege that preceded the conquest.

In the verses that follow today's reading God speaks of making an everlasting covenant with the whole people. Although this covenant is centred on the return of the Jews from exile, the chapter makes a universalistic promise of victory and glory to the whole world (verse 11), at which all can rejoice.

† 'I will thank you with my whole heart; I will sing joyfully before you, God. I will bow down towards your holy temple and I will give thanks for your loving-kindness and your truth' (Psalm 138:1-2).

For further thought

• Do you know someone bereaved whom you could telephone or visit and so bring to life the promise of comfort for mourners in these verses?

Saturday 21 November
Celebrate your return

Zephaniah 3:14-20

Sing, Daughter Zion; shout aloud, Israel! Be glad and rejoice with all your heart, Daughter Jerusalem!... The LORD your God is with you, the Mighty Warrior who saves. He will take great delight in you; in his love he will no longer rebuke you, but will rejoice over you with singing. (verses 14 and 17)

Again we read of God's promise via a prophet of the imminent return from the Babylonian exile. Verse 18 describes the grief of those who, because of the destruction of the Temple, were unable to celebrate the pilgrim festivals.

Zephaniah, like Isaiah in yesterday's reading, stresses not only the suffering of war and exile but also the shame suffered by those who, by losing the war, lost status and confidence. Zephaniah promises restoration and encourages singing and rejoicing so that they feel, rather than only know intellectually, their changed status now their punishment is over.

Like some of the other rejoicing passages read this week, I know that this passage has been interpreted by Christians in a way far from what I consider its literal meaning. I realise that, as a Jew, although I share many religious ideas with you who read these notes, I have a very different concept of Messiah and the Messianic Age. I believe the messiah hasn't yet come and hope for a future time of universal peace and happiness. Zalman Schachter Shalomi once told this story: The Messiah arrives. The Jews say, 'It's your first time here isn't it?' The Christians say, 'You've been before haven't you?' The Messiah says, 'I have been here hundreds of times but you were all too busy squabbling to notice!' (retold by Nancy Fuchs Kraemer in *Christianity in Jewish Terms*, ed. Tikva Frymer-Kensky: Westview Press, 2000).

† 'Hallelujah, for it's good to sing joyfully to our God; praise is beautiful and pleasant ... The Eternal delights in God-fearers and those who hope for God's loving-kindness' (Psalm 147: 1, 11).

For further thought

• Get involved in an interfaith activity in your area or try to find out more about the life and worship of people of another religion.

329

Rejoicing

2 Rejoicing in the New Testament

This week's notes are by **Kat Brealey**

Kat Brealey first developed a passion for justice and equality as an undergraduate theologian at the University of Manchester, where she studied feminism and liberation theologies. In 2012 she worked with Coventry Cathedral's reconciliation ministry team. More recently she has been exploring interfaith encounter in higher education, working at the University of Bristol Multifaith Chaplaincy. In her spare time she enjoys cycling, dystopian fiction and gospel music.

Sunday 22 November
Meeting

Luke 10:17-20

However, do not rejoice that the spirits submit to you, but rejoice that your names are written in heaven. (**verse 20**)

'The place God calls you to is the place where your deep gladness and the world's deep hunger meet.' So declares Frederick Buechner (*Wishful Thinking*, New York: HarperCollins, 1973), suggesting that joy – our theme this week – plays a key role in who we are and how we engage with the world.

So what do the writers of the New Testament have to say about this joy? The miracles in John's Gospel are commonly referred to as 'signs', pointing towards the coming kingdom. Here, in Luke, Jesus reminds his followers to look beyond outward manifestations, instead finding joy in what they usher in.

Similarly I often celebrate what feels like success in my work at the university chaplaincy – a new project, a fruitful discussion – and stop there. I fail to recognise the real cause for joy that lies beneath, which is that the kingdom of God is at hand, and my work is part of God's work! As we use our God-given skills and passions this week to meet the world's literal and metaphorical hunger, let's remember that '[y]our names are written in heaven'; that is, our highest calling is to point towards the kingdom.

† Loving God, in a world focused on pleasure but impoverished of joy, lead us to discover, experience and model your deep gladness in our lives.

November

330

Finding

Luke 15:1-10

Or suppose a woman has ten silver coins and loses one. Doesn't she light a lamp, sweep the house, and search carefully until she finds it? (**verse 8**)

I hate losing things. I don't do it very often, so when I have misplaced something I feel not just irritation but disbelief and ineptitude. The 'losers' in Jesus' story seem to handle their losses rather better, considering that in their case it wasn't merely a sentimental object that had disappeared but something of real value to their livelihood.

Lost sheep and silver coins are domestic images from the world of the Middle Eastern poor – a modern comparison might be the loss of a job, as opposed to a missing wedding ring. I wonder what the implications of this distinction are for us. If the analogy is that the repentant sinner is like the coin being found, this suggests God doesn't just like having us around, but that we have a key role to play. The important thing is not just that the objects in the parables were found, but what they were found for! Their relieved owners wouldn't have hidden them away for safe keeping; they were to be used, put back to work.

I'm encouraged by the notion that God's pursuit of us might not just be sentimental, but functional. Teresa of Avila wrote that Christ has 'no hands but yours', and God invites us into partnership in building the kingdom here on earth, in the many forms that takes.

And, finally, when the lost items are found, what happens? Friends and neighbours gather to share in the joy of the finder. Rejoicing takes place in a communal context – as we will see Paul explain to the Romans later this week.

† God of the lost and found, we thank you that you 'find' us for the greater purpose of working with you, in many different ways, to minister to those who are 'lost'.

For further thought

- What difference does it make to be needed by God, not just wanted? In what ways do you (or could you) partner in God's work?

November

Tuesday 24 November
Remaining

John 15:1-11

If you keep my commands, you will remain in my love, just as I have kept my Father's commands and remain in his love. I have told you this so that my joy may be in you and that your joy may be complete. (verses 10-11)

When these verses are read, the emphasis is often on our responsibility to 'remain' – that repeated injunction. If we keep our end of the bargain, John seems to say, Jesus will also remain in us – so cling on! In other contexts, though, remaining would be the default: if a friend asks us to wait for them outside a shop, we don't panic in case we accidentally walk off. It's a trivial comparison, but it belies a deeper insecurity many of us have about following Christ, encouraged by sentiments like, 'if God feels distant, who moved?!' We doubt our own commitment, continually checking ourselves for signs of rebellion.

The fatal flaw of this approach is that it assumes the responsibility to remain rests solely on us! New Testament scholar Rudolph Bultmann corrects this misapprehension, suggesting that Jesus speaks of 'not a being for but a being from – not holding but being held' (*The Gospel of John*, Westminster: John Knox, 1971). Without being much of gardener, I can see that this reading is more faithful to the agrarian image of the vine and branches. Branches grow from the central vine, and so it's the vine that holds the branches to itself, rather than them holding on for dear life! In some senses this is a relief – you may be familiar with the old cliché 'let go and let God'. However, in a society that prizes individualism and personal choice, is it actually more of a challenge to 'let God' hold us rather than the vice versa, without this devaluing our faith?

† Loving God, thank you that you hold us, and we remain in you. By your grace, wean us off the illusion that it is the other way round and grant us peace in that knowledge.

For further thought

- How secure are you in your identity as a follower of Christ? How do you measure this, and who do you allow to define it?

Wednesday 25 November
Suffering

Romans 5:2b-5

Not only so, but we also glory in our sufferings, because we know that suffering produces perseverance; perseverance, character; and character, hope. (verses 3-4)

While for many people this is an inspiring portion of scripture to turn to in hard times, it is also one that is frequently misused! All too often verses such as these have been used to suggest to those who are oppressed that the situation is the work of God, and to seek its end would be to challenge God's will. Yet the fact that we may learn lessons through hardship, lessons for which we are thankful, does not justify it. God's desire, as illustrated throughout the Bible, is to liberate people from oppression and suffering, not to inflict it. Hence suffering shouldn't be glorified nor silently endured.

That said, the testimony of many heroes of the faith demonstrates the power of suffering as a learning environment – from Job to Dietrich Bonhoeffer, to those we know personally who have endured trials and found their faith enriched. This nuance is a challenge. If the Christian faith is understood as centring on the pursuit of justice and an end to oppression, it can be difficult to recognise the valuable lessons learnt through hardship. It's a difficult line to walk, but one we need to navigate if we are to confront injustice without denying the voices of those who speak from an experience of it.

A Catholic friend is fond of encouraging me to 'enter into the mystery', and this phrase seems fitting here, as we wrestle with the relationship between suffering and joy, oppression and insight.

† God, help us be open to the lessons learned in suffering, without becoming closed to the pain that births them. May we enter into the mystery – not to find answers, but to find you.

For further thought

• How might our understanding of Jesus' suffering on the cross influence how we react to suffering in the lives of individual Christians – including our own?

November

Thursday 26 November
Sharing

Romans 12:11-15

Rejoice with those who rejoice; mourn with those who mourn. (verse 15)

This passage is one of my favourite bits of Paul's letters – one that my husband and I chose to have read at our wedding – mainly because it is great general advice for life as a Christian, whether in the context of marriage or not. Here we see again the communal joy illustrated in the parables above, this time being commended to the church in Rome as the way that Christians should live – sharing their lives, both in times of joy and sorrow.

In the age of social networking, we know more and more about the trivial details of other people's lives, and yet this facade of knowledge often conceals a lack of awareness about the things that truly matter. I imagine that Paul would have little time for this shallow engagement with one another. If we are to be an authentic community, as he wanted the recipients of his letters to be, then we need to make ourselves deliberately vulnerable in sharing both the ups and downs, as well as being ready to hear those things from others.

But while for some of us it seems natural to want to communicate news, good and bad, others prefer not to share the details of their lives more widely than necessary, often with good reason. This isn't about airing our dirty laundry in public though, nor just about boasting of grandchildren's latest successes! It is a demonstration of our commitment to each other as sisters and brothers in Christ. This emotional investment brings its share of deep sadness but it also expands our capacity for joy.

† Jesus, who attended weddings and cried at tombs, may we share in the raw, intense stuff of life and meet you there, plumbing fresh depths and reaching new heights in the service of your people.

For further thought

- How does your (lack of) openness to allowing others into your life, and entering into the lives of others, affect your experience of church?

Friday 27 November
Transforming

Acts 3:1-10

So the man gave them his attention, expecting to get something from them. Then Peter said, 'Silver or gold I do not have, but what I do have I give you. In the name of Jesus Christ of Nazareth, walk.' (verses 5-6)

The thing that strikes me about this encounter is the discrepancy between what the disabled man expected, and what he got! If people then were anything like people now, I don't doubt that often this man would sit at the temple gate for long periods without being given anything. However, when Peter and John came along, the way they addressed him created an expectation that he would receive something from them. And he did, but not in the manner he'd anticipated! His 'best case scenario' was to receive a few coins, rather than being ignored. But the disciples blew this out of the water, offering not financial support but physical healing.

Surely there is a lesson here for us. What are our expectations in terms of encounter with God? Do we have a 'best case scenario' that is shaped by a litany of disappointments over the years? Are we jaded, consciously or otherwise, by our experiences of the world? God doesn't want to drop a few coins in front of us and walk on. God wants to make eye contact, and speak into our situation in a way that transforms; perhaps starting by redefining our understanding of what it means for God to 'speak'!

This is not without challenge, though: the disabled man's livelihood was based on his physical circumstance. His healing meant finding a new way to make a living, and indeed building a new independent life. We too may find that an encounter with Jesus turns things upside down, but it's a risk worth taking.

† God, your kingdom is upside down and your intervention in our lives has a similar effect. Help us embrace this and surrender our own 'best case scenario' to your transformative vision for our lives.

For further thought
• Consider what transformation might look like in your life. What changes would you welcome? Which would you shy away from?

November

335

Saturday 28 November
Thanking

Revelation 19:1-9

Then I heard what sounded like a great multitude, like the roar of rushing waters and like loud peals of thunder, shouting: 'Hallelujah! For our Lord God Almighty reigns. Let us rejoice and be glad and give him glory!' (part of verses 6 and 7)

And so we reach Revelation. Amid the confusing talk of blood and prostitutes comes this statement: the wedding of the Lamb is here, rejoice! A number of Jesus' parables compare the kingdom of God to a wedding feast or banquet. Used again here, this image is intended to denote ultimate joy; creation is renewed and the nations live in peace, with Christ upon the throne. It is this fulfilment that all our present experiences of joy anticipate. With this in mind, we must recognise joy as a choice – not something that happens to us, but an orientation towards the world that we intentionally adopt. Indeed, to opt for joy is to make the kingdom of God present even now.

Books with titles like '1000 Places to See Before You Die' perpetuate the myth that real life, real joy, can be found only 'out there'. Everyday life is merely a hiatus, while we save up for our next experience. Instead, though, we should be seeking joy in the seemingly unremarkable things of life! It seems to me that the key is gratitude. Gratitude is described by Ann Voskamp as 'the manifestation of our Yes! to grace' (*One Thousand Gifts*, Zondervan, 2010). The challenge is to recognise and take responsibility for our own role in our joy. It's an attitude to be nurtured, that even amid difficult circumstances we can seek out opportunities to practise joy. What seemed unremarkable is transformed when we acknowledge it as God's gift to us, and in doing so, so are we.

† Generous God, forgive us for the times we fail to see the causes for joy that surround us. Open our eyes, our hands, our hearts to recognise and receive your gifts.

For further thought

• As Ann Voskamp suggests, nurture an attitude of thanksgiving by keeping a list of good things in your day-to-day life.

Readings in Luke

1 Preparing the people

This week's notes are by **John Birch**

John Birch is a Methodist Local Preacher based in South Wales. He spends a lot of time writing prayers, worship resources and Bible studies for his website faithandworship.com. He has written 700 prayers for leaders of worship who use the lectionary readings, and is constantly amazed at where in the world these resources are used and how God has blessed lives through them. John has also contributed to several denominational magazines, and even been translated into Swedish!

Sunday 29 November (Advent Sunday)
The enquiring mind

Luke 1:1-4

With this in mind, since I myself have carefully investigated everything from the beginning, I too decided to write an orderly account for you, most excellent Theophilus, so that you may know the certainty of the things you have been taught. (verses 3-4)

When my son studied history, he learned the crucial importance of referring to original sources of information wherever possible. Only by going back to those early accounts could he begin to form an unbiased opinion of historical events. I heard an academic say she had grown up with a particular story about a family friend, and had accepted this as true. It was only later, when her enquiring mind caused her to delve a little deeper, that she discovered that the real truth was somewhat different.

An enquiring mind is important for getting to the truth of Christianity. Relying on half-forgotten stories from Sunday school is not enough; they won't sustain us when faith is challenged. Over this week we will come across several people who asked questions of God and got life-changing answers.

So here is Theophilus, who had heard conflicting stories about Jesus, engaging the mind of Luke, a true historian, keen to investigate and make 'an orderly account' so that Theophilus (and all who read his words) might know the truth and a growing faith be strengthened. An enquiring faith is one that grows!

† Lord, grant us a real enthusiasm for exploring scripture so that we might draw closer to you, and our faith grow in confidence.

November

Meet the family!

Luke 1:5-20

Then an angel of the Lord appeared to him, standing at the right side of the altar of incense. When Zechariah saw him, he was startled and was gripped with fear. But the angel said to him: 'Do not be afraid, Zechariah; your prayer has been heard.' (verses 11-13a)

Luke in his research brings us a little of the backstory. To better understand Mary's role in the Advent narrative we need to meet cousin Elizabeth and her husband Zechariah.

We all have a backstory, quite often affecting who we are. It might be about the people who introduced our parents to each other, what they did for a living, where we were born or even social status. I am here because my father's cousin introduced him to her friend, which of course to me was God's timing, and I have become the person I am because of many people's influence on my life, some better than others, no doubt!

Luke's backstory is about ordinary people and God's timing. Here is a faithfully married couple who had endured the social stigma of childlessness for many years. We know how serious this was by the angel's words to Zechariah, and can only guess that their daily prayer for years had been for the gift of a child. Despite advancing years they had never entirely given up hope.

There are special places in our world where we seem to sense the real presence of God. For me it's often early in the morning, walking my dog in the countryside. For Zechariah, it was the inner court of the Temple, out of sight and with the scent of incense around him. That's where decades of prayer were finally answered and Zechariah was rendered speechless. That was God's timing!

'Do not be afraid,' says God. 'Your prayer has been heard' (verse 13).

† Lord, grant us patience in our prayer and the knowledge that all our prayers are heard by you, and in your good time will be answered.

For further thought

• Think about how easily you give in to the temptation of thinking God will never answer your prayers, and bring to mind Zechariah and Elizabeth.

Tuesday 1 December
The bigger picture

Luke 1:21-25

When his time of service was completed, [Zechariah] returned home. After this his wife Elizabeth became pregnant and for five months remained in seclusion. 'The Lord has done this for me,' she said. 'In these days he has shown his favour and taken away my disgrace among the people.'
(verses 23-25)

Much as I like to think I'm interested in world affairs, particularly in countries where people suffer daily hardship or persecution, I have to confess that most of the time I am more concerned about myself, and the day-to-day rhythm of my life. I have to stop now and then and remind myself that I am a small, but in God's eyes important, part of a bigger picture!

Take Elizabeth and Zechariah as an example. He was just one of thousands of priests, she a childless wife scorned for being barren. They longed for the child that would make their marriage complete in the eyes of their neighbours. There was nothing to make them stand out, other than they were part of God's plan for the salvation of humankind!

The bigger picture was about the fulfilment of God's purpose and promises for humankind, where Elizabeth's miraculous pregnancy would be an encouragement to Mary as she pondered her own obedience to God, and their son John would be the one who announced the coming of Jesus as Messiah.

Being faithful in service and persistent in prayer, these two ordinary people found that, although God acts on a large scale, he uses us and takes care of our small but important human concerns.

We are part of a bigger picture, however insignificant we might feel, but every selfless act, word of encouragement or giving of time brings a blessing into the world. And in giving, we are blessed.

† Gracious God, we thank you that each one of us is a part of your eternal plan.
   Use us in our daily walk of faith to bring a blessing to all those we meet.

For further thought

• If you struggle to see where you are in God's bigger picture, consider that where you are right now might be where God needs you!

Wednesday 2 December
How will this happen?

Luke 1:26-38

The angel went to her and said, 'Greetings, you who are highly favoured! The Lord is with you.' Mary was greatly troubled at his words and wondered what kind of greeting this might be. (verses 28-29)

Luke is moving the story forward now. Having introduced us to Elizabeth and Zechariah, we now meet Mary, an ordinary and faithful young girl for whom God has even bigger plans!

When I was working in industry, it was always with some trepidation that I answered a call from the boss that began with, 'John, we need to have a chat, please!' It either meant I'd done something wrong, or more likely that a task no one else wanted was about to drop on my desk. So I can empathise with Mary when faced with this greeting from God, and to what it might lead. Just as I might want reassurance from my boss that he was confident in my ability to complete what was being asked of me, so Mary wants to know how God plans to use her, considering that she is engaged to Joseph and, as yet, a virgin.

And it's that bigger picture again, because Mary's cousin Elizabeth is miraculously already five months pregnant. If Mary finds it difficult to envisage God working such a miracle in *her* life, then here's proof. With God, says the angel, nothing is impossible.

I never had much choice in accepting the tasks allotted to me but Mary could have refused despite the assurances she had been given. However, God had faith in her and, just as important, she had faith in God.

'I am the Lord's servant,' Mary answered. 'May your word to me be fulfilled.'

† May our response to your call on our lives, God, not be to hesitate or argue, but simply to accept that you do not ask anything of us that we cannot achieve.

For further thought
• How carefully do we plan out our lives? Do we welcome the possibility of God intervening and taking us on a different path?

Thursday 3 December
Comparing notes

Luke 1:39-45

At that time Mary got ready and hurried to a town in the hill country of Judea, where she entered Zechariah's home and greeted Elizabeth. When Elizabeth heard Mary's greeting, the baby leaped in her womb, and Elizabeth was filled with the Holy Spirit. In a loud voice she exclaimed: 'Blessed are you among women, and blessed is the child you will bear!'
(verses 39-42)

Those of us who rely on social media to keep in touch like nothing better than to log on and see photographs posted of loved ones on holiday or celebrating. They bring a family closer together in spirit, and we can share in the joy of the moment by leaving comments that can become a long-distance conversation.

It's a very human instinct to want to let others know good news. Not only does it allow the givers to share their joy with friends and relatives, but it brightens the day for those who are receivers.

Luke brings the strands of his backstory together today, as an excited Mary makes her way to Elizabeth's house to share her good news and compare notes and, in doing so, receives another affirmation that this is indeed a blessing from God. You can perhaps imagine the conversation that Luke doesn't give us – Elizabeth's excitement at hearing her cousin's news, Mary looking to Elizabeth for advice as to how she might best look after herself in pregnancy, and discussions perhaps about Joseph and his response to all that's happened. There would have been a lot to talk about!

But at the heart of their joy is the fact that both realise they are part of something much bigger, something wonderful that God is doing in their lives and for the whole world.

Our news might not be so groundbreaking but if God has blessed us we should be excited enough to share our joy!

† Lord, we rejoice in the joy of these two women, and all blessings received through the sharing of good news with those whom we love.

For further thought

• Are we sometimes hesitant to share good news? Why might that be, and do we have to be sensitive at times?

Friday 4 December
A song of joy

Luke 1:46-56

And Mary said: 'My soul glorifies the Lord and my spirit rejoices in God my Saviour, for he has been mindful of the humble state of his servant. From now on all generations will call me blessed...' (verses 46-48)

We are quite reserved in the West. In many cultures – particularly in the Middle East and Africa – where there's cause for joy, women will make a real song and dance about it. They know the meaning of celebration, and it's more than sending a congratulatory card!

So for Mary to break into song when sharing her joy with Elizabeth is an absolutely natural thing for her to do, and the song is full of Old Testament references that she would have been familiar with, particularly the song of Hannah in 1 Samuel 2 that celebrates the birth of Samuel and all that God was going to do through him.

Now these two women celebrate what God is going to do through the birth not only of Jesus but John as well. There's a lovely, almost throwaway, line at the end of this passage where Luke tells us that Mary stayed for three months, covering the time when Elizabeth would give birth. Is this the servant Mary that she sings about serving the needs of her cousin? If so, it's a lovely thought!

The expected birth of any baby is an occasion for joy, not only for a family, but because of the potential that lies within that child to become a part of the bigger picture of God's purposes for humankind. We know the story of John and Jesus, but what about the potential that lies within our own children and grandchildren?

† Eternal Father, we pray for all children born today that, wherever they are, the potential within them might be realised.

For further thought

• We need to ask ourselves as we grow older if as individuals we have become the people that God would have us be, and ask for grace to achieve our true potential.

Preparing the people

Luke 1:57-66

All the neighbours were filled with awe, and throughout the hill country of Judea people were talking about all these things. Everyone who heard this wondered about it, asking, 'What then is this child going to be?' For the Lord's hand was with him. (verses 65-66)

I am the father of two children, now grown up into adulthood, and grandfather to three little ones, and I'm beginning to find myself asking the same question I've asked before: 'What are these children going to grow up to be?'

Some parents 'hothouse' their children in a particular direction through education or even into particular careers. Others are much more relaxed and encourage them to discover their own strengths and weaknesses, allowing them to develop and find the career best suited to their skills and personalities.

Do we want our children to be 'successful' in the eyes of the world or are we content if they can simply grow up being happy, whether living in wealth or poverty? Being a parent can be stressful!

Elizabeth and Mary might have shared a smile when the neighbours began gossiping about this miraculous gift of a child. What indeed would he grow up to be? What these two women knew with certainty was that God's Spirit was in John and he would be used in a special way. This was a child who would prepare a nation for the coming of the Messiah, a child whose name would be remembered for all generations – not for worldly riches, as he was to become a hermit in the desert, but because of the riches of God's love evident in his life!

† Lord, how important John's role was to be, introducing a world to its Saviour! Grant us the faith and strength to do likewise when called to do so.

For further thought

• What do you consider 'success' in this life to be? Is it more than the accumulation of wealth?

Readings in Luke
2 A child is born

This week's notes are by **Sham P Thomas**

Revd Dr Sham P Thomas is an ordained priest of the Mar Thoma Church. He did his doctoral research in the area of Media and Religion at Edinburgh, Scotland, and was a Professor of Communication at the United Theological College, Bangalore, India. At present he serves the Mar Thoma Parish in Secunderabad, India and continues to lead retreats and conferences.

Sunday 6 December
Naming without being named

Luke 1:67-80

And you, child, will be called a prophet of the Most High; for you will go on before the Lord to prepare the way for him, to give knowledge of salvation through forgiveness of their sins... (verses 76-77)

Advent is a clarion call for preparation and proclamation of the child Jesus. Grateful and faith-filled expectation of the future flavours the present and makes life relevant. In this Advent season, may we be challenged to consider and proclaim God who came as a child and who will come again as Lord. This week highlights people who prayerfully and expectantly waited for the coming of the Messiah and themselves became part of God's salvific act in Jesus the Christ.

Despite the prophecy that Zechariah would be dumb until the birth of a son, Zechariah's first words ('God is gracious') came on naming his son John. As soon as his voice is restored he begins praising God. Once we experience God as gracious, we cannot but acknowledge it with our mouth. Zechariah relinquished his name and legacy by consciously opting to name his son John. He is not addressing the child as his son, but what he would become in relation to God almighty – that is, as the one who would pave the way for the Messiah. In other words, he wanted his son to gain a name for what he does for God and God's Messiah.

† Lord, in your continued favour lead us and guide us to walk the path of our ancestors. May our acts proclaim you rather than ourselves. All honour and glory be yours alone. Amen

No room for the child

Luke 2:1-7

And she gave birth to her firstborn, a son. She wrapped him in cloths, and placed him in a manger, because there was no guest room available for them. (verse 7)

Luke presents the birth of Jesus in a surprisingly brief manner. The entire Gospel is about Jesus, but details about his birth are inconspicuous. Contrary to popular imagination, Luke does not suggest that Jesus was born in a manger; interestingly, the place of his birth does not receive a mention. Does it mean that where Jesus was born was rather insignificant when compared to why he was born and how he had lived? Luke, however, mentions that Jesus was denied a space at his birth.

Luke does not suggest that there was no room in the inn. Probably the innkeeper had various constraints and considerations and thereby denied Joseph and Mary that requested space. The other occupants of the inn might have had concerns about taking in a woman in labour. Luke also suggests that Joseph and Mary were travelling to Bethlehem as Joseph belonged to the family of David. In short, the entire vicinity would have been occupied by Joseph's kith and kin yet the irony was that he was handicapped for space for the birth of his son. This probably places Jesus as a rejected child from his birth. This is not to romanticise all those who are born homeless but to emphasise the lack of sensitivity, and the selfish considerations, that denied space to Jesus and the many other children of this world. Jesus represents all homeless children on the one hand and on the other convicts us to give space for God in our lives.

† Lord God, you became a vulnerable and homeless babe for our sake. May we not deny you your rightful space in our lives and may we strive to abolish homelessness in this world. Amen

For further thought

- How do we understand the rejection of Jesus from the time of his birth? How can we celebrate Christmas meaningfully?

December

345

The breaking news: the birth

Luke 2:8-20

The shepherds said to one another, 'Let's go to Bethlehem and see this thing that has happened, which the Lord has told us about.' So they hurried off and found Mary and Joseph, and the baby, who was lying in the manger. (part of verses 15 and 16)

The birth of Jesus, which happened in the time of Emperor Augustus, was not announced in the Roman imperial manner. Heaven defied imperial protocol in breaking the news of the saviour's birth to a group of shepherds. This radical subversion in the sharing of news is indicative of the explosive and controversial content of the news itself. The angel declared that, contrary to the belief that Caesar was the saviour of the world and that the Roman Empire would establish peace, the vulnerable babe of the manger is the saviour who would enrol the whole world to the heavenly empire of joy and peace. Again, peace is portrayed as God's favour to chosen people, rather than as an achievement of the Roman emperor through might. Jesus, in other words, is the alternative emperor and he is initiating a new empire of salvation.

On receiving this news, the response of the shepherds was majestic. They put their livelihood at stake by setting aside the sheep under their watch in order to go to Bethlehem to visit the newborn saviour. By prioritising this journey of faith over their everyday sustenance, the shepherds had become members of the manger. They saw the saviour and savoured the meeting. They returned praising and witnessing to the wonder of Christmas. The manger is an invitation to meet God's messenger and become messengers by reflecting his message.

† You announce your Son in varied and unpredictable ways, O Lord! Help us to value the privilege of being recipients of this good news. May we seek to meet you where you are and reflect the resultant joy. Amen

For further thought

- Shepherds went to the manger to seek the saviour; soldiers were commissioned to slaughter him. What is our approach to the babe: stranglers or seekers?

Wednesday 9 December
Change-maker child!

Luke 2:21-35

Sovereign Lord, as you have promised, you may now dismiss your servant in peace. For my eyes have seen your salvation, which you have prepared in the sight of all nations... (verses 29-31)

Presentation of baby Jesus in the Temple and a prophecy about him lays the theme for today's biblical narrative. Like Zechariah, Jesus' parents named him as God commanded, relinquishing their prerogative in this matter. They brought him to the Temple to integrate him as part of the covenantal community of God. Their poverty limited them to offering the sacrifice prescribed for the poor (Leviticus 12:8). This did not deter them from making an effort to prepare the ground for their child to get connected to the faith resources and religious network.

While presenting the child, they received a prophecy about him. It is interesting to note that they have not received any direct messages from God since the child was born. Instead, it was communicated through the community of witnesses, like the shepherds at the manger and spirit-filled individuals like Simeon in the Temple. Whether parents would entertain receiving good news about their children from non-relatives and others is a challenge today!

Simeon, who affirmed the change-maker child, is a symbol of faith and hope. He affirmed the future of the world by upholding the sapling of God's salvation for the world. He did not see the fulfilment of God's plan, yet he was content to be a torchbearer of the great beginning.

Praising a child for his/her God-given future is an antidote to the cynicism that may set in for many people towards the end of their life. Affirming the children and empowering them for great things is the greatest blessing one can bestow on the future of the world.

† Lord, help us to internalise the cost of bearing salvation in the world. May our suffering for the Lord be a cause for blessing. Amen

For further thought
• What is the extra mile we can walk to ensure the spiritual growth of the next generation?

December

347

Thursday 10 December
An evangelist of the babe

Luke 2:36-40

Coming up to them at that very moment, she gave thanks to God and spoke about the child to all who were looking forward to the redemption of Jerusalem. (verse 38)

Seeing Jesus in the Temple, the prophet Anna also praised God. Simeon was privileged to have received a prophecy of seeing the Messiah in his lifetime, thus giving him hope to live on and a future to await. Even though Anna had the edge over Simeon because her tribe and father's name are mentioned, she was less fortunate as she did not have any promises or prophecy to bank upon. With her experience of widowhood after only seven years' marriage, Anna could have ended up embittered and broken.

However, she had transformed tragedy into a beautiful life by devoting her life to the Temple and engaging in fasting and prayer. For her, fasting and prayer were not for any particular agenda or on the basis of any promises. This has elevated Anna as a symbol of a life of prayer and faith without any particular assurances about an unknown future.

She recognised the child for what he would be and shared the good news. Anna seems to be the first evangelist who witnessed to Jesus even before he started his ministry. Her end days testify to the most fruitful life of faith.

† Lord of the unexpected, make our fragile life fruitful by enabling us to be faithful witnesses of your salvation. May we be faithful even when we have no assurances about the future. Amen

For further thought
• Can we attend worship, pray and fast without any particular agenda or goals? Are these an end in themselves?

Friday 11 December
Wonder Boy

Luke 2:41-52

'Why were you searching for me?' he asked. 'Didn't you know that I had to be in my Father's house?' (verse 49)

This story is the only incident reported from Jesus' childhood in the four Gospels, and it throws light on Jesus' life formation. Mary and Joseph followed certain religious practices and tried to inculcate such practices in their child as well. In this sense, they appear to be model parents in transmitting religious practices that are crucial for their identity formation. Jesus used this opportunity to be in the Temple, to hear and converse with the scholars and teachers about matters of faith. In the end he revealed his growing awareness of what he was and where he should be. Jesus realised his identity at the age of twelve. How wonderful it would it be if our children define themselves in relation to God even before they become teenagers!

This Temple episode of Jesus, however, is puzzling on many counts. Why is it that Jesus remained in the Temple without letting his parents know? Was he thinking that his parents should not have returned in search of him? More important, why did the parents simply assume that Jesus was travelling back with them? Could it be a warning that we should not take our younger generation for granted and assume that we all are on the same page? Is there a suggestion that, if Jesus' parents could make an apparent mistake with regard to their child, all other parents should be more alert and careful in bringing up their children?

† Lord God, help us to understand ourselves in relation to you. Enable us to recognise where we ought to be in each moment of our life. Amen

For further thought

- In what way do we take the young generation for granted? How can we avoid it?

Saturday 12 December
Preparation without pretension

Luke 3:1-20

The people were waiting expectantly and were all wondering in their hearts if John might possibly be the Messiah. John answered them all, 'I baptise you with water. But one who is more powerful than I will come, the straps of whose sandals I am not worthy to untie.' (part of verse 16)

As part of preparing the way for the Messiah, John became an itinerant preacher calling for repentance and fruitful living. Repentance, for John, is a radical examination of and retrospection on one's personal and public life. It is a required of all and no one would be barred from the impending judgements because of their ethnic or religious heritage. The faith of the ancestors will be honoured only when it is emulated by succeeding generations. People who claim great ancestry in faith should examine their lives closely.

Repentance, however, is only a part of life and hence needs to be complemented with a reorientation in life. In response to the crowd's question, John says: 'whoever has two shirts should share with the one who has none; and anyone who has food should do the same' (verse 11).

Perhaps John was advocating being generous with half of all one's resources. However, the radical nature of his call becomes clear when it is realised that John was asking the crowd to share whatever they possessed. Owning just two coats is not an excuse for not giving one to the needy. Sharing, thus, becomes a fundamental aspect of a fruitful life. John also suggested that a moral, ethical and simple lifestyle would bring in an era of corruption-free world.

† Lord, may we prepare your way rather than getting in your way. Help us to help others to become greater than us in your ministry. Amen

For further thought

- During Advent, how relevant is John's advice on sharing and contentment in life? How do these challenge a consumption-oriented and market-driven Christmas season?

Readings in Luke

3 Preparing the way

This week's notes are by **Anthony Loke**

Revd Dr Anthony Loke is an ordained minister with the Methodist Church in Malaysia. He lectures in the area of the Old Testament and is also Dean of Studies in the Seminari Theoloji Malaysia, the largest ecumenical seminary in the country. Anthony has written six books and is currently writing on the book of Judges. He is married to King Lang, who is a Doctor of Education candidate in Christian Education and teaches English. They have two adult children, Charis and Markus.

Sunday 13 December
The baptism of Jesus

Luke 3:21-38

As he was praying, heaven was opened and the Holy Spirit descended on him in bodily form like a dove. And a voice came from heaven: 'You are my Son, whom I love; with you I am well pleased.' **(part of verses 21-22)**

Jesus knew that the battles ahead of him would be intense. He would need to make preparations. One way was to identify himself fully with the people he came to save. When his cousin John the Baptist was baptising people in the river Jordan, Jesus came to him and submitted himself to a baptism that was not required of him. Was Jesus merely showing support for his cousin's ministry? In doing so, Jesus was identifying himself with the common people who had flocked to John. The religious leaders had stayed away. Jesus, in undergoing the baptism, was saying to the common people, 'I'm one of you'.

Yet there is a deeper meaning to Jesus' action. He was identifying himself with the whole of humankind. The one who was sinless chose to be one with sinners; he who never sinned and therefore did not need the water baptism chose to be baptised on our behalf. Right at the outset of his public ministry, Jesus had already identified himself with sinful humanity. The voice from heaven showed that God the Father was pleased with his Son and his upcoming ministry.

† Lord, thank you that Jesus came into this world and fully identified himself with all humanity. Amen

Monday 14 December
The temptations of Jesus

Luke 4:1-13

The devil said to Jesus, 'If you are the Son of God, tell this stone to become bread.' Jesus answered, 'It is written: "Man shall not live on bread alone."' (verses 3-4)

The temptations of Jesus represent his final preparation before a face-to-face encounter with his enemy, the devil. Victory would set the tone for the rest of his ministry; defeat here would signal a rout for God's plan of salvation. The Gospel accounts record three tests as Jesus was tempted by the devil. The first temptation represented the physical need of hunger. 'If you are the Son of God,' the devil suggests, 'would not God provide for your physical needs?' Jesus answers that there were more important things in life than just physical food, drawing from Deuteronomy 8:3. The second temptation represented the psychological need for power: 'If you worship me, all these things would be yours.' Jesus' answer that we should worship only God and no one else was drawn from Deuteronomy 6:13. The third temptation represented the emotional need for security. 'If you are the Son of God, throw yourself down and see whether God will carry you to safety.' Jesus' answer that one should not simply put God to the test was drawn from Deuteronomy 6:16.

Like the driving tests required of learners, one must pass all the tests before one can legally drive on the roads. Jesus passed the three temptations with flying colours and we are told that the devil left him until an opportune time. There is victory today but the battle continues to be long drawn.

† Lord, there is no freedom from temptations in this life, as there was not for Jesus. Give us the strength to overcome them, as Jesus did. Amen

For further thought

• Jesus had no other special resources to counter the devil's claims and lies but the word of God.

Tuesday 15 December
The homecoming of Jesus

Luke 4:14-30

The Spirit of the Lord is on me, because he has anointed me to proclaim good news to the poor. (part of verse 18)

Jesus' preparation was complete. Filled with the power of the Spirit, he returned to the district of Galilee and began preaching and teaching. It had been only a matter of time before he returned to his boyhood town of Nazareth. News of his ministry as a famed preacher and wonder worker had spread to the people of Nazareth and everyone was waiting to hear from the local boy who 'made good'.

The day came when Jesus went to the local synagogue, where he was invited to read and expound the scriptures. The text was taken from Isaiah 61:1-2. Jesus' comment that the scripture was fulfilled that day in their hearing elicited a strong response. At first, the townsfolk were amazed at the gracious words that came out of Jesus' mouth. But their response quickly turned ugly – Jesus had told them that he would not perform the very signs and wonders that they were hoping to witness.

Jesus had a good reason for not repeating what he was performing elsewhere in Galilee: his townsfolk were there only to see the spectacular and not to hear the gospel message that Jesus wanted to say to them. They took him to the brow of the hill and attempted to throw him off – but he walked right through their midst. They had rejected him, and he in turn rejected them.

† Lord, we know that we will face difficulties and rejections in our work for you. Help us to persevere in our task. Amen

For further thought

• It is never easy to minister in our hometown where everyone 'knows' us.

The authority of Jesus

Luke 4:31-37

'Be quiet!' Jesus said sternly. 'Come out of him!' Then the demon threw the man down before them all and came out without injuring him.
(verse 35)

In these verses, we see the other aspect of Jesus' earthly ministry: Jesus' powerful works through signs and wonders. These deeds are like signposts in that they point people to God. By themselves, signs and wonders are inadequate because the devil can also perform them. Signs and wonders need interpretation. Hence, they go together hand in hand with the preaching of the Word. The preaching tells people about God; signs and wonder authenticate the preaching.

In the synagogue at Capernaum, Jesus encountered a man who was possessed by a demon or evil spirit. Jesus' presence triggered a loud response from the spirit. In this particular case, the spirit responded openly because it recognised that Jesus had come into the world to destroy the works of the devil. The spirit knew his time living in the man was up.

Jesus' response is an example for us to follow. He discerned that the commotion was due to the presence of an evil spirit and not a case of insanity or mental illness. Jesus delivered the man in a simple but effective way – he commanded the spirit to be quiet and leave the man. Jewish exorcists tended to use long spells invoking the names of the Lord (see also Acts 19:13-16). Sometimes the simple but effective way is to speak on the authority of Jesus and command the spirits to be quiet and come out of the person.

† Lord, help me to be a channel through which Jesus' power and healing can flow to others in need. Amen

For further thought

- The evil spirit recognised the authority of Jesus as the Son of God. We are to minister in that same authority granted to us.

Thursday 17 December
The power of Jesus

Luke 4:38-44

So he bent over her and rebuked the fever, and it left her. She got up at once and began to wait on them. (verse 39)

In these next few verses, we see another aspect of the signs and wonders performed by Jesus: his miraculous healing of sickness and disease. The first incident concerned the healing of Peter's mother-in-law's high fever. Jesus rebuked the fever; we do not know whether or not the fever was due to the presence of an evil spirit that had to be rebuked. But the reaction was immediate – the fever left her and her temperature returned to normal. To show that the cure was complete and instantaneous, she got up and served a meal for Jesus and his disciples!

On that same day, many other people with various diseases and sicknesses were brought to Jesus to be healed. Occasionally, demons came out from the person shouting and revealing who Jesus was but were commanded to be quiet. Jesus chose to heal everyone who was brought to him on that day. On other days, he did not heal at all. In John 5, we read of how Jesus healed only one man who was paralysed from birth but left untouched the rest at the pool of Bethesda. This reminds us that healing comes from God; God chooses when to heal and whom to heal. We can't dictate to God the manner of healing or the extent of the healing. We are only the channels of God's mercy and grace.

† Lord, help me to preach the gospel message in words and deeds that all people may hear and see Jesus. Amen

For further thought
• Jesus' ministry was a holistic one that emphasised both words and deeds.

Friday 18 December
The calling of Jesus

Luke 5:1-11

When Simon Peter saw this, he fell at Jesus' knees and said, 'Go away from me, Lord; I am a sinful man!' ... Then Jesus said to Simon, 'Don't be afraid; from now on you will fish for people.' (verse 8 and part of verse 10)

We often separate the holy from the secular and mistakenly think that only the holy is good. We also think that God is not interested in our daily routine and secular jobs. God is supposed to be interested only in our 'holy' work. In today's story, we see that God is not only interested in a person's life but also in his or her daily work and routine. Jesus still calls each one of us to serve him and we do not have to leave our secular work to answer his call, as we can still serve him from where we are.

On this occasion, Jesus was preaching to a crowd that had gathered. Because of the size, he got into Simon's boat to create some space. When the sermon was over, Jesus challenged Simon to cast into the deep waters. Simon's first response was that it would be a waste of time as they had caught nothing the whole night. But he did what he was told and hauled in a large catch. The size of the catch evoked Simon's second response as he dropped to his knees, 'Go away from me, Lord; I am a sinful man' (verse 8). This caused Jesus to throw in a second challenge to Simon, 'Don't just catch fish from now on; catch people for the kingdom of God'. The effect was amazing – not only Simon but the other fishermen 'left everything and followed him' (verse 11).

† Lord, whatever our task is, help us to work wholeheartedly serving you and not pleasing others. Amen

For further thought

• Jesus calls us from our daily work in order to serve him by using our skills and talents.

Saturday 19 December
The compassion of Jesus

Luke 5:12-16

Jesus reached out his hand and touched the man. 'I am willing,' he said. 'Be clean!' And immediately the leprosy left him. (verse 13)

In the ancient world, leprosy can refer to a wide range of skin diseases, some of which were curable while others were not. Because of its contagious nature, leprosy was widely feared. It could spread throughout the whole community if left untreated. In those days, there was only one remedy for leprosy – quarantine, which was total isolation from the rest of the community. Leper colonies were formed far away from society and lepers were required to identify themselves if they came near to others. In ancient Jewish society, the priests were chosen to be the sole authority in judging cases of leprosy and also to pronounce a person was cured after a close inspection (see Leviticus 13–14).

A leper confronted Jesus one day and begged to be made clean (verse 12). The leper was covered with leprosy and he was not sure if Jesus was willing to heal him but Jesus stretched out his hand and touched him. By touching him, Jesus bridged the distance between the leper and himself. Jesus' touch was also significant because nobody had touched the leper for years. Jesus' touch was one of compassion and love that brought healing not only to the leper's body but also to his soul. Jesus told the leper to obey the ceremonial laws by presenting himself to the priest and making a thank offering for his healing. The crowd got hold of the news of this healing and it spread like wildfire.

† Lord, I need to touch others as I am touched by you. Amen

For further thought
• The healing of the leper becomes a powerful testimony to the priests and the leper's family and friends.

Readings in Luke
4 The beginnings of ministry

This week's notes are by **Bola Iduoze**

Bola is a qualified accountant with over 18 years' experience in the marketplace. Bola co-manages a business consultancy firm with her husband and has also coached individuals and helped organisations achieve better financial management. Bola writes a weekly blog at www.inspirationwithpb.com with the aim of encouraging and building faith. Bola co-pastors Gateway Chapel, a Pentecostal church in Kent, UK. She grew up in Ibadan, Nigeria.

Sunday 20 December
Jesus the healer

Luke 5:17-26

When Jesus saw their faith, he said, 'Friend, your sins are forgiven.' The Pharisees and the teachers of the law began thinking to themselves, 'Who is this fellow who speaks blasphemy? Who can forgive sins but God alone?' Jesus knew what they were thinking and asked, 'Why are you thinking these things in your hearts?' (verses 20-22)

A man who was ill had friends who were keen enough to take time off to bring him to Jesus. They soon realised that there were many people around who wanted to hear or see Jesus. As usual with crowds, people come from far and near with different objectives. These men, however, had a motive. Their objective was not just to marvel at great things done to other people. They had a friend who required the touch of Jesus. They found a way, despite the obstacles, to get their friend to Jesus, and Jesus saw their faith. It is amazing to note that faith could be visible. Jesus saw faith then, and still sees faith today. He saw their faith, then forgave and healed their friend. Their actions demonstrated their faith in Jesus' ability to heal their friend. They were not disappointed.

After Jesus performed this healing, the Pharisees and teachers of law became convinced that he was blaspheming because he forgave sins. The Bible says Jesus knew what they were thinking (verse 22) and he addressed their hearts. Jesus knows what we think, and can address our thoughts as well as our actions.

† Lord I pray that you will help me develop in faith, that my actions will reflect my belief in you, and that the thoughts of my heart will always be pleasing to you.

You are cordially invited...

Luke 5:27-39

After this, Jesus went out and saw a tax collector by the name of Levi sitting at his tax booth. 'Follow me,' Jesus said to him, and Levi got up, left everything and followed him. (verses 27-28)

Jesus went out and saw a man called Levi. In modern-day terms, he would be someone we would consider a sinner because tax collectors often levied on people a higher tax figure than they reported, taking the cut and becoming rich. They were usually wealthy and so was Levi. He is clearly seen as a sinner by the religious leaders in this society. For Jesus to call such a person to follow him was beyond the comprehension of any Pharisee or teacher of the law. They were not interested in the fact that Jesus was out reaching many more people: they were more concerned about what they thought their religion would permit, or forbid.

Levi, though new to Christ, was ready and willing. The Bible says he 'left everything' and followed Jesus. He seemed to have been waiting for someone to invite him and bring him closer to the truth. He left his past wealth, sin and work to follow Jesus. Not just that, he threw a party that was so great and attracted a large crowd of people. All of a sudden, he opened up his circle of influence to Jesus.

Through Levi, other people came in contact with Jesus: all because Jesus was ready to go out of his comfort zone to invite a new person into the kingdom.

We also should go ahead and invite someone to Jesus.

† Lord, help me not to be a stumbling block to people who want to come closer to you. Help me learn to introduce people within my circle of influence to your kingdom without judging them.

For further thought

- Levi was ready to follow Jesus – just waiting for the instruction. Someone around you might be waiting for the invitation, so extend the invitation to them.

Tuesday 22 December
Looking for a reason to accuse?

Luke 6:1-11

On another Sabbath he went into the synagogue and was teaching, and a man was there whose right hand was shrivelled. The Pharisees and the teachers of the law were looking for a reason to accuse Jesus, so they watched him closely to see if he would heal on the Sabbath. (verses 6-7)

When I was studying accountancy in Lagos, Nigeria, I remember having a roommate who, though a believer, was always out to see what either I or other Christians were not doing right. She was sure that God's grace could not be extended to Christians like us because we did not follow the law closely enough!

In just the same way, the Pharisees were out to find what Jesus was not doing right. From my knowledge of scripture, the Pharisees seemed to have been so used to following God in a particular way that they could just not see or accept Jesus' style. They constantly followed Jesus, not for their own benefit, but to see what he was not doing right and accuse him about all his actions. They made this their own mission for living.

In our Bible verses today, the Pharisees first accused his disciples and then, as soon as he healed the man with the shrivelled right hand, they once more thought about how Jesus must have broken the law. Though Jesus had a wise way of dealing with them, it would have been very exhausting to have people looking out for all the things they could find fault with. It is also a shame that they never enjoyed what Jesus had to offer because of this accusatory mindset. Having a mind to accuse others at all times could damage your faith and walk with God.

† Lord, I pray that you will help me walk in love with all the people around me, that I may see people as you see them without being judgemental or accusatory of your people.

For further thought

- An accusatory mind will prevent a Christian from benefitting from God's great work. If not addressed, it can develop into further negative actions.

Wednesday 23 December
The source of power!

Luke 6:12-19

One of those days Jesus went out to a mountainside to pray, and spent the night praying to God. (verse 12)

I once heard a very senior pastor mention the fact that, though God does great miracles through him, he was not particularly special, he just knew how to relate with the source of the power and spent a lot of time in prayer. That day, I saw the reason for his being a great pastor. He consistently spent time with God. He used to say 'A prayer that touches heaven changes the earth.'

Jesus was going to choose his team, and was also going to stand before a large crowd from far and near, but he never did any of that without first spending time with God so as to have an understanding of the source of the displayed power. After this time of prayer, Jesus was able to heal, help those with evil spirits and set many captives free. Later in our reading for today, Luke says 'Power was coming from him' (verse 19). His prayer time yielded a huge result. The same goes for us today. The more time we spend with God, the more waves we make here on earth.

If we want to make choices that we will not regret, we need to spend time with God first. In choosing business partners, a marriage partner, ministry partners and team members, we need to commit genuinely to earnest prayers that will in turn produce tremendous guidance and subsequent results.

Do not forget: a prayer that touches heaven will change the earth!

† Dear Lord, give me the grace to spend more time with you in the secret place of prayer, so that I will reflect your will in my daily choices and decisions.

For further thought

• Power came from Jesus to touch others because Jesus touched the source of all power in prayers. Let us embrace this habit and see changes around us.

Thursday 24 December
There are better days ahead!

Luke 6:20-26

Blessed are you who hunger now, for you will be satisfied. Blessed are you who weep now, for you will laugh. (verse 21)

One of the greatest and most remarkable stories I learnt as a young Christian in higher education was that of a woman who was rejected by her family because she converted from another religion to Christianity. Things got very tough for her and, according to her, there were many times when she wondered whether the benefits of her new conversion in fact outweighed the challenge of daily living. From a very comfortable financial status, being sponsored by her dad, overnight she became extremely poor. Her siblings were no longer allowed to contact her; but she stood her ground for Jesus because she came across this scripture. Her hope was built on God's promise of better days ahead of her.

Just like this woman, every disciple and believer can have this great assurance that brighter and better days are ahead. That is one of the great purposes of Jesus' coming to this world. We are not meant to be men and women without hope of a better tomorrow. We are not meant to build all we have on our experience here on earth. In fact, when we suffer because of our salvation, it should give us more joy, knowing that we will never suffer in vain.

Jesus told his disciples to rejoice in days of difficulties and sadness because great is their reward in heaven (verse 23). We can rejoice now because of our hope of a better tomorrow. We can choose to leap for joy because we have a God who specialises in giving good rewards to everyone who stands up for him and suffers any loss.

† Lord, help me to remember your promise of reward when I am going through difficulties; give me the grace to stand for you as I go through the hard times in life.

For further thought

• Do not seek everybody's acceptance. It is all right to be hated by others when you stand for Jesus. Stand up for Jesus because, ultimately, it will pay.

Friday 25 December (Christmas Day)
The greatest gift

Luke 6:27-38

Forgive, and you will be forgiven. Give, and it will be given to you. A good measure, pressed down, shaken together and running over, will be poured into your lap. For with the measure you use, it will be measured to you.
(verses 37b-38)

Christmas is commemorated by the exchange of gifts. The sign of your love and thought for someone on Christmas Day is one of the gifts you give them. There is always a lot of joy and excitement leading to Christmas because we give and receive gifts but there is a tendency for many of us to give gifts only to people whom we know have the capacity to give back to us. A gift I always wanted as a little girl, which I also received, was a ten-day trip with my dad around the northern part of Nigeria.

God on this day gave us an instruction that he himself followed in giving us the greatest gift ever. God gave his son to save and reconcile us to himself. In verse 35, Jesus instructed that 'we should love our enemies and do good to them'; he also said we should lend to them without expecting to get anything back. It takes a lot to give to people who do not have the capacity to give to you, and expect nothing in return, but Jesus said that is the way we should behave. Whether at Christmas or otherwise, give genuine gifts from your heart without expecting anything from those you have given to, but only from God.

God gave his son to us, knowing the outcome, and used that opportunity to reconcile humankind to himself. He gave the greatest gift of all; nothing should be too difficult for us to give or sacrifice for others.

† Dear Lord, this Christmas, give me a genuine heart that will love my enemies, bless those who curse me and give without reservation.

For further thought

• Giving to people without reservation opens the door for receiving from God without reservation. Take the position first, and then receive the reward.

Come, listen, and do!

Luke 6:39-49

Why do you call me, 'Lord, Lord,' and do not do what I say? As for everyone who comes to me and hears my words and puts them into practice, I will show you what they are like. (verses 46-47)

The most frustrating thing in parenting is having a child who will hear the parents' instruction but choose not to obey them. There is always a reason why a parent will give an instruction and there is also a level of expectation the parent has when giving instruction to the child. The expectation is that the child will carry out the instructions given.

God has an expectation of us as his children as well. He is happy that we come to him but frustrated that, though some of us come, and also call him Lord, we do not listen, nor do we do what he has asked us to do. The word 'Lord' indicates complete submission and surrender, so calling God 'Lord' means that we should be willing and ready not just to come and hear but also to do God's will, to become practitioners of God's word and ways.

God is not just looking for people to come without the evidence of our true follower-ship – which is complete obedience. If we are truly followers of Jesus, complete obedience is not optional. In his teaching, Jesus stated that complete obedience will make us like the wise builder – someone who has laid a foundation on the rock – when life's challenges come (which, by the way, come to everybody). Those who are fully obedient to God will still be standing after challenges because their foundation is built on a rock!

Be a true listener and doer of God's instruction. Do not just pay lip service to followership.

† Lord, help me to be a true Christian, who comes to you to hear your word and do your will at all times, even when it is not convenient.

For further thought

- The turmoil of life comes to us all, but there is an assurance of stability for the person who chooses to hear God's words and obey them.

Following the star of Bethlehem

This week's notes are by **Tom Arthur**

Tom Arthur lives in Cardiff, Wales. An American Presbyterian serving the United Reformed Church in the UK, he is now retired, teaching New Testament Greek, painting and drawing and enjoying his grandchildren. He is the author of *The Year of the Lord's Favor: Proclaiming Grace in the Year of Luke.*

Sunday 27 December
The Word made flesh – our flesh

John 1:1-14
To all who did receive him ... he gave the right to become children of God. (part of verse 12)

I remember when I was a kid watching *The Lone Ranger* on our old black-and-white television. As the Lone Ranger and his side-kick Tonto ride off into the sunset after yet another victory over the forces of evil, one of the locals invariably asks, 'Who was that masked man?'

Much Christian theology is dominated by a similar question about the identity of Jesus. Who was he? What I have always found captivating about these verses is how the answer to this question becomes an answer to another question: 'Who am I?' The 'word', or 'wisdom', is what lights up our own lives, not Jesus'. John tells the story of the virgin birth to tell continuing generations something very important. In our discipleship we are the ones who are putting flesh on the Word of God. The story of Jesus is not one of a hero's adventures, written for our entertainment, but the story of all those who feed the hungry, mend the broken and find the lost. John's Gospel invites us to get down on our knees and pray: 'Who am I?'

† Transfiguring God, let your word be born in me.

Monday 28 December
Jesus' hokey-cokey

Acts 11:27-30

The disciples, as each one was able, decided to provide help for the brothers and sisters living in Judea. (Acts 11.29)

I was presiding at worship a few weeks ago in the church we joined after I retired. It was an all-age service, so I prepared the bits of the service so that they would be accessible to our rather large group of youngsters. For instance, I rewrote the words to the 'hokey-pokey (which here in the UK we call the 'hokey-cokey). What I didn't know until we started singing it was that in the UK we know a chorus to the song that's not in the American version: 'Oh, the hokey-cokey,/Oh, the hokey-cokey,/Oh, the hokey cokey,/ Knees bend, arms stretch, ra ra ra!'

The congregation went wild, with enthusiastic bodies joining lyrics usually sung only in the pubs. I joined in as best as I could – in many ways the congregation took off without me. And they still talk about this as one of the most truly 'worshipful' moments they've had here. It was almost charismatic, and, I must confess, a bit scary.

My Hebrew professor in my seminary days described the Hebrew word for 'know' (*yadah*) as the Hebrew hokey-cokey: you 'put your whole self in'. This is what the disciples find themselves doing in our Acts reading. Each according to their means, they 'put their whole self in', enthusiastically, to the work of supporting the impoverished believers back in Jerusalem. This a moment of 'incarnation' for them, putting flesh on the Word of God by finding the centre of who they are in a compassionate relationship with others.

† Plant your Spirit in us, O God, that we might be knit together as the living presence of Christ in our world.

For further thought

• What was the most recent experience you had that you would call 'truly worshipful'?

Tuesday 29 December
Incarnate and transcendent

Romans 12.16-21

Live in harmony with one another ... if your enemy is hungry, feed him.
(verses 16 and 20)

My father suffered from Alzheimer's disease. One of the last things to disappear was his gifted imagination – his poetry, for instance. Not long before he had to move to the nursing home, he wrote this simple acrostic:

Hurt, we need a mother

Errant, we need a father

Alone, we need another

Lost, we need a star

In Matthew's version of the Christmas story we follow a star to discover God's presence in our humanity, a presence that continues, as Paul says in Romans, in those who live their lives together as the living body of Christ, in reconciliation, in lives that dismantle the barriers that divide us. This is incarnational life, an embeddedness of the Word in human community. But it is also breathtakingly transcendent. We need healing, and for that we require a vision and an imagination pointing beyond our isolated selves: a star.

† Open our lives to a world beyond our small vision for ourselves, that we might come together in peace and wholeness.

For further thought

• Make up your own acrostic poem, using a familiar Christmas word. Share it, if you like, on our Facebook group page www.facebook.com/freshfromtheword.

Wednesday 30 December
New clothes

Galatians 3:23-29

So in Christ Jesus you are all children of God through faith, for all of you who were baptised into Christ have clothed yourselves with Christ. (verses 26-27)

One of my favourite cartoons from *Mad* magazine has Fester Bestertester sitting at a kitchen table with his friend Karbuncle complaining that 'National Gorilla Suit Day' is just a gimmick invented by gorilla suit manufacturers to sell more gorilla suits. Then a woman comes through the door, throws off her 'woman' costume to reveal there is a real gorilla inside, then chases Fester Bestertester round the table and beats him to a pulp. Then a gorilla dressed in the woman's pinny comes to the door, throws off the gorilla suit to reveal again that there is a real gorilla inside, who chases Fester round the table and beats him to a pulp again. The cartoon goes through various hilarious permutations of this scene, always ending with a gorilla beating Fester Bestertester to a pulp. (*MAD's Maddest Artist: Don Martin Bounces Back*, Signet, 1963).

When Paul in Romans says in baptism we have clothed ourselves in Christ, does he mean we have put on a Jesus Christ suit similar to the costumes worn on National Gorilla Suit Day? Of course not. Paul may be making a liturgical reference to the new clothing we are given when we come up out of the baptismal pool. But he is also speaking, figuratively, of the whole person who, in conversion, exchanges a broken and partial identity for a Christlike wholeness. The Word becomes flesh in us, just as it did for Jesus. This is the depth of our identity, not just a matter of dressing up for the holidays.

† As I have died with Christ in my baptism, may I find the depth of who I am in being reborn in his likeness.

For further thought
• Today look out for signs of the word made flesh in your life and your community.

Thursday 31 December
Real and ordinary

Revelation 22:1-8

They will see his face, and his name will be on their foreheads. (verse 4)

Put yourself in the sandals of whatever committee it was who determined the canonical order of the Bible. You will see that they had little choice but to put the Book of Revelation at the end. With breathtakingly fantastic imagery, we are told how the world as we know it is transformed into a new heaven and a new earth.

Having reached this biblical end point, we close the book. It gradually dawns on us that nothing around us has really changed. We still live, as the twentieth-century American poet Wallace Stevens said, in that inescapable, indifferent 'old chaos of the sun' (from the poem 'Sunday Morning', *Harmonium*, Faber Poetry, 2001).

I remember a cold day in late December in Chicago contemplating the quiet emptiness of the days after Christmas. I was sitting in my church office. All the seasonal hoopla was over. Someone was in the sanctuary taking down the Christmas lights. I wrote a poem about the mood I was experiencing: ''Twas the day after Christmas when all through the house / not a creature was stirring, not even my spouse...' The magic was over. Or was it?

In his poem, 'The Work of Christmas Begins' (see http://tinyurl.com/logggseq), Howard Thurman speaks of the work of Christmas that begins only once we have finished playing with our toys and the glass baubles have been packed away for next year. Christ is born in our lives as we engage in finding the lost, healing the broken and making music in our hearts. The same thing happens when we turn over the last page of the Book of Revelation. The apocalyptic hoopla is over. We make it real and ordinary in how we live.

† Let the power of this vision fall on me, that I might live it out in the more prosaic world of my experience.

For further thought

• In the days ahead, how can you make Christmas real?

IBRA International Fund: would you help us?

Since the International Bible Reading Association was founded in 1882 our UK readers have been making donations to the IBRA International Fund (previously named the Missionary Fund), with the aim of supporting our overseas readers through the network of IBRA partners.

Our partners are based in 16 countries but the benefit flows over borders to at least 32 countries all over the world. Partners work tirelessly and often without pay to organise the translation, printing and distribution of IBRA Bible study notes and lists into many different languages from Ewe, Yoruba and Twi to Portuguese, Samoan and Telugu!

For over 130 years IBRA readers' donations have helped to support them and we guarantee that 100 per cent of your donations go to support our international brothers and sisters in Christ.

Making a difference

One of our partners in India, the All India Sunday School Association, ran three Sunday School Teacher Trainer Certificate programmes in 2013, in Poona, Nagpur and Agra, where IBRA notes were used as a resource.

The Congregational Christian Church in American Samoa told us:

"Every year the request comes from the community to print more copies to at least give another copy extra per household. Families have begun to use the material for their evening prayers at home."

In the Democratic Republic of Congo, the Baptist Community of the Congo River long to share the word of God with more people:

"People are really excited. ...In a country where the daily income is low, some are unable to buy [a] printed guide of daily Bible readings. They are expressing a deepest gratitude for free available IBRA material."

How your donations make a difference!

- **£5.00** prints 6 translated copies of *Fresh From the Word* in Ghana
- **£10.00** buys 14 translated copies for India
- **£25.00** sends 5 copies of *Fresh From the Word* (including the postage and packaging) to Nigeria
- **£50.00** would fund 1000 IBRA reading lists to be translated into Spanish, printed and distributed in Argentina.

Will you work with us and help us to enable Christians from different parts of the world to grow in knowledge and appreciation of the Word of God by making a donation of £5, £10 or even £50 to keep reaching people across the world with the word of God? The whole of your donation will support people overseas.

If you would like to make a donation, please use the envelope inserted in this book, send a cheque to International Bible Reading Association 1020 Bristol Road, Selly Oak, Birmingham B29 6LB or go online to shop.christianeducation.org.uk and click the donate button at the top of the page.

One person can make a difference

IBRA has been working in partnership with Dan Vaughan as our distributor in South Africa for over 20 years, but now Dan has decided the time has come to hand over to someone with fresh energy and new ideas. Dan began to support IBRA in 1993 while working for the South African Council of Churches.

He says: 'It's a ministry with an amazing impact on the lives of believers and I have enjoyed the opportunity immensely…. *Fresh From the Word* has been very enthusiastically received…. The IBRA notes are superb in challenging the reader – as no other notes can – to probe and pray for deeper insights in the reading of the Bible.'

We would like to thank Dan for his many years' devotion to the work of IBRA.

Thank you!

International Bible Reading Association Partners

A worldwide service of Christian Education at work in five continents

HEADQUARTERS
1020 Bristol Road
Selly Oak
Birmingham
B29 6LB
United Kingdom

www.christianeducation.org.uk
ibra@christianeducation.org.uk

and the following agencies:

NEW ZEALAND AND AUSTRALIA
Epworth Bookshop
157B Karori Road
Marsden Village
Karori
Wellington 6012

Mailing address:
PO Box 17255
Karori
Wellington 6147

sales@epworthbooks.org.nz

SAMOA
Congregational Christian Church
Central Office
Level 5, John Williams Building
Tamaligi
Apia

isalavao@cccs.org.ws

AMERICAN SAMOA
Congregational Christian Church in American
Samoa
PO Box 1537
1 Kananafou Street
Pago Pago
96799

cccasgs@efkas.org

FIJI
Methodist Bookstore
PO Box 354
Suva
Fiji

mbookstorefiji@yahoo.com

GHANA
IBRA Secretary
Asempa Publishers & IBRA
Box GP 919
Accra

gm@asempapublishers.com

NIGERIA
David Hinderer House
The Cathedral Church of St David
Kudeti
PMB 5298 Dugbe
Ibadan
Oyo State

SOUTH AND CENTRAL AFRICA
IBRA South Africa
6 Roosmaryn Street
Durbanville 7550

biblereading@evmot.com

DEMOCRATIC REPUBLIC OF THE CONGO
Communauté Baptiste du Fleuve Congo
Avenue Kalemie no 8
Kinshasa
BP 205 & 397
Kinshasa 1

ecc_cbfc@yahoo.fr

CAMEROON
Redemptive Baptist Church
PO Box 65
Limbe
Fako Division
South West Region

evande777@yahoo.com

INDIA
All India Sunday School Association
Plot No 8,
Threemurthy Colony
6th Cross, Mahendra Hills
PB no 2099
Secunderabad – 500 026
Andhra Pradesh

sundayschoolindia@yahoo.co.in

Fellowship of Professional Workers
Samanvay
Deepthi Chambers
Vijayapuri
Hyderabad – 500 017
Andhra Pradesh

fellowship2w@gmail.com

REPUBLIC OF KIRIBATI
KPC Bookstore
Po Box 80
Bairiki, Antebuka
Tarawa
Republic of Kiribati

IBRA scheme of readings 2016

Join us again next year when we shall be exploring the following themes:

Witness to the light
The heavens declare
Rulers brought down
Fulfilling all righteousness

Readings in Philippians
Grace to you, and peace
Finally, rejoice in the Lord

The Ten Commandments
The first seven Commandments
The final three Commandments

Navigating good and evil
Prologue: Where does evil come from?
What does evil look like today?
What does good look like today?
The way of the Cross
Practicalities of navigation

Readings in Luke 22–23
The passion of Jesus part 1
The passion of Jesus part 2

Feasting with God
Lord, stay with us!
Savouring a God of life
Jesus' table talk
Let us keep the festival

Exodus chapters 3–15
The call of Moses
The plagues on Egypt
Departure from Egypt

Seeing the Spirit of God
Seeing with the Spirit
Seeing aright
The gaze of love

Readings in Luke
Jesus in action: healing
Jesus' priorities: option for the poor

Living with illness
Spiritual crisis in illness
Spiritual resources in illness

Readings in 1 and 2 Chronicles

What's in a name?
Named people in the Old Testament
Named people in the New Testament
Nameless people in the Bible

God in action
Creating
Caring

1 John

Readings in Isaiah 40–55
The Creator God does a new thing
Israel's restoration
God's servant humiliated and vindicated

Prayer: relating to God
Patriachs and prophets
Psalms and personalities
In Christ Jesus

Readings in Luke
Following Jesus: being a disciple
Listening to Jesus' teaching
Teaching through stories

The Bible with the saints
Biblical saints
Saints from Christian tradition
Modern saints

Ephesians
Every spiritual blessing
Rooted and grounded in love
Be careful how you live
Living together in Christ

Readings in Matthew
Rejoicing in the Old Testament
Rejoicing in the New Testament